LAYER CAKES

WELCOME!

✦ ✦ ✦

CAKE LOVE STARTS HERE

SHEET CAKES

BUNDT CAKES

BROWNIES

CUPCAKES

PARTY CAKES

MUFFINS

FRUIT CRISP

COOKIES

FROSTINGS

. . . AND A WEDDING CAKE TOO!

Yellow Birthday Cake,
page 15

Bride's Cake,
page 18

Fresh Strawberry Cake,
page 22

Blueberry Muffin Cake,
page 26

Lemon Lover's Chiffon Cake,
page 31

Easy Orange Layer Cake,
page 35

Apricot Cake,
page 39

Coconut Cake,
page 42

Banana Cake,
page 46

Hummingbird Cake,
page 49

Classic Carrot Cake,
page 52

Snickerdoodle Cake,
page 56

German Chocolate Cake,
page 60

Chocolate Chip Layer Cake,
page 67

Devil's Food Cake,
page 64

Chocolate Chip Pistachio Cake,
page 70

Cookies and Cream Cake,
page 74

Chocolate Almond Torte,
page 78

Boston Cream Pie Your Way,
page 82

Chocolate Banana Cake,
page 85

A Gluten-Free Wedding Cake,
page 91

Almond Cream Cheese Pound Cake,
page 101

Kathy's Cinnamon Breakfast Cake,
page 104

Caramel Melted Ice Cream Cake,
page 107

Susan's Lemon Cake,
page 110

Fresh Orange Bundt Cake,
page 113

Banana Bread Cake,
page 117

Applesauce Cake,
page 120

Toasted Coconut Pound Cake,
page 123

Pumpkin Party Cake,
page 126

Southern Sweet Potato Pound Cake,
page 129

Chocolate Chip Cake,
page 132

Old-Fashioned Chocolate Pound Cake,
page 134

Chocolate Marbled Cappuccino Cake,
page 137

Darn Good Chocolate Cake,
page 140

Chocolate Chip Amaretto Cake,
page 143

Bacardi Rum Cake,
page 146

Kitchen Sink Gingerbread,
page 153

Easy One-Pan Caramel Cake,
page 156

Tres Leches Cake,
page 161

Honey Bun Cake,
page 158

Easy Fruit Crisp,
page 165

Fresh Apple and Pear Skillet Cake,
page 167

Lunchbox Applesauce Cake,
page 170

Pineapple Upside-Down Cake,
page 173

Hot Lemon Poke Cake,
page 175

Lemon Gooey Butter Cake,
page 178

Pumpkin Spice Cake,
page 181

Orange Cheesecake Squares,
page 184

Chocolate Zucchini Snack Cake,
page 187

Chocolate Sheet Cake,
page 190

Chocolate Espresso Buttermilk Cake,
page 193

Holy Cow Cake,
page 195

Favorite Yellow Birthday Cupcakes,
page 201

Pretty in Pink Strawberry Cupcakes,
page 205

Hartley's Coconut Cupcakes,
page 208

Georgia Peach Cupcakes,
page 211

Hawaiian Cupcakes,
page 214

Peanut Butter Cupcakes,
page 217

Chocolate Sour Cream Cupcakes,
page 220

Chocolate Chip Muffins,
page 223

Pumpkin Raisin Muffins,
page 227

New-Fashioned Banana Muffins,
page 230

Fresh Blueberry Muffins,
page 225

Lemon Buttermilk Poppy Seed Muffins,
page 233

Maple Corn Muffins,
page 236

Marbled Cream Cheese Brownies,
page 241

Peanut Butter Brownies,
page 244

Gluten-Free Magic Brownie Bars,
page 246

Gluten-Free Lemon Bars,
page 248

Slice and Bake Sugar Cookies,
page 250

Gingersnaps,
page 253

Gingerbread Boys and Girls,
page 255

Snickerdoodle Cookies,
page 258

Peanut Butter Cookies,
page 260

Almond Sugar Cookies,
page 264

Chocolate Cloud Cookies,
page 266

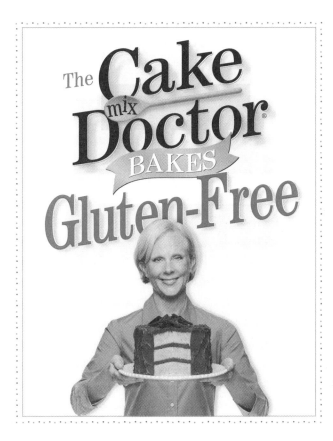

The Cake mix Doctor BAKES Gluten-Free

BY ANNE BYRN

Photography by Ben Fink

✦ ✦ ✦ ✦ ✦

WORKMAN PUBLISHING NEW YORK

Library of Congress Cataloging-in-Publication Data
Byrn, Anne.
  The cake mix doctor bakes gluten-free / by Anne Byrn.
    p. cm.
ISBN 978-0-7611-6098-4 (pb) – ISBN 978-0-7611-6107-3 (hc)
1. Gluten-free diet–Recipes. 2. Baking. I. Title.
RM237.86.B97 2010
641.5'638–dc22   2010032802

Cover design: David Matt
Interior design: Lisa Hollander
Author photograph: Gabrielle Revere
Interior photographs: Ben Fink
Cover cake styled by Sara Neumeier
Interior cakes styled by Cynthia Garcia-Vegas

Workman books are available at special discounts when purchased in bulk for premiums and sales promotions as well as for fund-raising or educational use. Special editions or book excerpts also can be created to specification. For details, contact the Special Sales Director at the address below or send an e-mail to specialsales@workman.com.

Workman Publishing Company, Inc.
225 Varick Street
New York, NY 10014-4381
www.workman.com
www.cakemixdoctor.com

Printed in the United States of America
First printing November 2010
10 9 8 7 6 5 4 3 2 1

Cover cake: If you'd like to bake the cover cake, see page 16.

Dedication

✦ ✦ ✦

For everyone who lives without gluten—
these cakes are for you.

Acknowledgments

✦ ✦ ✦

Thanks to all my readers, especially Cinde Shields, Lisa Bradley, and Hartley Steiner. I appreciate your recipe testing, dairy-free ideas, high-altitude advice, and the window into your gluten-free baking world. And thanks to my friends, especially Martha Bowden, and family who put aside wheat and embraced gluten-free cakes with enthusiasm.

Contents

✦ ✦ ✦

How to Bake a Cake and Eat It, Too

• • •

First things first: just what is gluten? Then, tips to help you go gluten-free with ease. How to bake gluten-free in a gluten-filled kitchen. Choosing the right equipment. And Gluten-Free Baking Dos and Don'ts.

GLUTEN-FREE
Layers

• • •

Universally loved, these elegant, dramatic cakes are no longer off-limits. For your next celebration, bake up a Snickerdoodle Cake, Chocolate Almond Torte, or Fresh Strawberry Cake with Strawberry Cream Cheese Frosting.

Make Your Own Gluten-Free Wedding Cake

• • •

A wedding cake for all—bride, groom, and guests. This towering confection is a match made in heaven: a rich, moist vanilla cake dazzles with a hint of almond and a divine cream cheese frosting. Cheers!

GLUTEN-FREE
Bundts

• • •

Comforting and easy classics, Bundts provide the perfect gluten-free ending to any meal. Serve up a slice of Almond Cream

*Bride's Cake
(page 18)*

Cheese Pound Cake, Caramel Melted Ice Cream Cake, or Applesauce Cake with Apple Cider Glaze.

Nostalgic and unfussy, scrumptious sheet cakes go straight from pan to plate with minimal prep and loads of taste. Try the Kitchen Sink Gingerbread, Chocolate Espresso Buttermilk Cake, Honey Bun Cake, or Orange Cheesecake Squares.

Chocolate Sheet Cake (page 190)

Whether for breakfast, dessert, or a midday snack, these decadent little confections take the cake. Satisfy your sweet tooth with Georgia Peach Cupcakes, Chocolate Sour Cream Cupcakes, Maple Corn Muffins, and more.

These are the bake sale standbys that will put a smile on everyone's face. No denying yourself at the next fund-raiser. Indulge without worry in Gluten-Free Magic Brownie Bars, Marbled Cream Cheese Brownies, Peanut Butter Cookies, and Chocolate Cloud Cookies.

No cake is complete without a luscious frosting, icing, or glaze on top. Spread a little love: Vanilla Buttercream Frosting. Cream Cheese Frosting, Fluffy Marshmallow Frosting. And Julie's Lemon Curd.

Welcome to Gluten-Free Baking

✦ ✦ ✦ ✦

An unexpected part of writing cookbooks is the dialogue I share with readers. The e-mails, letters, and comments I have received as the Cake Mix Doctor have opened my eyes to what goes on in everyday kitchens across the country. You have offered personal stories and predicaments, baking questions, and wonderful suggestions.

Apricot Cake with White Chocolate Cream Cheese Frosting (page 39)

I first received an e-mail about gluten-free cake baking about six years ago. Requests for gluten-free recipes trickled in up until about a year ago. Then readers became more vocal, more committed to encouraging me to write a gluten-free Cake Mix Doctor book. Their situations varied, from an older woman who needed to make gluten-free baked goods for her husband, to a young mom who had a daughter recently diagnosed with gluten intolerance, to a teenager who just wanted to be able to bake gluten-free cakes to feel normal. What they craved were the classic American desserts most of us take for granted: chocolate cupcakes, carrot cake, gingerbread, brownies, a yellow birthday cake. And what they needed—to bring cake baking into their homes—was a request I could not ignore.

It is estimated that 1 in 133 people in the United States and Canada suffers from celiac disease, an inability of their bodies to metabolize gluten, or the protein found in wheat, barley, and rye. Many more people are gluten-sensitive and need to avoid it in their diets. More still avoid gluten because they say they feel better without it. After these requests, I opened my eyes to the baking aisle and noticed, for the first time, the plethora of gluten-free cake mixes on the market. Then Betty Crocker unveiled a line of gluten-free cake mixes in the summer of 2009.

A Nationwide Need

I began reading about celiac disease. I talked about it with my friends and family and I learned that my children had classmates who followed gluten-free diets, that the daughter of my sister's neighbor was gluten-free, as was my literary agent's niece in Denver, and a friend I had been playing tennis with for more than two years was living gluten-free but she had never mentioned it. In Atlanta, two women were disappointed at having to pass up my samples of cinnamon cake at a Costco book signing and begged me to write a gluten-free cake book. In Memphis while recording a spot on local radio, I mentioned gluten-free baking and the host's face lit up. It turned out that seven of the twenty-two members of her Sunday school class have celiac disease and follow gluten-free diets. The list goes on, as if a web were being drawn and connecting us all. If we do not need to live gluten-free then someone in our close personal world does.

Across the country in Washington State, a reader named Cinde Shields was the most vocal and persistent about my writing this book. Cinde said she had had a personal goal of baking every Cake Mix Doctor recipe until her daughter was diagnosed with celiac disease two years ago. Cinde described the feeling of not being able to bake for her family and friends as upsetting and said she longed for quick, consistent, delicious cake mix recipes that started with a gluten-free mix.

I'd like to say this was the end of the story but, as I would find out, it was only the beginning. Neither having celiac disease nor being gluten intolerant, I had to educate myself about the disease and the gluten-free mixes on the market. After baking every mix I could get my hands on, I tried through trial and error various gluten-free add-ins to doctor up the mixes and make them more interesting. It was a challenge in the beginning because the mixes are made mostly of rice flour and are gritty in texture. In addition, because many people who are intolerant of gluten must also forgo casein, the protein found in milk, my recipes had to have dairy-free options as well.

This was pioneer territory. But what kept me going was one small success after another. When the Darn Good Chocolate Cake worked after half a dozen tries, it was a banner day! When I baked a perfect strawberry cake without gluten and a German chocolate cake that my family now prefers to the original Cake Mix Doctor version, there was no turning back. Other successes were around the corner. I was a from-scratch baker who raised the bar on conventional cake mixes, and now I am happy to help you make gluten-free mixes more interesting, bake Cake Mix Doctor favorites without hesitation, and bring baking traditions back into your home.

Enjoy these cakes, cookies, bars, and brownies, every one of them, for they are delicious, unexpected, warm, loving, and finally for you, gluten-free!

Anne Byrn
Nashville, Tennessee

✦ ✦ ✦

How to Bake a Cake and Eat It, Too

✦ ✦ ✦ ✦ ✦

If you're looking to bake gluten-free with great results, read on. Forget having to buy all the expensive ingredients for made-from-scratch gluten-free cakes. Instead you can begin with a gluten-free cake mix, add ingredients from your pantry, and without necessarily following package directions, arrive at a cake more wonderful than you ever imagined. Using a mix jump-starts the process, assures you the cake will rise, and best of all, allows you to bake well because these mixes are all-natural. Finally, you can bake a cake and eat it, too!

The baking basics in this book are the same as in my previous Cake Mix Doctor books. You need good pans, an oven that bakes at the right temperature, some creativity to flavor the cake as you like, and some practice in frosting a layer cake. You should read the recipes through completely before beginning to bake, just to make sure you've got all of the ingredients and equipment you'll need on hand.

But much is new, too, in the gluten-free cake world and I will lead you through the process. So, let's get baking gluten-free.

The Beginning

• • •

How in the world did a from-scratch baker wind up doctoring cake mixes? I had three children who made my world crazy but wonderful and I needed shortcuts. So how in the world did I wind up baking gluten-free cakes? My readers asked me to. And when Betty Crocker gluten-free cake mixes hit the baking aisle in my supermarket that got my attention.

So I baked the Betty Crocker mixes, as

What Is Gluten?

Gluten is the protein found in wheat, rye, and barley. It is a sticky substance and when used in baking helps hold bread, cakes, and pastries together and encourages them to rise as they bake. Gluten is not found in rice, corn, millet, amaranth, and teff. Oats, also, do not contain gluten, but because they are grown and transported in bulk, they may contain trace amounts of gluten from wheat, barley, or rye. To make sure the oats you eat will be gluten-free, look for proof of that on the package.

Although *gluten-free* has become something of a buzz word lately, many people have needed to avoid gluten for a long time. For people with celiac disease, gluten has a destructive effect on their intestines and digestive systems.

For others who are sensitive to gluten, it leads to digestive difficulties and other symptoms such as headaches, fatigue, and aching joints. Some people who suffer from intolerance to gluten develop a burning and itching rash called dermatitis herpetiformis. And parents of children with autism, Down syndrome, and ADHD attest that a gluten-free diet improves the health and well-being of their kids.

Why does it seem that more people today need to follow gluten-free diets? There are a number of theories, such as that our digestive systems are stressed, that there is more gluten than ever in our food supply, and that while gluten has long been in our food supply, people are more aware of the symptoms of celiac disease today.

well as the Gluten Free Pantry mixes, and a host of other mixes I found in supermarkets, health food stores, and online. These mixes ranged in size from fifteen ounces to nearly thirty ounces, but I found the fifteen-ounce mixes most compatible with my recipes. After baking them following the package instructions, I tried adding fruit, cream cheese, and more flavorings. I tried baking the mixes in two layer pans to create two-layer cakes. I baked them in Bundt pans and in small square pans. I made cupcakes and brownies, bars and cookies. I even baked a wedding cake. As with my previous cake mix doctoring, I wanted to improve the texture, flavor, and yield of these mixes. But these mixes were clearly different from the ones I had tested before.

What's in a Gluten-Free Cake Mix?

✦ ✦ ✦

Gluten-free cake mixes are mostly white rice flour. They also include a starch or a type of flour other than wheat gluten, such as tapioca, potato, or cornstarch, to improve the texture of the cake. The mixes might contain xanthan gum, which traps carbon dioxide gas and helps the cake rise. These mixes also contain flavorings and leavening. But they do not contain artificial ingredients or food colorings, a welcome change from conventional cake mixes. Here are a few

Hide and Seek

Gluten is hidden in all sorts of places, and some of these may surprise you. Here are a few.

✦ **Malt and malt flavoring**

✦ **Soy sauce**

✦ **Some soy milk products, so look at the labels**

✦ **Some modified food starch**

✦ **Some dextrin**

✦ **Some store-bought vanilla cake frosting**

✦ **Lipstick**

✦ **Play-Doh**

other things you should know about gluten-free mixes before you bake.

✦ Because the fifteen-ounce gluten-free cake mixes are smaller than flour-based cake mixes, they make slightly smaller cakes than you might be used to. I found the cake size quite nice and adequate for most families, serving ten to twelve.

✦ The gluten-free mixes cannot absorb as much liquid as mixes with gluten can, so take care when adding liquid should you want to doctor my recipes. Begin with a little liquid, say one half to three quarters of a cup, then add more as needed to make the batter smooth but thickened.

✦ I have found that, in general, three eggs is just the right amount for these mixes. A few of the recipes call for two eggs. And the cookies work best with one egg.

✦ Because gluten-free mixes are based on rice flour, they can be gritty. Adding instant pudding mix helps the mix rise higher in the pan and takes away some of the gritty texture. You can also use a little cocoa powder or almond flour instead of the pudding mix.

✦ Somehow sugar helps tenderize gluten-free cake mixes, which is why I add a little white sugar, brown sugar, or molasses to many of the recipes.

✦ To keep things simple, I based the recipes on yellow and chocolate gluten-free cake mixes. It was easy to turn the yellow cake mix into a spice cake by adding cinnamon and other spices.

✦ If you want a big cake for a large gathering, use two mixes and double the recipe.

Choosing the Right Equipment

• • •

While gluten-free cake mixes are different, the basic equipment needed to make cakes are the same—mixing bowls, baking pans, an electric mixer, wire cooling racks, rubber and metal spatulas for scraping bowls and spreading frosting, and those other handy utensils I love.

Mixing bowls: Stainless steel bowls of small, medium, and large sizes are not only handy to store nested one inside the other but they are lightweight and easy to lift when full of heavy batter. Plus, they can be hand washed or popped in the dishwasher. I also like a set of nesting glass mixing bowls because the glass bowls can be popped in the microwave oven should butter or cream cheese need softening.

Pans: A simple collection of baking pans will last you a lifetime. Buy three 9-inch shiny round cake layer pans and maybe a set of 8-inch round layers as well. You'll also need a Bundt pan, an 8-inch or 9-inch square baking pan for snack-size cakes, both a 13 by 9–inch metal and glass pan for sheet cakes, and at least two baking sheets. I baked the layers for this book in both 9-inch and 8-inch rounds and found the 8-inch pans made taller cakes, particularly nice for these smaller mixes. If you convert my 9-inch layer

How to Bake Gluten-Free in a Gluten-Filled Kitchen

People who have celiac disease are extremely sensitive to the presence of gluten. For other people who are gluten intolerant even a smidgen of gluten will make them feel bad. Take care when baking gluten-free in a kitchen where cakes and goodies are also prepared with wheat flour. Here are some suggestions.

✦ Always wash pans and utensils well with soap and hot water. Place pans and utensils that come into contact with wheat gluten in the dishwasher.

✦ Decrumb drawers that hold baking utensils so as not to cross-contaminate them.

✦ Or, set up a separate drawer or pantry for your gluten-free utensils.

✦ Set aside a separate cutting board for baking gluten-free.

✦ Have a separate sifter, spatulas, wooden spoons (older cracked spoons can hold flour in the cracks), and beaters for the electric mixer for gluten-free baking.

✦ Cover baking sheets with aluminum foil before making cookies.

---

recipes to 8-inch pans, increase the baking time by five minutes.

The mixer: If you know my books or have attended a cooking class, you know I can bake a whole cookbook's worth of recipes using an electric hand mixer. My KitchenAid stand mixer is helpful when making cookies, frosting (especially big batches), and larger cakes. I have a second set of beaters for the hand mixer and a second paddle for the KitchenAid, so I can bake two cakes before washing dishes.

Wire cooling racks: Essential for cooling cakes, you need two wire racks so two layers

can cool side by side when you are making a layer cake. As with the pans, invest in good racks—stainless steel racks don't rust.

Spoons and spatulas: Outside of the handy mixer, I rely on wooden spoons, rubber spatulas for frostings and to scrape batter out of a bowl, and metal icing spatulas for frosting cakes and cupcakes. For each of these I like a variety of sizes—small and large wooden spoons and rubber spatulas and a short as well as a long metal spatula.

Other handy things: Here are some of the little things that help make my baking life go smoothly.

✦ Glass as well as iSi Flex-it silicone measuring cups for liquids

✦ A stainless steel oil mister that I can fill with the vegetable oil of my choice and use to spray baking pans before adding the batter

✦ A serrated knife for slicing cake layers in half crosswise

✦ A wooden skewer, chopstick, or wooden craft stick for poking holes in cakes before pouring glaze over them

✦ A digital scale so I can weigh cake pans before baking to make sure I have the same amount of batter in each pan

✦ A Microplane grater for zesting lemons, limes, and oranges

✦ A medium-size ice cream scoop for scooping equal portions of batter into cupcake pans

Let's Bake

• • •

Ready to bake? Let's go through a quick checklist.

The oven: These recipes were baked in Thermador and General Electric ovens. Make sure your oven, whatever the brand, is calibrated correctly. As ovens age they tend to bake hotter. If you have moved to a new home and are baking with a new oven or you sense your cookies and cakes are baking too quickly, buy a small oven thermometer at a hardware store and place it at the back of your oven. If it takes longer than fifteen minutes for your oven to come to 350°F it is baking too cool. If it registers 375°F when you set the oven at 350°F it is baking too hot. Either have your oven recalibrated by an appliance repairman or lower or raise the oven temperature as needed when you bake. For best results, bake on a rack placed in the center of the oven.

The pan preparation: To ensure that a Bundt cake comes cleanly out of the pan each and every time, lightly mist the pan with vegetable oil spray and dust it with rice flour, cocoa powder, or cinnamon sugar. The same goes with layer pans, although they are a little more forgiving than Bundt pans. As for square and rectangular metal pans, you can mist these with oil and lightly dust them with rice flour or just mist them with oil if you will be serving the cake straight from the pan. For cupcakes and muffins, use paper liners if you want absolutely no cleanup. Or, if you are making muffins, mist the pans with vegetable oil spray and scoop in the batter. The muffins should pop right out and have a nice crunchy crust.

The method of mixing: Once again, I use the dump method of mixing these cakes, which means I place all the ingredients for the batter in the bowl and beat them with an electric mixer. That said, you can make this process a little easier on yourself and wind up with smoother batters if you remember a few things. For perfect blending, add the dry ingredients first and whisk them together by hand, using the beaters of an electric mixer. Then add the eggs and other wet ingredients, turn on the mixer, and continue with the recipe.

Take care when using butter or cream cheese to have them at room temperature. If the eggs are cold, you can add them, but if the recipe calls for water or milk you may want to warm it a little to offset the cold temperature of the eggs and to keep your butter and cream cheese from clumping. Temperature is a funny

Gluten-Free Cake Baking Dos and Don'ts

Do:

✦ Substitute liquid for liquid.

✦ Watch the amount of liquid and don't add too much.

✦ Beat cake batters for up to two minutes.

✦ Look for the usual signs of doneness: Cakes spring back when lightly pressed with a finger and yellow cakes turn golden brown when they are done.

✦ Let cakes cool in the pan for a slightly shorter time than regular cakes—five minutes for layers, ten minutes for Bundts—then turn them out and let them cool completely on racks before frosting.

Don't:

✦ Omit the eggs. Eggs provide structure in gluten-free cakes, and they help the cakes rise higher in the pan. You may use an egg substitute, such as Egg Beaters; follow the package directions.

✦ Bake gluten-free cakes too far in advance. They get gummy after three days. It's best to bake and eat them the same day, or one day later, or bake and freeze the layers up to a month ahead, then thaw them before frosting.

Love These Substitutes

You might not have been crazy about that substitute teacher in school, but you will love the way that with these recipes you can sub in different ingredients for those you don't like, don't have on hand, or cannot eat. Here are some suggestions.

Liquids: Instead of water or milk, use orange juice, apple juice, or almond milk.

Fruit: A cup of pureed fruit can be translated into mashed bananas, canned pumpkin, pureed soft pears, or applesauce.

Fat: For lower-fat versions, use yogurt instead of sour cream, applesauce instead of vegetable oil, and reduced-fat cream cheese and sour cream instead of full-fat cream cheese and sour cream.

Dairy: Most recipes in this book have suggestions for dairy-free substitutions, but as a general rule, you can use margarine, vegetable shortening, or butter-flavored spreads instead of butter; soy yogurt or coconut milk instead of sour cream; and a dairy-free cream cheese instead of cream cheese. And instead of cow's milk in cake batters and frostings, use almond milk, rice milk, coconut milk, or soy milk.

thing, and keeping the batter at a moderately warm temperature—not too hot and not too cold—will make it perfect every time.

The way to tell a cake is done: The more you bake, the better you will get at this crucial step. You will know by smell, sight, or touch, or all three, when a cake is done. If your oven has a window in the door, keep the light in the oven on as you bake, and take a peek inside when the cake has baked to the minimum baking time suggested. If it looks like the cake might be done, open the oven door and very carefully touch the center of the cake. If the cake springs back, it is done. If it does not, carefully close the oven door and let the cake continue to bake. You will be able to tell that yellow cake batters are done by seeing their color turn to golden brown. Chocolate cakes are a little trickier. You've got to use the spring test and also look to see if the cake is just beginning to pull away from the side of the pan. If so, it's done.

Finishing the Cake

• • •

Cooling: Once they are baked, transfer cakes to wire racks or to the top of your gas range so air flows around and underneath the cakes as they cool. I have found that gluten-free cakes can be removed from the pan a little sooner than their gluten cake counterparts. Layers need five minutes cooling time in the pan, Bundts about fifteen minutes. Some Bundts with chocolate and nuts in them need even longer to cool before they are ready to be turned out of the pan. In general, leave a cake in the pan as long as the recipe indicates.

When it's time to remove the cake from the pan, run a sharp knife around the edge of the pan. Give the cake a gentle shake or two to loosen it from the pan, and then invert it firmly onto a wire rack to finish cooling. Cake layers should be inverted twice so they cool right-side up.

Before frosting, make sure the cake is cool. There is nothing more frustrating than frosting a warm cake, especially in a warm kitchen. That cake will slide and you will have absolutely no control. Place a warm cake layer, or a warm sliding cake, right into the refrigerator to cool quickly before you finish frosting.

Making frosting: Should you top my gluten-free cakes with anything but homemade frosting? The answer, by the way, is no. While most canned frosting is gluten-free, it does not taste nearly as good as the frosting you make in your kitchen. Buttercreams and cream cheese frostings are the easiest to prepare. Ganache needs just two ingredients, chocolate and cream, and is a snap to make for your favorite chocolate cakes. And cooked icings, such as the Quick Caramel Frosting and the Chocolate Pan Frosting, are a taste of yesteryear. Once you start using

them you will be the go-to person for birthday cakes.

Don't want to make frosting? Whisk together a simple confectioners' sugar and milk glaze. Or make a glaze with confectioners' sugar and a little orange or lemon juice. Or just dust the cake with confectioners' sugar.

Frosting the cake: The layers, cupcakes, and some of the straight-from-the-pan cakes in this book need frosting. That leaves the Bundts, many snack cakes, some bars, and cookies should you have a fear of frosting. But fear no more! Frosting takes a little practice, and I promise you will get better at it. Here are some of my secrets for success (and also check out the box on page 275).

✦ Gently flatten cake layers as they cool by pressing down on them with a clean kitchen towel. Or just press down on one layer and let this be your bottom layer of the cake, leaving the top layer slightly domed. Flattened, or leveled, layers stack evenly and don't slip and slide when frosted, especially in warm weather.

✦ Frost cakes and cupcakes after they have cooled completely.

✦ Add just enough frosting between layers so they stick together but don't slip and slide.

✦ Frost the top so it looks pretty, then get to work on the side.

Storing Your Cake

• • •

Once your frosted or unfrosted cake is cool, it's either time to slice and serve it or to store it for enjoying later. The best way to store a frosted cake is under a glass dome or in a plastic cake saver. Unfrosted cakes can be stored with a draping of plastic wrap as they are more forgiving.

If unfrosted, most cakes can be stored on a kitchen counter for up to three days. Cakes frosted with a buttercream frosting can be stored on the counter in a cool kitchen for up to three days. Those frosted with cream cheese or whipped cream need to go into the fridge where they, too, can be stored for up to three days.

Freezing cakes: If you want to keep gluten-free cakes longer than three days, freeze the unfrosted layers or whole cake. Wrap them first in waxed paper and then wrap them in heavy-duty aluminum foil or place them in a resealable plastic bag and store them in the freezer for about a month. These cakes don't keep as long in the freezer as their gluten cake counterparts. But that's okay because that keeps you baking and serving fresh cake. When it's time to thaw the cake, place it on a kitchen counter, opening the bag or foil to let the moisture evaporate. Then you're ready to frost, slice, and serve. Freezing actually makes frosting a layer cake quite easy because, when you go to frost them, the layers will be cool and firm and will stack neatly and won't shift. Simple pleasures.

High-Altitude Gluten-Free Baking

• • •

I feel a little frustrated developing recipes at sea level knowing readers living at high altitudes (3,500 feet or more above sea level) may have some trouble baking them flawlessly. That is why I rely on a handful of experts who test my recipes at higher altitudes. For this book, I turned to gluten-free cook and baker Lisa Bradley of Santa Fe, New Mexico. Lisa lives at 7,000 feet, and she humorously says it has taught her "that cooking is as much an art as a science." She tested my Darn Good Gluten-Free Chocolate Cake and the Fresh Orange Bundt cake. (As a rule, Bundts do well at high altitudes because the pans give structure to the cake.)

What are the dilemmas of high altitude baking? The air pressure decreases as the elevation increases. Cake mixes contain leavening and at high altitudes this leavening causes the cakes to rise more quickly and then fall or to rise and spill over the pan. Even Bundts won't bake as high in the pan as they do at sea level. And layers need to be at least nine inches in diameter because cake batter will often flow over the side of a smaller pan.

Here are some high-altitude baking recommendations from Lisa Bradley, Mark Sciscenti, a Sante Fe pastry chef and high-altitude expert, and from *Living Without* magazine.

1. A slightly higher baking temperature helps. If the recipe calls for a 350°F oven, bake yellow cakes at 375°F and chocolate cakes at 365°F.

2. Because the oven temperature is higher, the baking time will be shorter. Count on five to eight minutes less for every thirty minutes of baking time. Take care not to overbake cakes. Cakes already taste drier at high altitudes, especially in desert areas.

3. The cake batters need a little extra moisture. Lisa thinks adding 4 to 5 tablespoons more to the liquid called for in the recipe is enough for Santa Fe's 7,000 foot elevation. For lower elevations count on an extra 1 to 2 tablespoons at 3,000 feet and another 1½ teaspoons of liquid for each additional 1,000 feet.

4. Using cream cheese, sour cream, and yogurt helps high-altitude cakes. They add moisture and structure. An extra egg white also adds structure and moisture.

5. Omit the added sugar in the recipes. While the sugar may tenderize cakes at sea level, high-altitude cakes don't need tenderizing. They need structure.

Gluten-Free Online: Where to Go for Help

• • •

The gluten-free world grows by the minute. Whether you want dietary information from a reputable website, are looking for an online forum to share recipes and baking tips with other gluten-free cooks, want to meet and share food with local cooks in your area, or shop for hard-to-find ingredients, there's a lot here. Please see pages 296 and 297 for a list of resources for living gluten-free.

✦ ✦ ✦

LAYERS

✦ ✦ ✦ ✦ ✦

I've said this before, and I'll say it once more—layer cakes tug at my heart. They are all that is good in this world. They are homespun. They are celebratory. And they are real. How many layer cakes have you eaten that were pencil straight, perfectly aligned, with the frosting professionally swirled? Well, maybe in photos they look like that, but in real life layer cakes are as imperfect as we are. A little heavier on the bottom layer, one side higher than the other . . . well, you know what I mean!

Classic Carrot Cake
with Cream Cheese Frosting
(page 52)

So, you see how much I love them, both with gluten and now especially without. I worried about this chapter and how layers would turn out when baked with gluten-free mixes. Would they rise? Would they stick to the pan? Would they look as happy and festive as cakes made with flour? My worries are no more. These layers bake up into a dazzling collection of recipes. A feast for the eye, they bring together my favorite layer cake flavors but in a gluten-free form. They are cakes you will be thrilled to bake, serve, and celebrate.

I do have some advice for you before you dive into these delicious recipes. The gluten-free mixes I used were fifteen ounces, about three ounces less than a conventional box of cake mix. So you will be baking a slightly smaller cake that will feed ten to twelve people max. To make the cakes appear taller, I offer a lot of tips throughout this chapter.

I learned in testing that it's important to place equal amounts of batter in the cake pans. Because there is less batter you will really notice if one layer is taller than the other once the cake is frosted and sliced. In most recipes you use from 1¾ to 2 cups of batter per cake pan. You can cup out the layers using a dry measuring cup or pour the batter into a 4-cup liquid measuring cup and then pour half into one pan and half into the other. Or, you can use a kitchen scale to weigh the batter in the pans. Should you want a large cake for a party, you can easily bake a cake using two gluten-free mixes. See the Bride's Cake, for example. When a two-cake-mix cake is filled and frosted, you can serve eighteen to twenty people and still have that layer cake look.

No more talk—get baking! I hope you love all these twenty recipes, from the carrot to the lemon chiffon to the strawberry to the blueberry muffin to chocolate chip to German chocolate to the flat-out decadent devil's food. I hope they tug at your heart. No one will ever guess you started with a gluten-free mix.

✦ ✦ ✦

Yellow Birthday Cake

✦ ✦ ✦

Knowing how much I wanted to include a family-favorite yellow layer cake recipe in this book, I started testing this cake early, but by the time my deadline was rolling around I still didn't have the cake perfected. I have learned that sometimes the seemingly simplest recipes are the toughest to develop. Because gluten-free mixes don't contain food coloring, the "yellow" had to come from added ingredients. In this recipe that is the egg yolks and butter. If you want an even more yellow color, substitute orange juice for 3 tablespoons of the milk and the cake will be even more delicious. To me this birthday cake is perfect—moist, rich, vanilla-flavored, and yellow. And I think it cries out for Chocolate Buttercream Frosting but my son prefers caramel, so you had better let the birthday boy or girl decide.

serves: **10 to 12**

prep: **30 minutes**

bake: **19 to 23 minutes**

cool: **25 minutes**

DAIRY FREE

Substitute water or orange juice for the milk in the cake. Use margarine or a half cup of vegetable oil instead of the butter. And for the Chocolate Buttercream Frosting, use margarine instead of butter and almond or rice milk instead of the milk.

How to Make the Cover Cake

To make our luscious three-layer cover cake, make a recipe and a half of the Yellow Birthday Cake. Bake in three 8-inch pans for 24 to 27 minutes. Frost with the Chocolate Buttercream Frosting.

Vegetable oil spray, for misting the pans
2 teaspoons rice flour, for dusting the pans
1 package (15 ounces) yellow gluten-free cake mix
¼ cup (half of a 3.4-ounce package) vanilla instant pudding mix
¾ cup milk (see Notes)
8 tablespoons (1 stick) unsalted butter, at room temperature
3 large eggs
1 tablespoon vanilla paste or pure vanilla extract (see Notes)
Chocolate Buttercream Frosting (page 287)

1. Place a rack in the center of the oven and preheat the oven to 350°F. Lightly mist two 9-inch round cake pans with vegetable oil spray, then dust them with the rice flour. Shake out the excess rice flour and set the pans aside.

2. Place the cake mix, pudding mix, milk, butter, eggs, and vanilla in a large mixing bowl and beat with an electric mixer on low speed until the ingredients are just incorporated, 30 seconds. Stop the machine and scrape down the side of the bowl with a rubber spatula. Increase the mixer speed to medium and beat the batter until smooth, 1 to 1½ minutes longer, scraping down the side of the bowl again if needed. The batter should look well blended. Divide the batter evenly between the 2 prepared cake pans, smoothing the tops with the rubber spatula. Place the pans in the oven side by side.

3. Bake the cake layers until they are golden brown and the tops spring back when lightly pressed with a finger, 19 to 23 minutes. Transfer the cake pans to wire racks and let the cake layers cool for 5 minutes. Run a sharp knife around the edge of each cake layer and give the pans a good shake to loosen the cakes. Invert each layer onto a wire rack, then invert it again onto another rack so that the layers are right side up. Let the layers cool completely, about 20 minutes longer.

4. Meanwhile, make the Chocolate Buttercream Frosting.

5. To assemble the cake, transfer one layer, right side up, to a serving plate. Spread the top with about 1 cup of the frosting. Place the second cake layer, right side up, on top of the first layer and frost the top and side of the cake, working with smooth, clean strokes.

NOTES: Use whatever milk you have on hand, but just so you know, whole and 2 percent milk will make a richer cake. To help keep the batter smooth, warm the milk slightly in a microwave on high power for 20 seconds before adding it to the mixing bowl.

Vanilla paste is sold in specialty food shops and natural food stores and has little flecks of the vanilla bean and a more pronounced vanilla flavor than vanilla extract. It is especially nice in this cake but don't go out and buy it just for this recipe; use regular vanilla extract. Most pure vanilla extract is gluten-free. Look for the gluten-free symbol or the words *gluten-free* on the vanilla you buy.

KEEP IT FRESH! Store the cake, lightly wrapped with aluminum foil or in a cake saver, on the kitchen counter for three days. Freeze only the cake layers, wrapped in aluminum foil, for up to one month. Let the layers thaw overnight on the counter before assembling and frosting the cake.

✦ ✦ ✦

The Cake Mix Doctor Says

Want a taller birthday cake? Bake this cake in 8-inch pans instead of the usual 9-inch pans. You'll need to bake the layers a little longer—about 5 minutes more. How to tell the size of your layer pans? Measure straight across from the inside edge of the rim. Another tip: Cakes look taller when you place them on cake stands.

recipe reminders

Made for:

Prep Notes:

Don't Forget:

Special Touches:

Bride's Cake

✦ ✦ ✦

serves: 18 to 20

prep: 40 minutes

bake: 35 to 40 minutes

cool: 35 minutes

The Bride's Cake is one of the more popular recipes from the first Cake Mix Doctor book. A vanilla cake with raspberry jam sandwiched between the layers and White Chocolate Cream Cheese Frosting all around, it is an elegant cake many people bake for small weddings, engagement parties, and bridal showers. Now here's the Bride's Cake in gluten-free form. To make it look substantial I used two packages of cake mix, plus sour cream and more egg whites. The layers are extra deep and after baking you split them crosswise and spread them with raspberry jam or preserves. See page 89 for directions on how to turn this cake into a supersize Bride's Cake—a wedding cake.

DAIRY FREE

Substitute plain soy yogurt or coconut milk for the sour cream in the cake. Omit the white chocolate and use a dairy-free cream cheese, such as Better Than Cream Cheese made by Tofutti, and margarine in place of the cream cheese and butter in the White Chocolate Cream Cheese Frosting.

For the cake

Vegetable oil spray, for misting the pans
2 teaspoons rice flour, for dusting the pans
2 packages (15 ounces each) yellow gluten-free
   cake mix
1 package (3.4 ounces) vanilla instant pudding mix
⅓ cup granulated sugar
1 cup reduced-fat sour cream
¾ cup vegetable oil
½ cup water
4 large egg whites
2 large eggs
2 tablespoons pure vanilla extract (see Note)
1 teaspoon pure almond extract

For the filling, frosting, and garnish

    1 jar (10 ounces) raspberry all-fruit preserves, about 1 cup
    White Chocolate Cream Cheese Frosting (page 280)
    1 pint fresh raspberries (optional)

1. Make the cake: Place a rack in the center of the oven and preheat the oven to 350°F. Take two 9-inch round cake pans that are at least 2 inches deep and lightly mist them with vegetable oil spray. Dust the cake pans with the rice flour, shake out the excess rice flour, and set the pans aside.

2. Place the cake mix, pudding mix, and sugar in a large mixing bowl and stir to combine. Add the sour cream, oil, water, egg whites, eggs, and vanilla and almond extracts, and beat with an electric mixer on low speed until the ingredients are just incorporated, 45 seconds. Stop the machine and scrape down the side of the bowl with a rubber spatula. Increase the mixer speed to medium and beat the batter until smooth, 1½ to 2 minutes longer, scraping down the side of the bowl again if needed. The batter should look well blended and will be thick. Divide the batter evenly between the 2 prepared pans, smoothing the tops with the rubber spatula. Place the pans in the oven side by side.

3. Bake the cake layers until they are lightly browned and the tops spring back when lightly pressed with a finger, 35 to 40 minutes. Transfer the cake pans to wire racks and let the cake layers cool for 5 minutes. Run a sharp knife around the edge of each cake layer and give the pans a good shake to loosen the cakes. Invert each layer onto a wire rack, then invert it again onto another rack so that the layers are right side up. Let the layers cool completely, about 30 minutes longer.

recipe reminders

Made for:

_____

_____

_____

_____

_____

Prep Notes:

_____

_____

_____

_____

_____

Don't Forget:

_____

_____

_____

_____

_____

Special Touches:

_____

_____

_____

_____

_____

_____

4. Meanwhile, prepare the filling and frosting: Stir the raspberry preserves and set aside. Make the White Chocolate Cream Cheese Frosting. Rinse and pat the fresh raspberries dry with paper towels.

5. To assemble the cake, using a serrated knife, slice each cake layer in half crosswise. Transfer the bottom half of one layer, cut side up, to a serving plate. Spread the cut side with ½ cup of the raspberry preserves, then place the top half over it, cut side down. Spread the top of this layer with 1 cup of the frosting. Place the bottom of the second layer, cut side up, on top of the first layer. Spread that layer with the remaining ½ cup of raspberry preserves. Place the top half of the second layer on top, cut side down. Frost the top and side of the cake with the remaining frosting, working with smooth, clean strokes. While the frosting is still soft, arrange the raspberries in a decorative pattern on top of the cake.

NOTE: Clear vanilla extract can be found where cake decorating supplies are sold. This helps keep the batter pale so that it bakes into a very white cake.

KEEP IT FRESH! If your kitchen is cool, store the cake, lightly wrapped with aluminum foil or in a cake saver, on the kitchen counter for twenty-four hours. Don't arrange the raspberries on the cake until just before serving. Or, store the cake in the refrigerator for three days. Freeze only the cake layers, wrapped in aluminum foil, for up to one month. Let the layers thaw overnight on the counter before assembling and frosting the cake.

✦ ✦ ✦

The Cake Mix Doctor Says

Not a fan of raspberry? Fill the layers with apricot all-fruit preserves and garnish the cake with edible apricot-colored pansies; use orange marmalade and the Candied Citrus Garnish (page 115); or use a filling of lemon curd, store-bought or homemade (page 294), and a garnish of fresh blueberries or strawberries.

Perfect Layers: 1, 2, 3

It's as easy as 1, 2, 3 to get cake layers to come out of cake pans cleanly each and every time. I have found gluten-free cakes don't stick to the pan as long as you follow these steps.

1. Prep the cake pans. Spray the layer pans with vegetable oil spray. Do not use an aerosol spray with propellant in it because it will cause the cake layers to darken and bake more quickly around the edges. Use vegetable oil in a spray container or brush the bottom of the pans with solid vegetable shortening or melted butter. Dust each pan with a teaspoon of rice flour or reserved cake mix. Or, for chocolate batters, dust each pan with a teaspoon of unsweetened cocoa.

2. Test for doneness. When the cake layers have been baking and are approaching doneness, take a peek inside the oven. I like to leave the oven light on while cakes bake so I can see them rise and gauge their doneness. When it gets close to the time, open the oven door carefully and lightly press the center of the layers with your finger. If the cakes spring back in the middle, they are done. Yellow cake layers will turn golden brown when baked to doneness.

3. Cool it. After you remove the cake layers from the oven, place the pans on wire racks and let the cakes cool for five minutes. Then, run a sharp knife around the edge of the cake layers, shake the pans gently to loosen the cakes, and invert the layers once and then again, so that they are right side up on the racks. Let the layers cool until they come to room temperature, about thirty minutes longer, before frosting them.

Fresh Strawberry Cake
with Strawberry Cream Cheese Frosting

✦ ✦ ✦

serves: **10 to 12**

prep: **35 minutes**

bake: **18 to 22 minutes**

cool: **25 minutes**

I can't imagine a spring birthday without a strawberry cake. It has been the cake of choice for my girls, and my guys love it, too. And we're all in favor of this gluten-free version. I think it's even more intensely strawberry flavored. Plus it's pretty, fancy, fun—all the right elements for a great party cake.

> Vegetable oil spray, for misting the pans
> 2 teaspoons rice flour, for dusting the pans
> 2 cups (16 ounces) fresh strawberries
> 1 package (15 ounces) yellow gluten-free cake mix
> 3 tablespoons strawberry gelatin
>   (half of a 3-ounce package)
> ½ cup vegetable oil
> 3 large eggs
> 2 teaspoons pure vanilla extract
> Strawberry Cream Cheese Frosting
>   (page 276)

1. Place a rack in the center of the oven and preheat the oven to 350°F. Lightly mist two 9-inch round cake pans with vegetable oil spray, then dust them with the rice flour. Shake out the excess rice flour and set the pans aside.

DAIRY FREE

When making the frosting, substitute a dairy-free cream cheese, such as Better Than Cream Cheese made by Tofutti, for the cream cheese and use margarine in place of the butter.

2. Rinse and drain the strawberries, then pat them dry with paper towels. Select the 6 prettiest berries for garnish and set them aside. Set aside one large strawberry to use in the Strawberry Cream Cheese Frosting. Cut the green caps off the remaining berries and mash the berries with a fork or place them in a food processor and pulse until you have a smooth puree, about 10 pulses. You need ¾ cup of pureed strawberries.

3. Place the cake mix and strawberry gelatin in a large mixing bowl and stir to combine. Add the strawberry puree, oil, eggs, and vanilla and beat with an electric mixer on low speed until the ingredients are just incorporated, 30 seconds. Stop the machine and scrape down the side of the bowl with a rubber spatula. Increase the mixer speed to medium and beat the batter until smooth, 1 to 1½ minutes longer, scraping down the side of the bowl again if needed. Divide the batter evenly between the 2 prepared cake pans, smoothing the tops with the rubber spatula. Place the pans in the oven side by side.

recipe reminders

Made for:

_____

_____

_____

_____

Prep Notes:

_____

_____

_____

_____

Don't Forget:

_____

_____

_____

_____

Special Touches:

_____

_____

_____

_____

_____

4. Bake the cake layers until they are golden brown and the tops spring back when lightly pressed with a finger, 18 to 22 minutes. Transfer the cake pans to wire racks and let the cake layers cool for 5 minutes. Run a sharp knife around the edge of each cake layer and give the pans a good shake to loosen the cakes. Invert each layer onto a wire rack, then invert it again onto another rack so that the layers are right side up. Let the layers cool completely, about 20 minutes longer.

5. Meanwhile, make the Strawberry Cream Cheese Frosting.

6. To assemble the cake, transfer one layer, right side up, to a serving plate. Spread the top with about 1 cup of the frosting. Place the second cake layer, right side up, on top of the first layer and frost the top and side of the cake, working with smooth, clean strokes. To make slicing easier, place the uncovered cake in the refrigerator until the frosting sets, 10 to 15 minutes.

7. Just before serving, garnish the cake with the 6 whole berries or slice the berries and pile them in the center of the cake. Or slice the berries lengthwise 2 or 3 times, slicing up to but not through the green stem end. Gently spread out the berries to form fans and arrange these on the top of the cake.

KEEP IT FRESH! If your kitchen is cool, store the cake, lightly wrapped with aluminum foil or in a cake saver, on the kitchen counter for twenty-four hours. Or, store it in the refrigerator for three days. Freeze only the cake layers, wrapped in aluminum foil, for up to one month. Let the layers thaw overnight on the counter before assembling and frosting the cake.

✦ ✦ ✦

Three Easy Garnishes

I am not a professional cake decorator so for me garnishes need to be simple, relate to the cake, and be visually interesting. Here are three of my favorites.

1. Slice three very thin slices of lemon or orange. Remove any seeds. Cut a slit from the rind to the center of each slice so you can twist it. Place one lemon or orange twist in the center of the cake. Place the second twist on top of the first but at a right angle to it to form a cross. And place the third on top of the second at a roughly 45 degree angle. If necessary you can use a toothpick to hold them in place, but if you stack them carefully they won't need securing.

2. Select six fresh raspberries, strawberries, or blueberries. Place one in the center of the cake and surround it with the remaining five berries. Dust the berries with confectioners' sugar just before serving.

3. Stick one sprig of mint or one beautiful edible flower, such as a pansy, in the center of the cake and nothing else is needed. If you are using a flower, be sure that it is pesticide-free.

The Cake Mix Doctor Says

How about a chocolate-covered strawberry cake? Bake the layers as directed but, instead of the strawberry frosting, use the Chocolate Buttercream Frosting (page 287) or Chocolate Pan Frosting (page 289). For the garnish, dip whole strawberries halfway in melted white or dark chocolate and let them cool on waxed paper until the chocolate hardens before arranging them on top of the cake.

Blueberry Muffin Cake

✦ ✦ ✦

serves: 10 to 12

prep: 40 minutes

bake: 19 to 24 minutes

cool: 25 minutes

At book signings, cooking classes, and on TV this was one of the most popular recipes in my most recent book. Maybe it's because the cake looks like a giant blueberry muffin with glaze trickling down the side. Who knows why the appeal, but this cake gets attention. So I could not wait to come up with a gluten-free version. And as much as I hate sending you out to buy a special ingredient, I did use a little soy flour in the topping, just to give it weight and crunch. You can use the leftover soy flour in other toppings or instead of rice flour when dusting pans before baking.

For the crunchy topping

    Vegetable oil spray, for misting the pans
    Parchment paper, for lining the pans
    ½ cup lightly packed light brown sugar
    ¼ cup soy flour (see Note)
    3 tablespoons unsalted butter, cold
    ½ cup finely chopped pecans

For the cake and glaze

1 large lemon

1 pint (2 cups) fresh blueberries

1 teaspoon soy flour

1 package (15 ounces) yellow gluten-free cake mix

¼ cup (half of a 3.4-ounce package) vanilla instant
pudding mix

¾ cup (6 ounces) lemon yogurt

¼ cup vegetable oil

¼ cup milk

3 large eggs

2 teaspoons pure vanilla extract

1½ cups confectioners' sugar, sifted

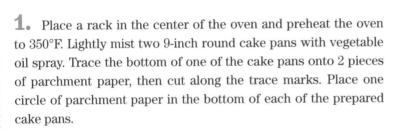

1. Place a rack in the center of the oven and preheat the oven to 350°F. Lightly mist two 9-inch round cake pans with vegetable oil spray. Trace the bottom of one of the cake pans onto 2 pieces of parchment paper, then cut along the trace marks. Place one circle of parchment paper in the bottom of each of the prepared cake pans.

2. Make the crunchy topping: Place the brown sugar and ¼ cup of soy flour in a small bowl and stir to combine. Cut the butter into 1-inch pieces and, using two sharp knives or a pastry blender, cut the butter into the sugar mixture until it is crumbly. Fold in the pecans. Spoon half of the topping mixture into each of the prepared cake pans, dividing it evenly between them and spreading it out evenly across the bottoms of the pans. Set the pans aside.

3. Make the cake: Rinse and pat the lemon dry with a paper towel, then grate 1 heaping teaspoon of the yellow zest onto a plate. Cut the lemon in half and squeeze the juice through a fine sieve, discarding the seeds. Place 2 tablespoons of lemon juice in a small mixing bowl and set it aside for the glaze. Measure

1 tablespoon of the remaining lemon juice and place it and the zest in a large mixing bowl.

4. Rinse and drain the blueberries, then pat them dry with paper towels. Measure 1½ cups of the berries and toss them with the 1 teaspoon of soy flour. Set these blueberries aside. Set aside the remaining ½ cup of blueberries for a garnish.

5. Place the cake mix and pudding mix in the large bowl with the lemon zest and juice and stir to combine. Add the yogurt, oil, milk, eggs, and vanilla and beat with an electric mixer on low speed until the ingredients are just incorporated, 30 seconds. Stop the machine and scrape down the side of the bowl with a rubber spatula. Increase the mixer speed to medium and beat the batter until smooth, 1 to 1½ minutes longer, scraping down the side of the bowl again if needed. Fold in the 1½ cups of blueberries. Divide the batter evenly between the 2 prepared cake pans, being careful not to disturb the topping and smoothing the tops with the rubber spatula. Place the pans in the oven side by side.

6. Bake the cake layers until they are golden brown and the tops spring back when lightly pressed with a finger, 19 to 24 minutes. Transfer the cake pans to wire racks and let the cake layers cool for 5 minutes. Run a sharp knife around the edge of each cake layer and give the pans a good shake to loosen the cakes. Invert each layer onto a wire rack and let them cool completely, topping side up, about 20 minutes longer.

7. Meanwhile, make the glaze: Add the confectioners' sugar to the reserved lemon juice and whisk until smooth, adding a little water or more lemon juice until the glaze is smooth but still runny enough that it will slowly drip down the side of the cake.

10 Steps to Sensational Gluten-Free Cakes

1. Read through recipes first, making sure you have all the right ingredients and equipment.

2. Prep the pan with vegetable oil spray and rice flour, or as the recipe directs.

3. Get creative with add-ins, such as chocolate chips, orange zest, or almond extract.

4. Mix the batter as directed in the recipe and, when making layer cakes, divide the batter evenly between the two layer pans so the layers will be done at the same time and will be even when stacked. You can cup out the batter, weigh it, or just use your eye.

5. Make sure your oven is baking at the right temperature.

6. Look for signs of doneness: The center of the cake will spring back when lightly touched. Yellow cakes will turn golden brown.

7. Cool cakes a little while in the pan, then let them finish cooling on a wire rack before frosting them.

8. Make a homemade frosting or glaze.

9. For pretty cakes, frost layers with a thin skim coating of buttercream or cream cheese frosting first and refrigerate the cake for the frosting to set. Then, spread a thicker layer of frosting over the first layer to finish.

10. Garnish your cake with a dusting of confectioners' sugar, a lemon twist, a handful of grated chocolate, or fresh blueberries to make it picture-perfect because you eat with your eyes first.

8. To assemble the cake, peel off and discard the parchment paper circles. Transfer one cake layer, topping side up, to a serving plate. Using a spoon, drizzle half of the glaze over the cake and allow it to drip over the edge. Place the second layer, topping side up, on top of the first layer and drizzle the remaining glaze over it. Garnish the top of the cake with the reserved ½ cup of blueberries.

NOTE: You can find soy flour at natural food stores and markets where gluten-free products are sold.

KEEP IT FRESH! Store the cake, lightly wrapped with aluminum foil or in a cake saver, on the kitchen counter for three days. Freeze only the cake layers, wrapped in aluminum foil, for up to one month. Let the layers thaw overnight on the counter before assembling and frosting the cake.

✦ ✦ ✦

The Cake Mix Doctor Says

If you are in a hurry, omit the crunchy topping for the Blueberry Muffin Cake and pour the lemon and blueberry batter into cake pans that have been misted with vegetable oil spray and dusted with rice flour. Assemble the cake with the lemon glaze as directed or frost it with the Lemon Cream Cheese Frosting (page 279). This is another layer cake that is especially pretty baked in 8-inch cake pans. If you use 8-inch cake pans the layers will need to bake for 25 to 30 minutes.

Lemon Lover's Chiffon Cake

✦ ✦ ✦

You'd think I was a fickle teenage girl the way I gushed about a favorite cake, yet a few days later, after I'd had another baking success, I'd started talking about how that recipe was my favorite. So, I hate to name favorites, but if I did, this cake would be right at the top. It would be my crush of the moment because the cake is moist and lemony, the filling is a snap to make, and the frosting is a wonderful combination of whipped cream and lemon curd, either homemade or from the supermarket. You'll love it, too.

serves: 10 to 12

prep: 30 minutes

bake: 18 to 22 minutes

cool: 25 minutes

For the cake

Vegetable oil spray, for misting the pans
2 teaspoons rice flour, for dusting the pans
1 extra large or 2 small lemons
3 large eggs
1 package (15 ounces) yellow gluten-free cake mix
¼ cup granulated sugar
⅔ cup orange juice (fresh or from a carton)
½ cup vegetable oil

For the filling and lemon whipped cream frosting

Julie's Lemon Curd (page 294) or 1 jar (10 ounces) gluten-free lemon curd
1 cup heavy (whipping) cream, chilled
1 tablespoon confectioners' sugar

DAIRY FREE

If it contains dairy products, omit the lemon curd. Substitute Vanilla Buttercream Frosting (page 271) for the lemon whipped cream frosting, using margarine instead of the butter and fresh lemon juice instead of the milk and omitting the vanilla. Use some of the frosting as the cake filling.

1. Make the cake: Place a rack in the center of the oven and preheat the oven to 350°F. Lightly mist two 9-inch round cake pans with vegetable oil spray, then dust them with the rice flour. Shake out the excess rice flour and set the pans aside.

2. Rinse and pat dry the lemon or lemons with paper towels, then grate the yellow zest onto a small plate. Measure 2 teaspoons for the cake batter and place it in a large mixing bowl. Cut the lemon in half and squeeze the juice through a fine sieve, discarding the seeds. Measure ¼ cup of lemon juice, pour it into the mixing bowl with the zest, and set the bowl aside.

3. Separate the eggs, placing the whites in another large mixing bowl and the yolks in the mixing bowl with the lemon zest and juice. Beat the whites with an electric mixer on high speed until stiff peaks form, 3 to 4 minutes. Set the beaten egg whites aside.

4. Place the cake mix, sugar, orange juice, and oil in the bowl with the egg yolks and lemon and beat with an electric mixer on low speed until the ingredients are just incorporated, 30 seconds. Stop the machine and scrape down the side of the bowl with a rubber spatula. Increase the mixer speed to medium and beat the batter until smooth, 1 to 1½ minutes longer, scraping down the side of the bowl again if needed. Using a rubber spatula and giving the bowl quarter turns, gently fold the egg whites into the batter until no traces of whites remain and the batter has lightened. Divide the batter evenly between the 2 prepared cake pans, smoothing the tops with the rubber spatula. Place the pans in the oven side by side. Place a large mixing bowl and electric mixer beaters in the refrigerator to chill.

5. Bake the cake layers until they are golden brown and the tops spring back when lightly pressed with a finger, 18 to 22 minutes. Transfer the cake pans to wire racks and let the cake layers cool for 5 minutes. Run a sharp knife around the edge of each cake layer and give the pans a good shake to loosen the cakes. Invert each layer onto a wire rack, then invert it again onto another rack so that the layers are right side up. Let the layers cool completely, about 20 minutes longer.

6. Meanwhile, make the filling and frosting: Measure ⅔ cup of lemon curd for the filling and set it aside in a small microwave-safe glass bowl. Pour the cream into the chilled mixing bowl. Using the refrigerated mixer beaters, beat the cream with an electric mixer on high speed until stiff peaks form, 3 minutes. Fold in the confectioners' sugar and ¼ cup of lemon curd. Beat again on low speed until the lemon curd is incorporated, 30 seconds. Refrigerate the frosting until ready to use.

7. To assemble the cake, place the glass bowl with lemon curd for the filling in a microwave oven and microwave on high power for 10 seconds to warm it. Transfer one cake layer, right

recipe
reminders

Made for:

Prep Notes:

Don't Forget:

Special Touches:

I'm Thinking Key Lime Chiffon

Use bottled key lime juice in the cake and substitute grated Persian or key lime zest for the lemon zest. Use a lime curd in between the layers and in the frosting.

side up, to a serving plate. Spread the top with the warmed lemon curd. Place the second layer, right side up, on top of the first and frost the top and side of the cake with the lemon whipped cream frosting. Refrigerate the cake until time to serve.

KEEP IT FRESH! Store the cake in a cake saver in the refrigerator for up to three days. Freeze only the cake layers, wrapped in aluminum foil, for up to one month. Let the layers thaw overnight on the kitchen counter before assembling and frosting the cake.

✦ ✦ ✦

The Cake Mix Doctor Says

Because you get more volume from room temperature eggs, here is a quick trick. Bring chilled eggs right from the fridge to room temperature by placing them, uncracked, in a small bowl and add hot tap water to cover. Let them sit for 6 to 8 minutes, then dry them, crack and separate them, and whip the whites high!

Make the cake even prettier with strips of Candied Citrus Garnish (page 115) arranged in the top center.

Easy Orange Layer Cake

✦ ✦ ✦

The easiest way to doctor up any cake mix is to use orange juice instead of water. That trick makes this pretty layer cake a breeze to make because you just pour refrigerated orange juice into a measuring cup. If you have two oranges, zest one for the cake and one for the frosting and use the fresh juice. But the idea is to keep this cake easy and to use what you have. Orange cakes appeal to all ages, so they make great birthday cakes. They're festive and as suitable at a summer barbecue as they are for a Thanksgiving dinner.

serves: **10 to 12**

prep: **25 minutes**

bake: **19 to 24 minutes**

cool: **25 minutes**

Vegetable oil spray, for misting the pans
2 teaspoons rice flour, for dusting the pans
1 package (15 ounces) yellow gluten-free cake mix
¼ cup granulated sugar
⅔ cup plus 1 tablespoon orange juice (fresh or from a carton)
8 tablespoons (1 stick) unsalted butter, at room temperature
3 large eggs
1 teaspoon pure vanilla extract
1 teaspoon orange zest (optional, see Note)
Orange Cream Cheese Frosting (page 278)

1. Place a rack in the center of the oven and preheat the oven to 350°F. Lightly mist two 9-inch round cake pans with vegetable oil spray, then dust them with the rice flour. Shake out the excess rice flour and set the pans aside.

DAIRY FREE

Use ½ cup of vegetable oil in the cake batter instead of the butter. And instead of making the Orange Cream Cheese Frosting, make a dairy-free orange buttercream by blending 6 tablespoons of soft margarine, 2 to 3 cups of confectioners' sugar, and 2 to 3 tablespoons of orange juice.

2. Place the cake mix, sugar, orange juice, butter, eggs, vanilla, and orange zest, if using, in a large mixing bowl and beat with an electric mixer on low speed until the ingredients are just incorporated, 30 seconds. Stop the machine and scrape down the side of the bowl with a rubber spatula. Increase the mixer speed to medium and beat the batter until smooth, 1 to 1½ minutes longer, scraping down the side of the bowl again if needed. Divide the batter evenly between the 2 prepared cake pans, smoothing the tops with the rubber spatula. Place the pans in the oven side by side.

3. Bake the cake layers until they are golden brown and the tops spring back when lightly pressed with a finger, 19 to 24 minutes. Transfer the cake pans to wire racks and let the cake layers cool for 5 minutes. Run a sharp knife around the edge of each cake layer and give the pans a good shake to loosen the cakes. Invert each layer onto a wire rack, then invert it again onto another rack so that the layers are right side up. Let the layers cool completely, about 20 minutes longer.

4. Meanwhile, make the Orange Cream Cheese Frosting.

5. To assemble the cake, transfer one layer, right side up, to a serving plate. Spread the top with about 1 cup of the frosting. Place the second cake layer, right side up, on top of the first layer and frost the top and side of the cake, working with smooth, clean strokes. To make slicing easier, place the uncovered cake in the refrigerator until the frosting sets, 10 to 15 minutes.

NOTE: If you have two oranges and are squeezing them for the juice in this recipe, first rinse, dry, and grate 1 teaspoon of the zest of one orange into the cake batter and save the zest of the second orange for the frosting. But if you have just one orange, save its orange zest for the frosting. Slice the orange and squeeze its juice into a measuring cup. What you lack in fresh juice for this recipe make up by adding OJ from a carton.

Candied Orange Wheels

It's easy to make beautiful candied orange slices to garnish your favorite cake. Thin-skinned oranges are the best for candying. To do this, preheat the oven to 200°F. Make a simple syrup by placing 1 cup of sugar and 1 cup of water in a heavy saucepan over medium heat and bringing them to a boil, stirring constantly until the sugar dissolves. Reduce the heat to low and let the simple syrup simmer.

Meanwhile, using a sharp knife, cut a medium-size orange into very thin slices. Remove any seeds. Using tongs, carefully dip the orange slices into the hot syrup and hold them there until well coated, 30 seconds. Remove the orange slices from the syrup, let the excess syrup drip off, and arrange the orange slices on a silicone baking mat placed on top of a baking sheet. Bake the coated orange slices until they are crisp and golden, 20 minutes.

Remove the baking sheet from the oven and let the candied orange slices cool completely on the baking sheet. Once they are cool, carefully remove the orange slices from the baking sheet and store them in an airtight container. They will keep for two weeks. You can also use this method to candy lemon and lime slices.

KEEP IT FRESH! If your kitchen is cool, store the cake, lightly wrapped with aluminum foil or in a cake saver, on the kitchen counter for twenty-four hours. Or, store it in the refrigerator for three days. Freeze only the cake layers, wrapped in aluminum foil, for up to one month. Let the layers thaw overnight on the counter before assembling and frosting the cake.

✦ ✦ ✦

The Cake Mix Doctor Says

This cake is even prettier made as an 8-inch cake. Bake the 8-inch round layers for 24 to 29 minutes. And turn this cake into an adult orange rum cake by brushing the layers with dark rum after they come out of the oven. Frost as directed, adding a few Candied Orange Wheels (see above). Yum.

8 Crazy-Good Birthday Party Cakes for Kids

Apricot Cake
with White Chocolate
Cream Cheese Frosting

✦ ✦ ✦

I f you want an elegant cake this is it, perfect for birthdays and parties and all things special. I don't know what I like better—the pale apricot color of the cake or the apricot preserves between the layers or the white chocolate frosting. They are great together and beg to be served for a springtime party or a cozy winter dinner with friends.

serves: **10 to 12**

prep: **45 minutes**

bake: **18 to 22 minutes**

cool: **25 minutes**

Vegetable oil spray, for misting the pans
2 teaspoons rice flour, for dusting the pans
1 can (15.25 ounces) apricot halves packed in heavy syrup
1 package (15 ounces) yellow gluten-free cake mix
¼ cup (half of a 3.4-ounce package) vanilla instant pudding mix
½ cup vegetable oil
3 large eggs
1 teaspoon pure vanilla extract
½ teaspoon pure almond extract
⅔ cup to 1 cup apricot all-fruit preserves (see Note)
White Chocolate Cream Cheese Frosting (page 280)

DAIRY FREE

O mit the white chocolate and substitute a dairy-free cream cheese, such as Better Than Cream Cheese made by Tofutti, and margarine for the cream cheese and butter in the White Chocolate Cream Cheese Frosting.

1. Place a rack in the center of the oven and preheat the oven to 350°F. Lightly mist two 9-inch round cake pans with vegetable oil spray, then dust them with the rice flour. Shake out the excess rice flour and set the pans aside.

recipe reminders

Made for:

_____

_____

_____

_____

Prep Notes:

_____

_____

_____

_____

Don't Forget:

_____

_____

_____

_____

Special Touches:

_____

_____

_____

_____

2. Drain the apricots over a glass measuring cup. Set the apricot liquid aside. Place the drained apricots in a food processor fitted with a steel blade and process until smooth, 8 to 10 pulses. You should have about ¾ cup of pureed apricots. If not, add enough of the reserved apricot liquid to the pureed fruit to make ¾ cup. Set the apricot puree aside. Discard the remaining apricot liquid.

3. Place the cake mix and pudding mix in a large mixing bowl and stir to combine. Add the pureed apricots, oil, eggs, and vanilla and almond extracts and beat with an electric mixer on low speed until the ingredients are just incorporated, 30 seconds. Stop the machine and scrape down the side of the bowl with a rubber spatula. Increase the mixer speed to medium and beat the batter until smooth, 1 to 1½ minutes longer, scraping down the side of the bowl again if needed. Divide the batter evenly between the 2 prepared cake pans, smoothing the tops with the rubber spatula. Place the pans in the oven side by side.

4. Bake the cake layers until they are golden brown and the tops spring back when lightly pressed with a finger, 18 to 22 minutes. Transfer the cake pans to wire racks and let the cake layers cool for 5 minutes. Run a sharp knife around the edge of each cake layer and give the pans a good shake to loosen the cakes. Invert each layer onto a wire rack, then invert it again onto another rack so that the layers are right side up. Let the layers cool completely, about 20 minutes longer.

5. Meanwhile, put the apricot preserves in a small bowl and stir it to soften. Make the White Chocolate Cream Cheese Frosting.

6. To assemble the cake, using a serrated knife, slice each cake layer in half crosswise. Transfer the bottom half of one layer, cut side up, to a serving plate. Spread the cut side with half of the apricot preserves, then place the top half over it, cut side down. Spread the top of this layer with 1 cup of the frosting. Place the bottom of the second layer, cut side up, on top of the first layer. Spread that layer with the remaining apricot preserves. Place the top half of the second layer on top, cut side down. Frost the top and side of the cake with the remaining frosting, working with smooth, clean strokes. To make slicing easier, place the uncovered cake in the refrigerator until the frosting sets, 15 minutes.

NOTES: Use as much or as little apricot preserves as you like between the cake layers. In my opinion, more is better!

For a really festive cake, garnish with white chocolate curls (see Curly Q&A, page 83) and fresh apricot slices.

KEEP IT FRESH! If your kitchen is cool, store the cake, lightly wrapped or in a cake saver, on the kitchen counter for twenty-four hours. Or, store it in the refrigerator for three days. Freeze only the cake layers, wrapped in aluminum foil, for up to one month. Let the layers thaw overnight on the counter before assembling and frosting the cake.

✦ ✦ ✦

The Cake Mix Doctor Says

I found with testing that different brands of canned apricot halves, even when the can is the same size, contain different amounts of apricots. Some brands have more apricots and some have more liquid. As long as you have ¾ cup of pureed apricots, even if you have to thin the puree a little with the liquid in which they were packed to make ¾ cup, this is fine. The apricots make this a very moist cake.

Coconut Cake
with Fluffy Marshmallow Frosting

✦ ✦ ✦

serves: 18 to 20

prep: 45 minutes

bake: 35 to 40 minutes

cool: 35 minutes

I come from coconut cake country—the South—and this coconut cake was a big hit down here. No one suspected it contained a gluten-free mix. Well, okay, they had an idea because my kitchen had been devoted to gluten-free baking for several months. But I will bet if you place this cake on a Southern dining room sideboard during the winter holidays people will ooh and aah. Like the Bride's Cake, this is another big cake made from two packages of cake mix. It's perfect for large gatherings. The frosting is my quick version of the more time-consuming seven minute frosting. And the topping is simple—a pile of flaked coconut.

Vegetable oil spray, for misting the pans

2 teaspoons rice flour, for dusting the pans

2 packages (15 ounces each) yellow gluten-free
    cake mix

1 package (3.4 ounces) vanilla instant pudding mix

⅓ cup granulated sugar

1 cup reduced-fat sour cream

¾ cup light coconut milk (see Notes)

¾ cup vegetable oil

4 large egg whites

2 large eggs

1 tablespoon pure vanilla extract (see Notes)

2 teaspoons gluten-free coconut extract
    (see Notes)

Fluffy Marshmallow Frosting (page 282)

1 package (7 ounces, 2⅔ cups; see Notes)
    sweetened flaked coconut

DAIRY FREE

Substitute plain soy yogurt or full-fat coconut milk for the sour cream in the cake.

1. Place a rack in the center of the oven and preheat the oven to 350°F. Take two 9-inch round cake pans that are at least 2 inches deep and lightly mist them with vegetable oil spray. Dust the cake pans with the rice flour, shake out the excess rice flour, and set the pans aside.

2. Place the cake mix, pudding mix, and sugar in a large mixing bowl and stir to combine. Add the sour cream, coconut milk, oil, egg whites, eggs, and vanilla and coconut extracts and beat with an electric mixer on low speed until the ingredients are just incorporated, 45 seconds. Stop the machine and scrape down the side of the bowl with a rubber spatula. Increase the mixer speed to medium and beat the batter until smooth, 1 to 1½ minutes longer, scraping down the side of the bowl again if needed. The batter should look well blended. Divide the batter evenly between the 2 prepared pans, smoothing the tops with the rubber spatula. Place the pans in the oven side by side.

Love the Lime in the Coconut Cake

This cake is for coconut purists. If you want a more tropical rendition, spread lime curd between the layers and frost the top and side of the cake with the White Chocolate Cream Cheese Frosting (page 280). Garnish the top with 1 cup of flaked coconut, lightly toasted in a 350°F oven for 5 to 6 minutes.

3. Bake the cake layers until they are lightly browned and the tops spring back when lightly pressed with a finger, 35 to 40 minutes. Transfer the cake pans to wire racks and let the cake layers cool for 5 minutes. Run a sharp knife around the edge of each cake layer and give the pans a good shake to loosen the cakes. Invert each layer onto a wire rack, then invert it again onto another rack so that the layers are right side up. Let the layers cool completely, about 30 minutes longer.

4. Meanwhile, make the Fluffy Marshmallow Frosting.

5. To assemble, using a serrated knife, slice each cake layer in half crosswise. Transfer the bottom half of one layer, cut side up, to a serving plate. Spread the cut side with a heaping 1 cup of frosting. Sprinkle ½ cup of the coconut on top. Place the top half over it, cut side down, then frost the top of this layer with a heaping 1 cup of frosting and sprinkle ½ cup of the coconut over it. Repeat with the second layer, making sure to reserve enough frosting to generously frost the side and top of the cake. Sprinkle the remaining coconut, about 1 cup, on top of the cake for garnish.

NOTES: Canned light coconut milk is sold in supermarkets with other ingredients for Thai cooking. If you like, you can omit the coconut milk and just add water.

If you use clear vanilla extract, sold where you buy cake decorating supplies, this will keep the batter white, but it's not really necessary. And be sure to read the label on the coconut extract. Some is imitation coconut flavoring and some is pure coconut extract, which is more expensive. Either should be gluten-free, but read the label to make sure.

To make sure you've got enough coconut to decorate this cake, know that there are about 2⅔ cups sweetened flaked coconut in a 7-ounce bag and about 5⅓ cups coconut in a 14-ounce bag.

KEEP IT FRESH! Store the cake in a cake saver in the refrigerator for up to three days. Freeze only the cake layers, wrapped in aluminum foil, for up to one month. Let the layers thaw overnight on the kitchen counter before assembling and frosting the cake.

✦ ✦ ✦

The Cake Mix Doctor Says

Because this is a tall cake, it is easier to assemble if the layers are flat, not domed. You can level the ¼-inch of dome off the top of each baked and cooled layer by slicing it off using a serrated knife, or you can lightly press down on the layers with a clean kitchen towel immediately after they come out of the oven.

recipe reminders

Made for:

_____

_____

_____

_____

Prep Notes:

_____

_____

_____

_____

Don't Forget:

_____

_____

_____

_____

Special Touches:

_____

_____

_____

_____

_____

Banana Cake
with Quick Caramel Frosting

✦ ✦ ✦

serves: **10 to 12**

prep: **25 minutes**

bake: **18 to 22 minutes**

cool: **25 minutes**

DAIRY FREE

The cake is dairy-free, but there are butter and milk in the Quick Caramel Frosting. Substitute one of the cream cheese frostings, making it with dairy-free cream cheese and margarine. Or make a glaze with orange juice and confectioners' sugar and stack the banana layers, placing a spoonful of glaze between them and pouring the remainder over the top of the cake.

L ittle surprise that mashed ripe bananas make this an awesome cake. Fruit works so well in gluten-free recipes. I am not sure whether it's the moisture it adds or the natural acidity but whenever fruit is in the batter, be it banana, apricot, or strawberry, the result is a great cake. Anytime you bake with bananas try to use very ripe ones. I mean so ripe and black no one wants to eat one—that's when they're perfect for baking! Frost the cake with my caramel frosting. It seals the sweet deal.

Vegetable oil spray, for misting the pans
2 teaspoons rice flour, for dusting the pans
1 package (15 ounces) yellow gluten-free cake mix
1 heaping cup mashed bananas
    (from 3 small very ripe bananas)
½ cup vegetable oil
3 large eggs
2 teaspoons pure vanilla extract
1 teaspoon ground cinnamon
Quick Caramel Frosting (page 285)

1. Place a rack in the center of the oven and preheat the oven to 350°F. Lightly mist two 9-inch round cake pans with vegetable oil spray, then dust them with the rice flour. Shake out the excess rice flour and set the pans aside.

2. Place the cake mix, bananas, oil, eggs, vanilla, and cinnamon in a large mixing bowl and beat with an electric mixer on low speed until the ingredients are just incorporated, 30 seconds. Stop the machine and scrape down the side of the bowl with a rubber spatula. Increase the mixer speed to medium and beat the batter until smooth, 1 to 1½ minutes longer, scraping down the side of the bowl again if needed. Divide the batter evenly between the 2 prepared cake pans, smoothing the tops with the rubber spatula. Place the pans in the oven side by side.

3. Bake the cake layers until they are golden brown and the tops spring back when lightly pressed with a finger, 18 to 22 minutes. Transfer the cake pans to wire racks and let the cake layers cool for 5 minutes. Run a sharp knife around the edge of each cake layer and give the pans a good shake to loosen the cakes. Invert each layer onto a wire rack, then invert it again onto another rack so that the layers are right side up. Let the layers cool completely, about 20 minutes longer.

4. Meanwhile, make the Quick Caramel Frosting and keep it warm.

5. To assemble the cake, transfer one layer, right side up, to a serving plate. Spread the top with about 1 cup of the frosting. Place the second cake layer, right side up, on top of the first layer and frost the top and side of the cake, working with smooth, clean strokes. The frosting will look thin when it is warm but it will harden and set as it cools. If it gets too hard to work with a spatula, place the pan back over low heat and stir the frosting with a wooden spoon until it softens then resume frosting. If the frosting is still too stiff, add a tablespoon of milk and stir over low heat until smooth.

recipe reminders

Made for:

_____

_____

_____

Prep Notes:

_____

_____

_____

Don't Forget:

_____

_____

_____

Special Touches:

_____

_____

_____

_____

KEEP IT FRESH! Store the cake, lightly wrapped or in a cake saver, on the kitchen counter for three days. Freeze only the cake layers, wrapped in aluminum foil, for up to one month. Let the layers thaw overnight on the counter before assembling and frosting the cake.

✦ ✦ ✦

The Cake Mix Doctor Says

If you like, you can scatter ½ cup of chopped toasted pecans on top of the cake to garnish it while the frosting is still warm. If you have extra chopped pecans, press them along the bottom of the cake. And if you want to turn this into a chocolate-covered banana cake, frost it with the Chocolate Pan Frosting on page 289.

Hummingbird Cake
with Lighter Cream Cheese Frosting

✦ ◆ ✦

Banana and pineapple taste so good together you just want to hum. And that is the only explanation I can give for the name of this quirky and wonderful cake. You hum like a hummingbird when you eat it. When frosted with a lighter version of my cream cheese frosting and topped with toasted pecans it's not just a hummingbird cake, it's a humdinger!

Vegetable oil spray, for misting the pans
2 teaspoons rice flour, for dusting the pans
1 can (8 ounces) crushed pineapple
1 package (15 ounces) yellow gluten-free cake mix
1 cup mashed bananas (from 2 medium-size very ripe
  bananas, see Note)
½ cup vegetable oil
3 large eggs
2 teaspoons pure vanilla extract
1 teaspoon ground cinnamon
Lighter Cream Cheese Frosting (page 274)
½ cup chopped toasted pecans (optional; see box, page 172),
  for the garnish

1. Place the rack in the center of the oven and preheat the oven to 350°F. Lightly mist two 9-inch round cake pans with vegetable oil spray, then dust them with the rice flour. Shake out the excess rice flour and set the pans aside.

serves: **10 to 12**

prep: **30 minutes**

bake: **18 to 22 minutes**

cool: **25 minutes**

DAIRY FREE

When making the Lighter Cream Cheese Frosting, substitute a dairy-free cream cheese, such as Better Than Cream Cheese made by Tofutti, for the cream cheese and use margarine instead of the butter.

2. Drain the can of pineapple and set the liquid aside for another use (see The Cake Mix Doctor Says) or discard it. Place ½ cup of the drained pineapple in a large mixing bowl. Add the cake mix, mashed banana, oil, eggs, vanilla, and cinnamon and beat with an electric mixer on low speed until the ingredients are just incorporated, 30 seconds. Stop the machine and scrape down the side of the bowl with a rubber spatula. Increase the mixer speed to medium and beat the batter until smooth, 1 to 1½ minutes longer, scraping down the side of the bowl again if needed. Divide the batter evenly between the 2 prepared cake pans, smoothing the tops with the rubber spatula. Place the pans in the oven side by side.

3. Bake the cake layers until they are golden brown and the tops spring back when lightly pressed with a finger, 18 to 22 minutes. Transfer the cake pans to wire racks and let the cake layers cool for 5 minutes. Run a sharp knife around the edge of each cake layer and give the pans a good shake to loosen the cakes. Invert each layer onto a wire rack, then invert it again onto another rack so that the layers are right side up. Let the layers cool completely, about 20 minutes longer.

4. Meanwhile, make the Lighter Cream Cheese Frosting.

5. To assemble the cake, transfer one layer, right side up, to a serving plate. Spread the top with about 1 cup of the frosting. Place the second cake layer, right side up, on top of the first layer and frost the top and side of the cake, working with smooth, clean strokes. Scatter the pecans on top of the cake as a garnish, if desired. To make slicing easier, place the uncovered cake in the refrigerator until the frosting sets, 10 to 15 minutes.

NOTE: This cake and any cake made with bananas tastes best when the bananas are very ripe. The blacker the banana skins, the better the flavor!

KEEP IT FRESH! If your kitchen is cool, store the cake, lightly wrapped or in a cake saver, on the kitchen counter for twenty-four hours. Or, store it in the refrigerator for three days. Freeze only the cake layers, wrapped in aluminum foil, for up to one month. Let the layers thaw overnight on the counter before assembling and frosting the cake.

✦ ✦ ✦

The Cake Mix Doctor Says

Use the leftover pineapple liquid to make a speedy buttercream frosting. Beat 8 tablespoons (1 stick) of soft butter with 3 cups of confectioners' sugar and 2 to 3 tablespoons of pineapple liquid until smooth and light. This frosting allows the cake to be stored at room temperature.

recipe reminders

Made for: _____

_____

_____

_____

_____

Prep Notes: _____

_____

_____

_____

_____

Don't Forget: _____

_____

_____

_____

_____

Special Touches: _____

_____

_____

_____

_____

Classic Carrot Cake
with Cream Cheese Frosting

✦ ✦ ✦

serves: 10 to 12

prep: 35 minutes

bake: 24 to 27 minutes

cool: 25 minutes

What is a cake book without a carrot cake recipe? This is the moist cake of our childhoods, likely the first cake we baked all by ourselves for a dinner party, and little surprise, it's the cake that our kids love, too. But a gluten-free version? Is this possible? You bet. I packed not just freshly shredded carrots—not the ones from the bag—but also golden raisins, applesauce, and spices into this recipe. Covered with the customary cream cheese frosting, this cake is timeless.

Vegetable oil spray, for misting the pans

2 teaspoons rice flour, for dusting the pans

2 medium-size carrots

½ cup golden raisins

1 package (15 ounces) yellow gluten-free cake mix

¼ cup (half of a 3.4-ounce package) vanilla instant
   pudding mix

¾ cup unsweetened applesauce

½ cup vegetable oil

3 large eggs

2 teaspoons ground cinnamon

¼ teaspoon ground nutmeg

1 teaspoon pure vanilla extract

Cream Cheese Frosting (page 273)

½ cup chopped walnuts (optional), for the garnish

DAIRY FREE

When making the Cream Cheese Frosting, substitute margarine for the butter and a dairy-free cream cheese, such as Better Than Cream Cheese made by Tofutti, for the cream cheese.

1. Place a rack in the center of the oven and preheat the oven to 350°F. Lightly mist two 9-inch round cake pans with vegetable oil spray, then dust them with the rice flour. Shake out the excess rice flour and set the pans aside.

2. Peel the carrots and grate them to yield 1 heaping lightly packed cup. Place the carrots in a small bowl. Coarsely chop the raisins and add them to the carrots. Measure 1 tablespoon of the cake mix and toss this with the carrots and raisins. Set the carrot mixture aside.

3. Place the remaining cake mix in a large mixing bowl. Stir in the pudding mix. Add the applesauce, oil, eggs, cinnamon, nutmeg, and vanilla and beat with an electric mixer on low speed until the ingredients are just incorporated, 30 seconds. Stop the machine and scrape down the side of the bowl with a rubber spatula. Increase the mixer speed to medium and beat the batter until smooth, 1 to 1½ minutes longer, scraping down the side of the bowl again if needed. The batter should look well blended. Stir in

recipe reminders

Made for:

_____

_____

_____

_____

Prep Notes:

_____

_____

_____

_____

Don't Forget:

_____

_____

_____

_____

Special Touches:

_____

_____

_____

_____

the carrot mixture until well combined. Divide the batter evenly between the 2 prepared cake pans, smoothing the tops with the rubber spatula. Place the pans in the oven side by side.

4. Bake the cake layers until they are golden brown and the tops spring back when lightly pressed with a finger, 24 to 27 minutes. Transfer the cake pans to wire racks and let the cake layers cool for 5 minutes. Run a sharp knife around the edge of each cake layer and give the pans a good shake to loosen the cakes. Invert each layer onto a wire rack, then invert it again onto another rack so that the layers are right side up. Let the layers cool completely, about 20 minutes longer.

5. Meanwhile, make the Cream Cheese Frosting.

6. To assemble the cake, transfer one layer, right side up, to a serving plate. Spread the top with about 1 cup of the frosting. Place the second cake layer, right side up, on top of the first layer and frost the top and side of the cake, working with smooth, clean strokes. Scatter the walnuts, if using, on top of the cake or press them into the frosting around the side of the cake. To make slicing easier, place the uncovered cake in the refrigerator until the frosting sets, 10 to 15 minutes.

KEEP IT FRESH! If your kitchen is cool, store the cake, lightly wrapped or in a cake saver, on the kitchen counter for twenty-four hours. Or, store it in the refrigerator for three days. Freeze only the cake layers, wrapped in aluminum foil, for up to one month. Let the layers thaw overnight on the counter before assembling and frosting the cake.

✦ ✦ ✦

7 Elegant Cakes for a Grown-Up Birthday Party

The Cake Mix Doctor Says

To make a really beautiful carrot cake, apply a thin skim coat of frosting on the top and side and chill the cake for 10 minutes. Then, remove the cake from the refrigerator and apply a more generous layer with the remaining frosting to finish the cake.

Snickerdoodle Cake

✦ ✦ ✦

serves: **10 to 12**

prep: **30 minutes**

bake: **18 to 22 minutes**

cool: **25 minutes**

If you are on a gluten-free diet and adore cinnamon, what's there for you? This cake, named for the classic American cinnamon cookie (see page 258 for the gluten-free version), is packed with cinnamon, from the crunchy layer that goes into the bottom of the pans, to the batter poured on top, to the cream cheese frosting spread over the baked layers. This is like one big cinnamon cookie calling your name. Smells like one, too!

For the crunchy topping

Vegetable oil spray, for misting the pans
Parchment paper, for lining the pans
¾ cup lightly packed light brown sugar
½ teaspoon ground cinnamon
3 tablespoons unsalted butter, slightly chilled

For the cake

1 package (15 ounces) yellow gluten-free cake mix
¼ cup (half of a 3.4-ounce package) vanilla instant pudding mix
1 teaspoon ground cinnamon
¾ cup milk
8 tablespoons (1 stick) unsalted butter, melted
3 large eggs
2 teaspoons pure vanilla extract

For the cinnamon cream cheese frosting

- 4 ounces (half of an 8-ounce package) reduced-fat cream cheese, at room temperature
- 4 tablespoons (½ stick) unsalted butter, at room temperature
- 2½ cups confectioners' sugar, sifted
- 2 teaspoons pure vanilla extract
- ¼ teaspoon ground cinnamon

1. Place a rack in the center of the oven and preheat the oven to 350°F. Lightly mist two 9-inch round cake pans with vegetable oil spray. Trace the bottom of one of the cake pans onto 2 pieces of parchment paper, then cut along the trace marks. Place one circle of parchment paper in the bottom of each of the prepared cake pans.

2. Make the crunchy topping: Place the brown sugar and ½ teaspoon of cinnamon in a small bowl and stir to combine. Cut the butter into 1-inch pieces and, using 2 sharp knives or a pastry blender, cut the butter into the brown sugar mixture until it is crumbly. Spoon half of the topping mixture into each of the prepared cake pans, dividing it evenly between them and spreading it out evenly across the bottoms of the pans. Set the pans aside.

3. Make the cake: Place the cake mix, pudding mix, and 1 teaspoon of cinnamon in a large bowl and stir to combine. Add the milk, melted butter, eggs, and 2 teaspoons of vanilla and beat with an electric mixer on low speed until the ingredients are just incorporated, 30 seconds. Stop the machine and scrape down the side of the bowl with a rubber spatula. Increase the mixer speed to medium and beat the batter until smooth, 1 to 1½ minutes longer, scraping down the side of the bowl again if needed. Divide the batter evenly between the 2 prepared cake pans, spreading the batter over the topping and smoothing the tops with the rubber spatula. Place the pans in the oven side by side.

4. Bake the cake layers until they are golden brown and the tops spring back when lightly pressed with a finger, 18 to 22 minutes. Transfer the cake pans to wire racks and let the cake layers cool for 5 minutes. Run a sharp knife around the edge of each cake layer and give the pans a good shake to loosen the cakes. Invert each layer onto a wire rack and let them cool completely, topping side up, about 20 minutes longer.

5. Meanwhile, make the cinnamon cream cheese frosting: Place the cream cheese and butter in a medium-size mixing bowl and beat with an electric mixer on low speed until combined, 30 seconds. Stop the machine. Add the confectioners' sugar a bit at a time, beating with the mixer on low speed until the sugar is well incorporated, 1 minute. Add the 2 teaspoons of vanilla and ¼ teaspoon of cinnamon, then increase the mixer speed to medium and beat the frosting until fluffy, 1 minute longer.

6. To assemble the cake, peel off and discard the parchment paper circles. Transfer one cake layer, topping side up, to a serving plate. Spread the top with about 1 cup of the frosting. Place the second cake layer, topping side up, on top of the first layer and frost only the side of the cake. To make slicing easier, place the uncovered cake in the refrigerator until the frosting sets, 10 minutes.

KEEP IT FRESH! If your kitchen is cool, store the cake, lightly wrapped with aluminum foil or in a cake saver, on the kitchen counter for twenty-four hours. Or, store it in the refrigerator for up to three days. Freeze only the cake layers, wrapped in aluminum foil, for up to one month. Let the layers thaw overnight on the counter before assembling and frosting the cake.

✦ ✦ ✦

The Cake Mix Doctor Says

A Snickerdoodle Cake was in my first cookbook and remains a favorite. Ground cinnamon is easy to add to cake batters, enlivening yellow cakes and giving an exotic touch to chocolate cakes.

German Chocolate Cake

✦ ✦ ✦

serves: **10 to 12**

prep: **45 minutes**

bake: **18 to 22 minutes**

cool: **25 minutes**

DAIRY FREE

Use water instead of milk in the cake, and prepare a simple buttercream frosting, either chocolate (page 287) or vanilla (page 271), made with margarine in place of the butter and water in place of the milk.

Up until now, I loved the flavor of my German chocolate cake made with a conventional cake mix. But now, using a gluten-free mix and flavoring the batter with melted German's chocolate, this cake takes the cake. Bake two layers then split them into four and sandwich them with the classic coconut and pecan frosting. This is a rich and festive cake just right for holidays. You can make it a day ahead because it stays moist in the fridge—that is if it lasts that long!

For the cake

Vegetable oil spray,
   for misting the pans
2 teaspoons rice flour, for dusting the pans
1 bar (4 ounces) German's sweet chocolate
1 package (15 ounces) yellow gluten-free cake mix
¼ cup (half of a 3.4-ounce package) vanilla instant
   pudding mix
¾ cup milk (see Note)
½ cup vegetable oil
3 large eggs, lightly beaten
2 teaspoons pure vanilla extract

For the coconut pecan frosting

- 1 cup evaporated milk
- 1 cup granulated sugar
- 8 tablespoons (1 stick) unsalted butter
- 3 large egg yolks
- 1 teaspoon pure vanilla extract
- 1 package (7 ounces, 2⅔ cups) sweetened flaked coconut (see The Cake Mix Doctor Says, page 63)
- 1 cup chopped pecans (see The Cake Mix Doctor Says, page 63)

1. Make the cake: Place a rack in the center of the oven and preheat the oven to 350°F. Lightly mist two 9-inch round cake pans with vegetable oil spray, then dust them with the rice flour. Shake out the excess rice flour and set the pans aside.

2. Melt the chocolate by breaking it into squares, placing it in a heavy saucepan over very low heat, and stirring constantly, about 5 minutes. Or place the chocolate squares in a medium-size microwave-safe glass bowl and microwave on high power for 45 seconds to 1 minute, then stir until the chocolate has melted completely. Scrape the melted chocolate into a large mixing bowl.

3. Place the cake mix, pudding mix, milk, oil, eggs, and 2 teaspoons of vanilla in the mixing bowl with the chocolate and beat with an electric mixer on low speed until the ingredients are just incorporated, 30 seconds. Stop the machine and scrape down the side of the bowl with a rubber spatula. Increase the mixer speed to medium and beat the batter until smooth, 1 to 1½ minutes longer, scraping down the side of the bowl again if needed. The batter should look well blended. Divide the batter evenly between the 2 prepared pans, smoothing the tops with the rubber spatula. Place the pans in the oven side by side.

4. Bake the cake layers until the tops spring back when lightly pressed with a finger, 18 to 22 minutes.

Deep in the Heart of Texas

There is nothing German about the German Chocolate Cake, the dazzling layer cake that made the rounds at Texas and Oklahoma parties in the 1950s and is still popular today.

According to *The Dallas Morning News,* the first recipe for the cake—based on Baker's German's sweet chocolate—came from a Texas homemaker and was printed in that newspaper in 1957. Amazingly, the recipe drove Texas sales of German's chocolate through the roof. U.S. sales of German's chocolate shot up 73 percent that year.

The chocolate was named for Samuel German—an Englishman who emigrated to Boston and worked at the Walter Baker Chocolate Company in the mid-1800s. German was intrigued by chocolate, and he developed his own particular style. It would be named for him, but manufactured by Baker.

5. While the cakes bake, make the coconut pecan frosting: Place the evaporated milk, sugar, butter, and egg yolks in a large saucepan over medium heat. Cook, stirring constantly with a wooden spoon, until thickened and golden brown in color, 10 to 12 minutes. Remove the pan from the heat and stir in the vanilla. Let the frosting cool to room temperature for a spreading consistency, 30 minutes, then fold in the coconut and pecans.

6. When the cakes test done, transfer the cake pans to wire racks and let the cake layers cool for 5 minutes. Run a sharp knife around the edge of each cake layer and give the pans a good shake to loosen the cakes. Invert each layer onto a wire rack, then invert it again onto another rack so that the layers are right side up. Let the layers cool completely, about 20 minutes longer.

7. To assemble the cake, using a serrated knife, slice each cake layer in half crosswise. Transfer the bottom half of one

Stack and Frost: Layer Cake Poetry

When cake layers are cool to the touch,
You can stack and frost your cake.
Place the flattest layer on a pretty plate,
Add a cup of frosting, smoothing it over the top,
And put the second layer on top of the first.
Run a thin layer of frosting around the side,
And you're nearly done.
Slather more frosting on the side but leave plenty
for the top.
Make swirls, curls, and luscious designs
with a knife or spoon,
Then slice and fork into deliciousness,
And share with friends.

layer, cut side up, to a serving plate. Spread the cut side with 1 cup of the frosting, then place the top half over it, cut side down. Spread the top of this layer with 1 cup of the frosting. Place the bottom of the second layer, cut side up, on top of the first layer. Spread that layer with another 1 cup of frosting. Place the top half of the second layer on top, cut side down. Pile the remaining frosting on top of the cake, spreading it out evenly and leaving the side of the cake bare. To make slicing easier, place the uncovered cake in the refrigerator until the frosting sets, 20 to 30 minutes.

NOTE: Use whatever milk is in your refrigerator or use ½ cup of the evaporated milk that will be left over from a 12-ounce can when you make the coconut pecan frosting, adding ¼ cup of milk or water to make the ¾ cup needed for the cake. I love not wasting ingredients!

KEEP IT FRESH! If your kitchen is cool, store the cake, lightly wrapped with aluminum foil or in a cake saver, on the kitchen counter for twenty-four hours. Or, store it in the refrigerator for three days. Freeze only the cake layers, wrapped in aluminum foil, for up to one month. Let the layers thaw overnight on the counter before assembling and frosting the cake.

✦ ✦ ✦

The Cake Mix Doctor Says

The flavor of the frosting will be so much better if you first toast the pecans and coconut until they are browned and fragrant. Leave the oven on at 350°F when you take out the cake layers. Chopped pecans will be toasted in 2 to 3 minutes and sweetened flaked coconut in 5 to 6 minutes.

recipe reminders

Made for:

_____

_____

_____

_____

Prep Notes:

_____

_____

_____

_____

Don't Forget:

_____

_____

_____

_____

Special Touches:

_____

_____

_____

_____

Devil's Food Cake
with Vanilla Buttercream Frosting

✦ ✦ ✦

serves: 10 to 12

prep: 30 minutes

bake: 20 to 24 minutes

cool: 25 minutes

DAIRY FREE

Substitute water or soy milk for the buttermilk in the cake. For the Vanilla Buttercream Frosting, use margarine instead of the butter and almond milk or orange juice instead of the milk.

This may be my favorite birthday cake of all time, a dark devil's food paired with a white and creamy frosting. You just can't beat it. And in the gluten-free version it's a snap to make. Moist and rich, the cake is a good keeper if you want to bake it a day ahead. Vary the frosting if you like, using the Cream Cheese Frosting (page 273) or the Chocolate Pan Frosting (page 289). Any way you top it, this cake is a winner.

Vegetable oil spray, for misting the pans
2 teaspoons unsweetened cocoa powder or
   rice flour, for dusting the pans
1 package (15 ounces) chocolate gluten-free
   cake mix
½ cup buttermilk
½ cup vegetable oil
3 large eggs
1 tablespoon pure vanilla extract
Pinch of ground cinnamon
Vanilla Buttercream Frosting (page 271)

1. Place a rack in the center of the oven and preheat the oven to 350°F. Lightly mist two 9-inch round cake pans with vegetable oil spray, then dust them with the cocoa or rice flour. Shake out the excess cocoa or rice flour and set the pans aside.

2. Place the cake mix, buttermilk, oil, eggs, vanilla, and cinnamon in a large mixing bowl and beat with an electric mixer on low speed until the ingredients are just incorporated, 30 seconds. Stop the machine and scrape down the side of the bowl with a rubber spatula. Increase the mixer speed to medium and beat the batter until smooth, 1 to 1½ minutes longer, scraping down the side of the bowl again if needed. The batter should look well blended. Divide the batter evenly between the 2 prepared cake pans, smoothing the tops with the rubber spatula. Place the pans in the oven side by side.

3. Bake the cake layers until the tops spring back when lightly pressed with a finger, 20 to 24 minutes. Transfer the cake pans to wire racks and let the cake layers cool for 5 minutes. Run a sharp knife around the edge of each cake layer and give the pans a good shake to loosen the cakes. Invert each layer onto a wire rack, then invert it again onto another rack so that the layers are right side up. Let the layers cool completely, about 20 minutes longer.

recipe reminders

Made for: _____

_____

_____

_____

_____

Prep Notes: _____

_____

_____

_____

_____

Don't Forget: _____

_____

_____

_____

_____

Special Touches: _____

_____

_____

_____

4. Meanwhile, make the Vanilla Buttercream Frosting.

5. To assemble the cake, transfer one layer, right side up, to a serving plate. Spread the top with about 1 cup of the frosting. Place the second cake layer, right side up, on top of the first layer and frost the top and side of the cake, working with smooth, clean strokes.

KEEP IT FRESH! Store the cake, lightly wrapped with aluminum foil or in a cake saver, on the kitchen counter for three days. Freeze only the cake layers, wrapped in aluminum foil, for up to one month. Let the layers thaw overnight on the counter before assembling and frosting the cake.

✦ ✦ ✦

The Cake Mix Doctor Says

Frosting dark cake layers with a white frosting can be a chore because crumbs keep dragging into the frosting. Two easy ways to solve this problem are either to first freeze the layers, then frost them while they are still frozen and let the frosted cake thaw on the kitchen counter. Or spread a thin skim coat of frosting all over the cake, then chill it for 10 to 15 minutes. When you spread a thicker finishing coat of frosting over the skim coat no crumbs will drag into the frosting.

For a pretty finishing touch, top the cake with a scattering of shaved dark chocolate (see The Cake Mix Doctor Says, page 69).

Chocolate Chip Layer Cake

✦ ✦ ✦

True confessions time: I have this drawer in my kitchen island that is deep and handy and just the place to stash the baking ingredients like vanilla that I use a lot. But if you open the drawer and look inside, you'll mostly see chocolate chips. That's because I'm a little obsessed with them, trying new brands whenever I see them—just to taste test, of course! I'm partial to the Ghirardelli bittersweet chocolate chips for baking and munching. I buy big bags of Nestlé semisweet chips at Costco to save money. And I need the miniature chips for folding into recipes such as this one. Mini chips don't sink to the bottom of the pan; they suspend beautifully in the batter. This is just a great basic, all-American layer cake, and it's irresistible spread with the Chocolate Buttercream Frosting. But then, I am a little partial to chocolate chips.

Vegetable oil spray, for misting the pans
2 teaspoons rice flour, for dusting the pans
1 package (15 ounces) yellow gluten-free cake mix
¼ cup (half of a 3.4-ounce package) vanilla instant
    pudding mix
½ cup milk
½ cup vegetable oil
3 large eggs
1 tablespoon pure vanilla extract
1 cup miniature semisweet chocolate chips
Chocolate Buttercream Frosting (page 287)

serves: 10 to 12

prep: 30 minutes

bake: 19 to 24 minutes

cool: 25 minutes

DAIRY FREE

Substitute water or orange juice for the milk in the cake batter. Use the Enjoy Life brand of dairy-free semisweet chocolate chips. And for the Chocolate Buttercream Frosting, use Earth Balance butter-flavored spread instead of the butter and brewed coffee or water instead of the milk. If you are making a dairy-free frosting, double the amount because the spread does not achieve the volume that butter does.

recipe reminders

1. Place a rack in the center of the oven and preheat the oven to 350°F. Lightly mist two 9-inch round cake pans with vegetable oil spray, then dust them with the rice flour. Shake out the excess rice flour and set the pans aside.

2. Place the cake mix, pudding mix, milk, oil, eggs, and vanilla in a large mixing bowl and beat with an electric mixer on low speed until the ingredients are just incorporated, 30 seconds. Stop the machine and scrape down the side of the bowl with a rubber spatula. Increase the mixer speed to medium and beat the batter until smooth, 1 to 1½ minutes longer, scraping down the side of the bowl again if needed. The batter should look well blended. Fold in the chocolate chips. Divide the batter evenly between the 2 prepared cake pans, smoothing the tops with the rubber spatula. Place the pans in the oven side by side.

3. Bake the cake layers until they are golden brown and the tops spring back when lightly pressed with a finger, 19 to 24 minutes. Transfer the cake pans to wire racks and let the cake layers cool for 5 minutes. Run a sharp knife around the edge of each cake layer and give the pans a good shake to loosen the cakes. Invert each layer onto a wire rack, then invert it again onto another rack so that the layers are right side up. Let the layers cool completely, about 20 minutes longer.

4. Meanwhile, make the Chocolate Buttercream Frosting.

5. To assemble the cake, transfer one layer, right side up, to a serving plate. Spread the top with about 1 cup of the frosting. Place the second layer, right side up, on top of the first layer and frost the top and side of the cake, working with smooth, clean strokes.

KEEP IT FRESH! Store the cake, lightly wrapped with aluminum foil or in a cake saver, on the kitchen counter for three days. Freeze only the cake layers, wrapped in aluminum foil, for up to one month. Let the layers thaw overnight on the counter before assembling and frosting the cake.

✦ ◆ ✦

The Cake Mix Doctor Says

You don't have any miniature chocolate chips? Run a grater over a bar of semisweet chocolate to make 1 cup of lightly packed chocolate shavings. Or, take a sharp knife and cut the bar into thin shavings. You will need 4 to 6 ounces of chocolate to make a cup of shavings.

To make this cake extra special, garnish the top with a stencil pattern. Chill the cake until the frosting has set. Place a stencil (found at baking supply stores) on top. Sift confectioners' sugar over the entire stencil, then carefully lift off the stencil, and voilá!

Round vs. Square Pans

Use the cake pans you have: If I call for round but you have the same size square, you can use those pans. But be forewarned that cakes in square pans tend to bake more quickly at the corners and along the sides and that the center of the cake really domes up. This can make stacking the two layers a little more challenging. Feel free to level the bottom layer with a serrated bread knife by cutting a quarter inch off of the domed top. Do keep the domed top on the top layer as it improves the appearance of the cake.

Chocolate Chip Pistachio Cake

✦ ✦ ✦

serves: **10 to 12**

prep: **45 minutes**

bake: **18 to 22 minutes**

cool: **25 minutes**

When my daughter's English class was studying *Othello* and the "green-eyed monster," jealousy, I baked a cake for them. Remembering the pistachio-flavored and green-hued cakes of the seventies, I added pistachio pudding mix to a cake mix. Working on this book, I tried the trick with a gluten-free mix and the results were yummy. You can intensify the pistachio flavor by folding in finely chopped pistachios along with the chocolate chips before the cake goes into the oven, but that's up to you. Do cover the cake with my signature Chocolate Pan Frosting. For garnish, what else? Chopped dry-roasted pistachios.

DAIRY FREE

Substitute water for the milk in the cake. When making the Chocolate Pan Frosting, use margarine instead of butter and use rice or almond milk instead of the milk.

Vegetable oil spray, for misting the pans
2 teaspoons rice flour, for dusting the pans
1 package (15 ounces) yellow gluten-free cake mix
¼ cup (half of a 3.4-ounce package) pistachio instant pudding mix
¾ cup milk
½ cup vegetable oil
3 large eggs
2 teaspoons pure vanilla extract
⅔ cup miniature semisweet chocolate chips
Chocolate Pan Frosting (page 289; see The Cake Mix Doctor Says, page 72)
½ cup chopped salted dry-roasted pistachios (optional), for garnish

1. Place a rack in the center of the oven and preheat the oven to 350°F. Lightly mist two 9-inch round cake pans with vegetable oil spray, then dust them with the rice flour. Shake out the excess rice flour and set the pans aside.

2. Place the cake mix, pudding mix, milk, oil, eggs, and vanilla in a large mixing bowl and beat with an electric mixer on low speed until the ingredients are just incorporated, 30 seconds. Stop the machine and scrape down the side of the bowl with a rubber spatula. Increase the mixer speed to medium and beat the batter until smooth, 1 to 1½ minutes longer, scraping down the side of the bowl again if needed. The batter should look well blended. Fold in the chocolate chips. Divide the batter evenly between the 2 prepared cake pans, smoothing the tops with the rubber spatula. Place the pans in the oven side by side.

3. Bake the cake layers until they are golden brown and the tops spring back when lightly pressed with a finger, 18 to 22 minutes. Transfer the cake pans to wire racks and let the cake layers cool for 5 minutes. Run a sharp knife around the edge of each cake layer and give the pans a good shake to loosen the cakes. Invert each layer onto a wire rack, then invert it again onto another rack so that the layers are right side up. Let the layers cool completely, about 20 minutes longer.

4. Meanwhile, make the Chocolate Pan Frosting.

5. To assemble the cake, transfer one layer, right side up, to a serving plate. Ladle 1 cup of warm frosting over the top, spreading it evenly. Place the second layer, right side up, on top of the first layer

recipe reminders

Made for: _____

_____

_____

_____

_____

Prep Notes: _____

_____

_____

_____

_____

Don't Forget: _____

_____

_____

_____

_____

Special Touches: _____

_____

_____

_____

_____

and frost the top and side of the cake, working with smooth, clean strokes. If desired, garnish the top of the cake with the chopped pistachios while the frosting is still soft to the touch.

KEEP IT FRESH! Store the cake, lightly wrapped with aluminum foil or in a cake saver, on the kitchen counter for three days. Freeze only the cake layers, wrapped in aluminum foil, for up to one month. Let the layers thaw overnight on the counter before assembling and frosting the cake.

✦ ✦ ✦

The Cake Mix Doctor Says

The Chocolate Pan Frosting is a wonderful fudgy confection unlike any other. It needs to go on while still slightly warm, so make the frosting during the last 10 minutes the cake is cooling. The frosting sets up quickly and, if it gets hard too soon, place it back over low heat and stir it until it softens.

Holiday Perfect Cakes by the Calendar

Do you feel the urge to bake a cake when a holiday or special day rolls around? This should give you an idea as to how to match these layer cakes with holiday meals.

✦ Valentine's Day—Fresh Strawberry Cake with Strawberry Cream Cheese Frosting, page 22

✦ St. Patrick's Day—Chocolate Chip Pistachio Cake, page 70

✦ Easter—Coconut Cake with Fluffy Marshmallow Frosting, page 42

✦ Mother's Day—Lemon Lover's Chiffon Cake, page 31

✦ Father's Day—German Chocolate Cake, page 60

✦ Fourth of July—Hummingbird Cake with Lighter Cream Cheese Frosting, page 49

✦ Halloween—Devil's Food Cake with Vanilla Buttercream Frosting, page 64

✦ Christmas or Hanukkah—Easy Orange Layer Cake, page 35

✦ New Year's Eve—Chocolate Almond Torte, page 78

Butter Got the Lumps?

When butter is just too cold or something in the batter, such as the eggs or orange juice, is too cold, the more you beat, the more those pesky little flecks of butter remain. I have found a remedy, however. Fill the kitchen sink to a two-inch depth with very warm water. Place the mixing bowl of batter in the sink and leave it for ten to fifteen minutes. Remove the mixing bowl from the sink, dry off the bottom of the bowl, and beat the batter until smooth. It will come together beautifully in less than a minute.

Cookies and Cream Cake

✦ ✦ ✦

serves: **10 to 12**

prep: **45 minutes**

bake: **18 to 22 minutes**

cool: **25 minutes**

This is birthday cake around our house—who can pass up a cake that contains crushed gluten-free chocolate sandwich cookies? The cake is designed to use up the entire package, so no stealing any cookies! Some crushed cookies go into the vanilla cake batter and more go on top of the cake. The frosting is just the right complement, a chocolate-flavored whipped cream. A refrigerator cake, it stays fresh in the fridge for three days—perfect for party planning because you can bake it ahead and check it off your list!

For the cake

Vegetable oil spray, for misting the pans
2 teaspoons rice flour, for dusting the pans
1 package (10.6 ounces) chocolate gluten-free sandwich cookies (see Note)
1 package (15 ounces) yellow gluten-free cake mix
¼ cup (half of a 3.4-ounce package) vanilla instant pudding mix
1 cup milk
½ cup vegetable oil
3 large eggs
1 tablespoon pure vanilla extract

For the chocolate whipped cream frosting

2 cups heavy (whipping) cream, chilled

1 tablespoon confectioners' or granulated sugar

1 teaspoon unsweetened cocoa powder

1. Make the cake: Place a rack in the center of the oven and preheat the oven to 350°F. Lightly mist two 9-inch round cake pans with vegetable oil spray, then dust them with the rice flour. Shake out the excess rice flour and set the pans aside.

2. Set aside 3 whole cookies to garnish the top of the cake. Place the remaining cookies in a plastic bag and crush them with a rolling pin or crush them in a food processor. Measure 1 cup of cookie crumbs for the cake batter and set aside the remaining 1¼ cups of cookie crumbs for scattering over the frosted cake.

3. Place the cake mix, pudding mix, milk, oil, eggs, and vanilla in a large mixing bowl and beat with an electric mixer on low speed until the ingredients are just incorporated, 30 seconds. Stop the machine and scrape down the side of the bowl with a rubber spatula. Increase the mixer speed to medium and beat the batter until smooth, 1 to 1½ minutes longer, scraping down the side of the bowl again if needed. The batter should look well blended. Fold in the 1 cup of chocolate cookie crumbs. Divide the batter evenly between the 2 prepared pans, smoothing the tops with the rubber spatula. Place the pans in the oven side by side. Place a large mixing bowl and electric mixer beaters in the refrigerator to chill.

4. Bake the cake layers until they are golden brown and the tops spring back when lightly pressed with a finger, 18 to 22 minutes. Transfer the cake pans to wire racks and let the cake layers cool for 5 minutes. Run a sharp knife around the edge of each cake layer and give the pans a good shake to loosen the cakes. Invert each layer onto a wire rack, then invert it again onto another rack

recipe reminders

Made for:

_____

_____

_____

_____

Prep Notes:

_____

_____

_____

_____

Don't Forget:

_____

_____

_____

_____

Special Touches:

_____

_____

_____

_____

When You're the Only Gluten-Free Eater in the House

No one needs to eat an entire cake, so here are three suggestions for avoiding that temptation.

Share: Cut the cake into quarters, give three quarters away to friends, and save one quarter (three slices) for yourself.

Freeze: Wrap three quarters of the cake in waxed paper and then in heavy-duty aluminum foil, place them in a resealable plastic bag, and freeze them for later.

Make cupcakes: Turn any of the cake recipes into cupcakes. They will make eighteen to twenty cupcakes when the pans are filled two-thirds full. Save a few cupcakes for yourself and take the rest into the office or to school.

so that the layers are right side up. Let the layers cool completely, about 20 minutes longer.

5. Meanwhile, make the chocolate whipped cream frosting: Pour the cream into the chilled mixing bowl. Using the refrigerated mixer beaters, beat the cream with an electric mixer on high speed until soft peaks form, 1 to 1½ minutes, then add the sugar and cocoa. Continue beating on high until stiff peaks form, 1½ minutes longer. Refrigerate the frosting until ready to use.

6. To assemble the cake, transfer one layer, right side up, to a serving plate. Spread the top with 1¾ to 2 cups of the frosting. Place the second layer, right side up, on top of the first layer and liberally frost the top and side of the cake. Scatter the reserved 1¼ cups of cookie crumbs on the top of the cake and arrange three cookies, either whole or cut in half, on top of the cake as garnish.

NOTE: I used a 10.6-ounce bag of Glutino chocolate gluten-free sandwich cookies. You can find these gluten-free cookies online and also at Whole Foods.

KEEP IT FRESH! Store the cake, in a cake saver, in the refrigerator for three days. Freeze only the cake layers, wrapped in aluminum foil, for up to one month. Let the layers thaw overnight on the counter before assembling and frosting the cake.

✦ ✦ ✦

The Cake Mix Doctor Says

To make a four-layer cake, bake and cool the cake layers as directed. Using a serrated knife, slice each of the cake layers in half crosswise. Transfer the bottom half of one layer, cut side up, to a serving plate. Spread the cut side with 1 cup of the frosting, then place the top half over it, cut side down. Spread the top of this layer with 1 cup of frosting. Place the bottom of the second layer, cut side up, on top of the first layer. Spread that layer with another 1 cup of frosting. Place the top half of the second layer on top, cut side down. Pile the remaining frosting on top of the cake and frost the top and side of the cake, working with smooth, clean strokes. Sprinkle the top of the cake liberally with the reserved cookies crumbs and arrange the whole cookies as a garnish.

Chocolate Almond Torte

✦ ✦ ✦

serves: **10 to 12**

prep: **45 minutes**

bake: **18 to 22 minutes**

cool: **25 minutes**

Rising beautifully, and with such an interesting combination of flavors of almonds and chocolate, this torte resembles a fancy cake you might find in a European pastry shop. So you'd never think for a moment that it's made with anything other than wheat flour. It's a good keeper, too, what with the chocolate frosting that glides on and seals in the moisture of the cake.

For the cake

Vegetable oil spray, for misting the pans
2 teaspoons unsweetened cocoa powder or rice flour, for dusting the pans
½ cup whole shelled almonds
1 package (15 ounces) chocolate gluten-free cake mix
¼ cup granulated sugar
1 cup reduced-fat sour cream
⅓ cup vegetable oil
¼ cup water
3 large eggs
1 teaspoon pure vanilla extract
1 teaspoon pure almond extract

For the filling

⅓ cup almond paste (see Note)

8 tablespoons (1 stick) butter, at room temperature

2½ cups confectioners' sugar, sifted

1 tablespoon milk or heavy (whipping) cream

For the ganache

8 ounces (1⅓ cups) semisweet chocolate chips

¾ cup heavy (whipping) cream

1 teaspoon pure vanilla extract

1. Make the cake: Place a rack in the center of the oven and preheat the oven to 350°F. Lightly mist two 9-inch round cake pans with vegetable oil spray, then dust them with the cocoa. Shake out the excess cocoa and set the pans aside.

2. Place the almonds in a food processor fitted with a steel blade and process them in short pulses until finely ground, 30 to 45 seconds. Transfer the ground almonds to a large mixing bowl.

3. Place the cake mix and granulated sugar in the bowl with the almonds and stir to combine. Add the sour cream, oil, water, eggs, 1 teaspoon of vanilla extract, and the almond extract and beat with an electric mixer on low speed until the ingredients are just incorporated, 30 to 45 seconds. Stop the machine and scrape down the side of the bowl with a rubber spatula. Increase the mixer speed to medium and beat the batter until smooth, 1 to 1½ minutes longer, scraping down the side of the bowl again if needed. The batter should look well blended. Divide the batter evenly between the 2 prepared pans, smoothing the tops with the rubber spatula. Place the pans in the oven side by side.

4. Bake the cake layers until the tops spring back when lightly pressed with a finger, 18 to 22 minutes. Transfer the cake pans

---

DAIRY FREE

Use coconut milk instead of the sour cream in the cake. Use margarine and almond milk instead of the butter and milk in the filling. And instead of frosting the cake with chocolate ganache, spread thawed frozen dairy-free whipped topping on the top and side of the cake.

to wire racks and let the cake layers cool for 5 minutes. Run a sharp knife around the edge of each cake layer and give the pans a good shake to loosen the cakes. Invert each layer onto a wire rack, then invert it again onto another rack so that the layers are right side up. Let the layers cool completely, about 20 minutes longer.

5. Meanwhile, make the filling: Place the almond paste in a small glass bowl and heat on high power in a microwave for 10 to 15 seconds. Spoon the warm paste into a medium-size mixing bowl and add the butter. Beat with an electric mixer on medium speed until the lumps are gone, 1½ to 2 minutes. Add the confectioners' sugar and milk and beat again on medium speed until the filling is smooth and creamy, 1 to 2 minutes longer. Set the filling aside.

6. Make the ganache: Place the chocolate chips in a medium-size stainless steel mixing bowl. Pour the cream into a heavy saucepan, place it over medium heat, and bring to a boil, stirring. Remove the cream from the heat and pour it over the chocolate. Using a wooden spoon, stir until the chocolate is melted. Stir in the 1 teaspoon of vanilla, and set the ganache aside to cool slightly. Ganache needs to be thick enough to spread like soft butter. If your kitchen is cool the ganache will reach this consistency in 10 to 15 minutes. If the kitchen is warm you can place the ganache in the refrigerator for 2 to 3 minutes to speed up the process.

7. To assemble the cake, using a serrated knife, slice each cake layer in half crosswise. Transfer the bottom half of one layer, cut side up, to a serving plate. Thinly spread the cut side with ½ cup of the filling, then place the top half over it, cut side down. Spread the top of this layer with ½ cup of the filling. Place the bottom of the second layer, cut side up, on top of the first layer. Spread that layer with ½ cup of the filling. Place the top half of the second layer on top, cut side down. Once the ganache has cooled to frosting consistency, frost the top and side of the cake liberally with it, working with smooth, clean strokes.

NOTE: Almond paste is a mixture of ground almonds and sugar and often another ingredient or two for flavoring or texture. It is used mostly as a filling in pastries, either on its own or combined with other ingredients. You can find cans of the Solo brand in the baking aisle of most supermarkets. And you can also find almond paste sold in handy tubes so you can use some and refrigerate the leftovers.

KEEP IT FRESH! Store the cake, in a cake saver, on the kitchen counter for three days. Freeze only the cake layers, wrapped in aluminum foil, for up to one month. Let the layers thaw overnight on the counter before assembling and frosting the cake.

✦ ✦ ✦

The Cake Mix Doctor Says

Garnish the top with almond brittle. Mist a baking sheet with vegetable oil and set aside. Place 1 cup granulated sugar in a heavy medium-size pan over medium heat, and let the sugar melt without stirring it. Move the pan around in circles until the sugar is dissolved and a deep caramel color. Turn off the heat. Add 1 cup whole almonds, and continue moving the pan to coat the almonds. Immediately pour the almond brittle onto the prepared baking sheet, and shake the baking sheet so the almonds are in a single layer. Cool completely, chop the brittle as desired, and place on top of the cake as a garnish.

Boston Cream Pie Your Way

✦ ✦ ✦

serves: **8 to 12**

prep: **25 minutes**

bake: **43 to 47 minutes**

cool: **45 minutes**

DAIRY FREE

A s this cake needs cow's milk to make the pudding filling set, it is not possible to make the cake dairy-free.

O ne of the first desserts I made as a beginning baker was this Boston Cream Pie. It begins with a round yellow cake that is split into two layers and filled with vanilla pudding. While I cover the cake with a rich chocolate glaze, food historians differ on whether the chocolate glaze is a departure from the classic dessert. Some say once you add the glaze the cake should be called a "Parker House chocolate pie," named after the Boston hotel where the cake was first made with the chocolate glaze. All pretty confusing but delicious stuff, especially since the "pie" is really a cake, and in the end you are the one to decide how you will prepare it—glazed or unglazed. I say bake it as you like (see my Cake Mix Doctor variations on page 84), cut the cake into wedges, and savor a timeless American dessert.

For the cake

Vegetable oil spray, for misting the pan
1 teaspoon rice flour, for dusting the pan
1 package (15 ounces) yellow gluten-free cake mix
¼ cup (half of a 3.4-ounce package) vanilla instant
    pudding mix (see Note)
1 cup whole or 2 percent milk
½ cup vegetable oil
3 large eggs
1 tablespoon pure vanilla extract

For the pudding layer

¼ cup (the other half of the 3.4-ounce package)
   vanilla instant pudding mix
1 cup cold whole milk

For the chocolate glaze

Half recipe Chocolate Pan Frosting
   (page 290), or confectioners' sugar

1. Make the cake: Place a rack in the center of the oven and preheat the oven to 350°F. Lightly mist a 9-inch round baking pan with vegetable oil spray, dust it with the rice flour, and set the pan aside.

2. Place the cake mix, ¼ cup of pudding mix, 1 cup of milk, and the oil, eggs, and vanilla in a large mixing bowl and beat with an electric mixer on low speed until the ingredients are just incorporated, 30 seconds. Stop the machine and scrape down the side of the bowl with a rubber spatula. Increase the mixer speed to medium and beat the batter until smooth, 1½ to 2 minutes longer, scraping down the side of the bowl again if needed. Pour the batter into the prepared pan, smoothing the top with the rubber spatula, and place the pan in the oven.

3. Bake the cake until it is golden brown and the top springs back when lightly pressed with a finger, 43 to 47 minutes. Transfer the cake pan to a wire rack and let the cake cool for 10 minutes.

4. Meanwhile, make the pudding: Place the ¼ cup of pudding mix in a small bowl and whisk in the cold milk. Continue to whisk the pudding for 2 minutes, then place it in the refrigerator to chill.

5. Run a sharp knife around the edge of the cake and give the pan a good shake to loosen the cake. Invert the cake onto a wire

Curly Q&A

Q: How can I make chocolate curls to top this cake?

A: Buy the biggest piece of white chocolate you can find. Let it come to room temperature. Drag a sharp vegetable peeler across the top of the white chocolate. Store the curls in a cool place until ready to use them. You can make regular chocolate curls using the same method.

recipe reminders

Made for:

_____

_____

_____

_____

Prep Notes:

_____

_____

_____

_____

Don't Forget:

_____

_____

_____

_____

Special Touches:

_____

_____

_____

_____

rack, then invert it again onto another rack so that it is right side up. Let the cake cool until cool to the touch, 15 minutes longer.

6. Meanwhile, prepare the Warm Chocolate Glaze and let it cool.

7. To assemble the cake, slice it in half crosswise. Place the bottom half on a serving plate, cut side up, and spread the pudding evenly over it. Place the top half over the pudding, cut side down. Spoon the chocolate glaze, if using, over the cake and place it uncovered in the refrigerator for at least 20 minutes before slicing and serving. Or dust the top of the cake with confectioners' sugar.

NOTE: The Jell-O brand of instant pudding is gluten-free. The vanilla pudding comes in a 3.4-ounce box. Trader Joe's makes a delicious gluten-free instant vanilla pudding that comes in a 3.39-ounce box.

KEEP IT FRESH! Store the cake, loosely covered with plastic wrap or in a cake saver, in the refrigerator for three days. Freeze only the cake layer, wrapped in aluminum foil, for up to one month. Let the cake layer thaw overnight on the counter before filling and glazing it.

✦ ✦ ✦

The Cake Mix Doctor Says

Love chocolate and bananas? Thinly slice a large banana and arrange the slices on top of the cake before pouring the chocolate glaze over it. Or how about a strawberry cream pie? Omit the chocolate glaze and spoon 2 cups of sweetened sliced strawberries over the top of the cake with the pudding filling. Want a peaches and cream pie? Omit the chocolate glaze and spoon 2 cups of sweetened sliced peaches over the top of the cake.

Chocolate Banana Cake
with Peanut Butter Frosting

✦ ✦ ✦

Close your eyes and imagine banana, creamy peanut butter, and chocolate. I could eat them every afternoon, and often, I do. So once I got the hang of baking with gluten-free mixes and saw how well pureed fruit performed in them, I knew I had to make a chocolate cake with mashed bananas. And after I did, I knew there would be only one frosting—peanut butter. Okay, there are a number of frostings that would work great on this cake, but peanut butter and chocolate and banana are old friends. They are meant to be together in our mouths and in our kitchens.

serves: **10 to 12**

prep: **30 minutes**

bake: **20 to 25 minutes**

cool: **25 minutes**

Vegetable oil spray, for misting the pans

2 teaspoons unsweetened cocoa powder or rice flour, for dusting the pans

1 package (15 ounces) chocolate gluten-free cake mix

1 cup mashed ripe bananas (from 3 small very ripe bananas)

½ cup buttermilk

⅓ cup vegetable oil

3 large eggs

1 tablespoon pure vanilla extract

Peanut Butter Frosting (page 283)

DAIRY FREE

Substitute water or soy milk for the buttermilk in the cake. For the Peanut Butter Frosting, use margarine instead of the butter and rice milk instead of the milk.

1. Place a rack in the center of the oven and preheat the oven to 350°F. Lightly mist two 9-inch round cake pans with vegetable oil spray, then dust them with the cocoa. Shake out the excess cocoa and set the pans aside.

2. Place the cake mix, bananas, buttermilk, oil, eggs, and vanilla in a large mixing bowl and beat with an electric mixer on low speed until the ingredients are just incorporated, 30 seconds. Stop the machine and scrape down the side of the bowl with a rubber spatula. Increase the mixer speed to medium and beat the batter until smooth, 1 to 1½ minutes longer, scraping down the side of the bowl again if needed. The batter should look well blended. Divide the batter evenly between the 2 prepared cake pans, smoothing the tops with the rubber spatula. Place the pans in the oven side by side.

3. Bake the cake layers until the tops spring back when lightly pressed with a finger, 20 to 25 minutes. Transfer the cake pans to wire racks and let the cake layers cool for 5 minutes. Run a sharp knife around the edge of each cake layer and give the pans a good shake to loosen the cakes. Invert each layer onto a wire rack, then invert it again onto another rack so that the layers are right side up. Let the layers cool completely, about 20 minutes longer.

4. Meanwhile, make the Peanut Butter Frosting.

5. To assemble the cake, transfer one layer, right side up, to a serving plate. Spread the top with about 1 cup of the frosting. Place the second cake layer, right side up, on top of the first layer and frost the top and side of the cake, working with smooth, clean strokes.

KEEP IT FRESH! Store the cake, lightly wrapped with aluminum foil or in a cake saver, on the kitchen counter for three days. Freeze only the cake layers, wrapped in aluminum foil, for up to one month. Let the layers thaw overnight on the counter before assembling and frosting the cake.

✦ ✦ ✦

The Cake Mix Doctor Says

Dust the top with cocoa powder and place fresh banana slices in the center right before serving.

✦ ✦ ✦

Chocolate Banana Chip Muffins

To make morning muffins and afternoon snacks, follow the chocolate banana cake recipe, then:

1. Lightly mist two 2½-inch cupcake pans with vegetable oil spray or line them with 18 paper cupcake liners.

recipe reminders

Made for:

_____

_____

_____

_____

Prep Notes:

_____

_____

_____

_____

Don't Forget:

_____

_____

_____

_____

Special Touches:

_____

_____

_____

_____

2. In Step 2, once the batter is smooth, fold in ½ cup miniature semisweet chocolate chips.

3. Using an ice cream scoop, scoop the batter into the cupcake cups, filling them about two-thirds full. The recipe will make about 18 muffins.

4. Bake the muffins at 375°F until done, 18 to 22 minutes.

5. If desired, dust with confectioners' sugar before serving.

Chocolate Banana Cupcakes with Peanut Butter Frosting

Party cupcakes are just a recipe away. Follow the chocolate banana cake recipe but:

1. Lightly mist two 2½-inch cupcake pans with vegetable oil spray or line them with 18 paper cupcake liners.

2. Using an ice cream scoop, scoop the batter into the cupcake cups, filling them about two-thirds full. The recipe will make about 18 cupcakes.

3. Bake the cupcakes at 350°F until done, 20 to 25 minutes.

4. Frost the cupcakes with the Peanut Butter Frosting (page 283).

Gluten-Free
WEDDING CAKE

✦ ✦ ✦ ✦

When this book was in the idea phase—in my head—I thought I'd like to develop a wedding cake recipe. The more I considered it, the more I knew I had to come up with a gluten-free wedding cake because a wedding cake is, after all, one of the most sacred, most celebratory cakes of all. But true to my nature, I tucked that idea out of my mind until the layer cake testing was underway. Then I received an e-mail. It was from my friend Jenny Mandel at Workman Publishing who said Gillian Lay, a book sales manager in New York who was following a gluten-free

Let Everyone Eat Cake

This wedding cake will feed forty to forty-five guests unless the bride and groom want to keep the top layer for their first anniversary; then it will feed about thirty-five. Should you want to bake a larger cake, add a 16-inch layer to the bottom of the cake and the servings increase to nearly one hundred. You'll need a second full recipe of batter for this layer. To cover this additional cake, make a little more frosting by adding one more 8-ounce package of cream cheese, plus an additional 4 tablespoons of butter, 1 teaspoon of vanilla, and 4 cups of confectioners' sugar. Need still more cake? You'll need an additional 8-inch round cake pan. To fill it, bake an additional quarter recipe (1 package cake mix, ½ package pudding mix, 2½ tablespoons sugar, ½ cup sour cream, 6 tablespoons oil, ¼ cup water, 2 egg whites, 1 egg, 1 tablespoon vanilla extract, ½ to ¼ teaspoon almond extract). This is enough to fill another 8-inch round pan. Stack the two 8-inch rounds on top of each other (glued together with a little frosting, of course) and you have a taller middle layer, adding 16 more servings. Or, bake sheet pans of cake. Each 18 by 13—inch pan will yield about fifty servings, and for each pan you will need one full recipe of batter.

diet, was getting married in the fall. Did I, by chance, have a gluten-free wedding cake recipe? Now the idea of a wedding cake had a real person attached to it. Someone was planning the biggest day of her life and she needed my cake recipe to make it complete. I had better get busy.

So this recipe came to life. Beginning with four boxes of Betty Crocker yellow gluten-free cake mix, along with two boxes of instant pudding mix, some sugar, sour cream, oil, eggs, extra egg whites, and a generous addition of vanilla and almond extract, I baked a three-tiered wedding cake and frosted it with a glorious cream cheese frosting. After garnishing the wedding cake with one last yellow flower, we cut into it, served up slices, and everyone oohed and aahed over the moist texture and hint of almond. We didn't have a bride and groom to cut the cake, but we had a new and promising beginning—a gluten-free wedding cake!

✦ ✦ ✦

A Gluten-Free Wedding Cake

✦ ◆ ✦

Just because you or someone you love is following a gluten-free diet doesn't mean you need to go without wedding cake. Gluten-free cake mix makes this recipe for the cake easy to assemble, and with my additions the cake is moist, flavorful, and interesting.

Supplies

One 12-inch round cake pan, at least 2 inches deep

One 8-inch round cake pan, at least 2 inches deep

One 6-inch round cake pan, at least 2 inches deep

Parchment paper, for lining the pans

Large mixing bowls

Handheld electric mixer or restaurant-size stand mixer

2 large wire racks for cooling the 12-inch layer or 4 smaller wire racks that you can push together, plus racks for the 8- and 6-inch layers

Space in the refrigerator for the 12-inch, 8-inch, and 6-inch layers to chill after frosting

3 cardboard cake rounds: one 12 inches in diameter, one 8 inches, and one 6 inches

Double-sided tape or masking tape

15- to 16-inch round cake plate or cake base (see Notes)

Plastic drinking straws

Pastry bag with #4 or #10 and small star tips

Fresh flowers of your choice (see Notes)

serves: 40 to 45

prep: 35 to 40 minutes

bake: 50 to 55 minutes

cool: At least 1 hour and 10 minutes

assemble: 2 to 3 hours

DAIRY FREE

Use a dairy-free substitute such as coconut milk for the sour cream in the cake. When making the frosting, use butter-flavored Crisco vegetable shortening sticks instead of the butter and a dairy-free cream cheese, such as Better Than Cream Cheese made by Tofutti, for the cream cheese.

For the cake

Vegetable shortening, for greasing the pans
Rice flour, for dusting the pans
4 packages (15 ounces each) yellow gluten-free cake mix
2 packages (3.4 ounces each) vanilla instant pudding mix
⅔ cup granulated sugar
2 cups reduced-fat sour cream
1½ cups vegetable oil
1 cup water
8 large egg whites
4 large eggs
4 tablespoons pure vanilla extract
2 to 3 teaspoons pure almond extract

For the frosting

3 packages (8 ounces each) cream cheese, at room temperature
12 tablespoons (1½ sticks) butter, at room temperature
1 tablespoon pure vanilla extract
14 cups confectioners' sugar, sifted
2 tablespoons meringue powder (see Notes)
Unsweetened dried coconut flakes (optional)

1. Make the cake: Place a rack in the center of the oven and preheat the oven to 325°F. Generously grease the side of each of the cake pans and dust them with rice flour. Shake out the excess rice flour. Lightly grease the bottoms of the pans. Trace the bottom of each of the cake pans onto pieces of parchment paper, then cut along the trace marks. Place one circle of parchment paper in the bottom of each of the prepared cake pans. Set the pans aside.

2. Place the cake mix, pudding mix, and granulated sugar in a large mixing bowl and toss with a large wooden spoon to combine. Set the bowl aside.

3. Place the sour cream, oil, water, egg whites, eggs, 4 table-spoons of vanilla, and the almond extract in a very large mixing bowl and beat with an electric mixer on low speed until the egg yolks are incorporated, 15 seconds. Add the cake mix mixture, about 3 cups at a time, beating on low speed until just incorporated, about 15 seconds each time. When all of the cake mix mixture has been added, increase the mixer speed to medium and beat the batter until smooth, 1½ to 2 minutes longer.

4. Using a glass measuring cup, measure 2 cups of batter and place this in the prepared 6-inch pan. Measure 3½ cups of batter and place this in the prepared 8-inch pan. Place the remaining batter in the 12-inch pan. The batter will be about 1 inch below the top of the pans. Smooth the top of the batter in all 3 pans with a rubber spatula. Place the pans in the oven. If your oven is not large enough to hold 3 pans on one rack, place 2 pans on the center rack and place the third pan in the center of the highest rack. Or, bake the 2 smaller layers first, letting the 12-inch layer rest on a counter and baking it after the first 2 layers come out of the oven.

5. Bake the cake layers until they just begin to pull away from the side of the pans and the tops are lightly browned. A toothpick inserted in the center of the layers should come out clean. (Although I usually don't advise using a toothpick to test for doneness, these cake layers are denser and thicker than usual.) The

Change It Up!

Forgo the almond extract in the wedding cake batter and use a tablespoon of grated lemon zest. Make homemade lemon curd (see page 294) or find one without gluten and use this as a filling; you'll need 3 cups of lemon curd. Then, using a serrated knife, slice the cooled cake layers in half crosswise before frosting them. Sandwich a thin layer of lemon curd between the two halves of each layer. Add a little lemon zest to the frosting, if desired.

Or go the coffee route and brush the cake layers with Kahlúa after they are baked. Make a mocha cream cheese frosting by adding espresso powder to taste—start with 1 tablespoon and go from there.

12-inch layer will bake the quickest and be done after 48 to 53 minutes and the thicker 8-inch and 6-inch layers will be done after 50 to 55 minutes. Transfer the cake pans to wire racks to cool. Immediately press down gently on the top of each layer for 10 to 15 seconds with your hands or with the bottom of a saucepan that is the same size as the layer (make sure the bottoms of the pans are clean). This will level the layers and make them easier to stack. Let the layers cool in the pans for 10 minutes. Run a knife around the edge of each cake layer and gently shake the pans to loosen the cakes. Invert each layer onto a wire rack, then again onto another rack so that the cakes are right side up.

6. Let the cake layers cool to room temperature, 1 hour longer. Then, wrap them well in plastic wrap and store them at room temperature for up to 1 day before frosting them. Or wrap the layers first in plastic wrap and then in heavy-duty aluminum foil and freeze them for up to 1 month. In warm weather, make sure the cake layers are cold before frosting them. Place them in the freezer to chill if needed.

7. Make the frosting: Place the cream cheese and butter in a very large mixing bowl and beat with an electric mixer on medium-low speed until creamy, 1 to 1½ minutes. Set 2 cups of the confectioners' sugar aside for the piping frosting. Add the 1 tablespoon of vanilla and the remaining 12 cups of confectioners' sugar, 2 cups at a time, beating on low speed until all of the sugar is incorporated. Stop the machine and scrape down the side of the bowl with a rubber spatula. Increase the mixer speed to medium and beat the frosting until it is fluffy, 1 to 2 minutes longer. Place the frosting in the refrigerator to chill for 30 minutes.

8. Frost the cake: Dab 2 tablespoons of frosting onto each cardboard cake round and spread it over the top in a thin layer. Place the 12-inch cake layer on top of the 12-inch round, the 8-inch layer on top of the 8-inch round, and the 6-inch layer on top of the 6-inch round. The dab of icing will keep the layers from sliding. Frost the top and side of the cake layers with a long, thin metal icing spatula. Begin by spreading a thin coat all the way around the side to seal in the crumbs, then go back and apply a thicker coat, using the cake round as a guide for the spatula. Frost the 12-inch and 8-inch layers flat across the top. Frost the 6-inch layer more generously as it will be placed on top of the cake. Place the cake layers, uncovered, in the refrigerator to chill. You should have about 4 cups of frosting remaining. If you will be transporting the cake, set aside about 1 cup of frosting in a plastic container and place it in the refrigerator to use to repair spots in the frosting when you arrive. The remaining frosting will be used to pipe decorations onto the cake.

9. Make the piping frosting: Add the reserved 2 cups of confectioners' sugar and the 2 tablespoons of meringue powder to the remaining frosting and beat with an electric mixer on medium-low speed until incorporated, 30 seconds. Increase the mixer speed to medium-high and beat the frosting mixture until it stiffens, 30 seconds to 1 minute longer. Place the piping frosting in the refrigerator to chill for 15 to 20 minutes.

10. Assemble the cake: Place a few pieces of double-sided tape or loops of masking tape in the center of a cake plate or cake base. Place the 12-inch cake layer still on its cardboard base on the cake plate or base; the tape will hold it securely. Position the empty 8-inch baking pan upside down on top of and in the center of the 12-inch cake layer so that it leaves an indentation in the frosting. This marks where you'll place the 8-inch layer. Insert a drinking straw vertically into the center of the 12-inch layer and mark where the top of the cake meets the straw. Remove the straw and cut it and 6 more straws into pieces of this length. To support the next layer, insert 1 of the cut straws back into the center of the 12-inch cake layer and insert the remaining 6 pieces of straw in an evenly spaced spoke pattern around it, halfway between the

recipe reminders

Made for:

_____

_____

_____

_____

Prep Notes:

_____

_____

_____

_____

Don't Forget:

_____

_____

_____

_____

Special Touches:

_____

_____

_____

_____

A Wedding Checklist

One month before

_____

_____

_____

_____

_____

_____

_____

_____

_____

Two weeks to go

_____

_____

_____

_____

_____

_____

_____

_____

_____

center of the cake layer and the outline of the 8-inch pan. Carefully place the 8-inch layer with its cardboard base on top of the 12-inch layer, centering it on the outline of the pan.

11. Position the empty 6-inch baking pan upside down on top of and in the center of the 8-inch layer to mark it. Insert a straw into the center of the 8-inch layer and mark where the top of the cake meets the straw. Remove the straw and cut it and 5 more pieces of straw to this length. Insert 1 of the cut straws back into the center of the 8-inch cake layer and insert the remaining 5 pieces of straw in an evenly spaced spoke pattern around it, halfway between the center of the cake layer and the outline of the 6-inch pan. Carefully place the 6-inch layer with its cardboard base on top of the 8-inch layer, centering it on the outline of the pan. Set the cake aside.

12. Remove the piping frosting from the refrigerator. Spoon a generous cup into a pastry bag fitted with a round tip (either #4 for a thin line or #10 for a thicker one). Pipe a line of frosting around the bottom of each cake layer to cover the cardboard rounds. If you need to go back and pipe another line of frosting, either above or below this line, do so. Using a small star tip, pipe small stars at 1-inch intervals on the piped line or pipe small dots or place edible pearls along the line. To get the hang of it, first practice piping stars onto a plate. The cooler the frosting is, the better formed the stars will be. Feel free to be as decorative as you like with the frosting, adding whatever embellishments you wish, such as tiny dots on the bottom layer. You will have plenty of frosting with which to work.

13. For the top of the cake, press dried, unsweetened coconut flakes onto the top and sides of the top layer, if desired. Place one or two large orchids or roses on the side of the cake, resting on the large layer. Feel free to decorate the sides of the cake and the base of the plate with more flowers.

14. The cake is now finished. Store it in the refrigerator until time to serve; it will keep for up to 24 hours, but the flowers should be added just before the reception begins.

NOTES: Meringue powder is gluten-free. I use it to add to the frosting that will be used for decorating to make it stiffer so when it is piped onto the cake, in a thin line or decorative dots, the frosting will hold its shape. Meringue powder and the cardboard cake rounds needed for this cake can be found at baking supply stores.

The cake plate or cake base needs to be 3 to 4 inches larger in diameter than the largest cake layer—15 to 16 inches in diameter.

When decorating the cake, flowers make a fresh and easy garnish. But be careful that the blooms you use are free from pesticides and organically grown. Match the flowers on the cake with the bride's colors for her big day.

SECRET FOR SUCCESS: My friend Martha Bowden and I baked the layers a day ahead and froze them. Then the next day, we took the layers out of the freezer and let them thaw on a counter for a few hours. The frosting, too, was made the day ahead. It is much easier to assemble this cake with cooled layers.

A One-Week Countdown

Seven days _____

_____

_____

Six days _____

_____

_____

Five Days _____

_____

_____

Four days _____

_____

_____

Three days _____

_____

_____

Two days _____

_____

_____

One day more _____

_____

_____

The Big Day _____

_____

_____

BUNDTS

✦ ✦ ✦ ✦

It's no wonder the Bundt pan has been *the* baking pan to turn to for the past thirty years. Cupcakes may be the current darling of the American kitchen, but the Bundt is your reliable best friend. The benefits of Bundts are many, whether or not the cake contains gluten. First of all, the Bundt is a simple pan. There's no stacking, no frosting—no fuss. Even if your cake dips once it comes out of the oven—which often happens at high altitudes—once the Bundt is inverted onto the cake plate, who will ever know? And Bundts are attractive, with those signature grooves along the sides. Those grooves conveniently serve as slicing guides, another benefit!

Susan's Lemon Cake (page 110)

Cakes that bake well in Bundts have sturdy batters, often containing fruit or nuts or chocolate. They keep well, freeze well, and best of all, they are good travelers. This is the cake to take to a potluck, bake sale, or dinner party. And let us not forget two other important benefits of the Bundt pan: even baking and compatibility with a reduced-sugar diet. The design of the pan ensures that the batter bakes consistently throughout. And because there is no frosting to make, these cakes contain less sugar. Serve them with fresh fruit or nothing at all.

Please be sure to check the baking times carefully before beginning for you will find that the slightly smaller gluten-free mixes make a little less batter and so the cakes need less time in the oven. While the recipes call for a 12-cup Bundt pan, you can also use a decorative 10-cup Bundt pan. Rest assured that even though there is less batter than from a regular cake mix, it still bakes up into an impressive cake.

From the simple Cake Mix Doctor classic recipes, such as Kathy's Cinnamon Breakfast Cake and Susan's Lemon Cake, to new cakes

5 Fast Toppers for a Bundt Cake

1. Confectioners' sugar dusted over the top through a small sieve

2. Sliced sweetened peaches or strawberries, or the fruit of your choice

3. All kinds of chocolate shavings

4. Chopped toasted pecans, almonds, or walnuts

5. Crushed peppermint candy or peanut brittle

such as a Banana Bread Cake with Caramel Glaze, Southern Sweet Potato Pound Cake, and a Chocolate Marbled Cappucino Cake, there is a Bundt for everyone here. Make the Pumpkin Party Cake in October and the Old-Fashioned Chocolate Pound Cake with Peppermint Drizzle on birthdays. And have fun exploring all the delicious gluten-free benefits of Bundts.

✦ ✦ ✦

Almond Cream Cheese Pound Cake

✦ ✦ ✦

Our family has been making this cream cheese pound cake with a regular mix for years. We love it as a Bundt, as layers, and as cupcakes. You can frost it with chocolate, with vanilla, with orange—you name it. And, now, you can make it gluten-free!

serves: 10 to 12

prep: 15 minutes

bake: 35 to 40 minutes

cool: 25 to 30 minutes

For the cake

Vegetable oil spray, for misting the pan

1 tablespoon rice flour, for dusting the pan

1 package (15 ounces) yellow gluten-free cake mix

¼ cup almond flour (see Note)

¼ cup granulated sugar

4 ounces (half of an 8-ounce package) reduced-fat cream cheese, at room temperature

½ cup vegetable oil

3 large eggs

1 teaspoon pure vanilla extract

1 teaspoon pure almond extract

For the orange and almond glaze

1 cup confectioners' sugar, sifted

3 tablespoons orange juice (fresh or from a carton)

½ teaspoon pure almond extract (optional)

DAIRY FREE

Substitute dairy-free cream cheese, such as Better Than Cream Cheese made by Tofutti, for the cream cheese in the cake batter.

Sticky Situation: How to Prep a Bundt Pan so the Cake Doesn't Stick

Nothing is as frustrating as a cake stuck to the pan. You shake, you pry, you pray! And still that cake sticks and you end up patching it back together and pouring loads of glaze on top. My best advice is to prep the pan with a little extra care so the cake doesn't stick next time. With most lightweight Bundt pans, those with the nonstick coating, you just need a generous misting of a vegetable oil spray and a dusting of either rice flour, soy flour, unsweetened cocoa, a cinnamon-sugar mix, or cake mix. But for heavier Bundt pans, especially those decorative Bundts with lots of grooves, you should paint the pan with vegetable oil shortening using a small pastry brush. Then dust it with rice or soy flour, cocoa, or cinnamon sugar. Make sure you don't let the cake cool in the pan too long—just ten minutes for Bundts and five minutes for layers is enough with these gluten-free mixes. Loosen the edges of the cake with a long, sharp knife or metal spatula, then give it a few good shakes before inverting it onto a cake rack to cool completely.

1. Make the cake: Place a rack in the center of the oven and preheat the oven to 350°F. Lightly mist a 12-cup Bundt pan with vegetable oil spray, then dust it with the rice flour. Shake out the excess rice flour and set the pan aside.

2. Place the cake mix, almond flour, granulated sugar, cream cheese, oil, eggs, vanilla extract, and the 1 teaspoon of almond extract in a large mixing bowl and beat with an electric mixer on low speed until the ingredients are just incorporated, 30 seconds. Stop the machine and scrape down the side of the bowl with a rubber spatula. Increase the mixer speed to medium and beat the batter until smooth, 1½ to 2 minutes longer, scraping down the side of the bowl again if needed. Pour the batter into the prepared Bundt pan, smoothing the top with the rubber spatula, and place the pan in the oven.

3. Bake the cake until it is golden brown and the top springs back when lightly pressed with a finger, 35 to 40 minutes. Transfer the Bundt pan to a wire rack and let the cake cool for 10 minutes. Run a long, sharp knife around the edge of the cake, shake the pan gently, and invert the cake onto a wire rack.

4. Make the glaze: Place the confectioners' sugar, orange juice, and ½ teaspoon of almond extract, if desired, in a small mixing bowl and whisk until the glaze is smooth. Transfer the cake to a serving plate. Spoon the glaze over the top of the cake, then let the cake cool completely, 15 to 20 minutes longer, before slicing and serving.

NOTE: You can find finely ground almond flour at natural food stores and Whole Foods. Keep it refrigerated.

KEEP IT FRESH! Store the cake in a cake saver at room temperature for up to three days. Freeze the unglazed cake, wrapped in aluminum foil, for up to one month. Let the cake thaw overnight on the kitchen counter before glazing.

✦ ✦ ✦

The Cake Mix Doctor Says

If you love almonds, make them a bigger part of this cake. After misting the pan with vegetable oil spray, scatter ¼ cup of sliced almonds in the bottom of the pan, then pour in the batter. For a more intense orange flavor, add 1 teaspoon of grated orange zest to the batter. And for a finishing touch, sprinkle the top with sliced almonds.

recipe reminders

Made for:

Prep Notes:

Don't Forget:

Special Touches:

Kathy's Cinnamon Breakfast Cake

✦ ✦ ✦

serves: **10 to 12**

prep: **25 minutes**

bake: **35 to 40 minutes**

cool: **25 to 30 minutes**

DAIRY FREE

Substitute water for the milk in the cake batter and glaze.

A favorite Cake Mix Doctor recipe, this cake is perfect for baking for others, especially out-of-town guests. The gluten-free version is a little lighter than the original recipe but it still has the signature cinnamon streusel running through the middle of the cake and the glaze trickling down the sides. It's up to you whether to add the toasted pecans because the cake is equally good with or without them. Thanks to friend Kathy Sellers for sharing this recipe many years ago.

For the cinnamon streusel

⅓ cup lightly packed light brown sugar
1 teaspoon ground cinnamon
⅓ cup finely chopped pecans (optional)

For the cake

Vegetable oil spray, for misting the pan
1 tablespoon cinnamon sugar (see box, page 118),
    for dusting the pan
1 package (15 ounces) yellow gluten-free cake mix
¼ cup (half of a 3.4-ounce package) vanilla
    instant pudding mix
1 cup milk
½ cup vegetable oil
3 large eggs
2 teaspoons pure vanilla extract

For the glaze

⅓ cup confectioners' sugar, sifted

1 to 2 tablespoons milk

Dash of pure vanilla extract

1. Make the cinnamon streusel: Place the brown sugar, cinnamon, and pecans, if desired, in a small mixing bowl and stir to mix. Set the streusel mixture aside.

2. Make the cake: Place a rack in the center of the oven and preheat the oven to 350°F. Lightly mist a 12-cup Bundt pan with vegetable oil spray, then dust it with the cinnamon sugar. Shake out the excess cinnamon sugar, and set the pan aside.

3. Place the cake mix, pudding mix, the 1 cup of milk, and the oil, eggs, and the 2 teaspoons of vanilla in a large mixing bowl and beat with an electric mixer on low speed until the ingredients are just incorporated, 30 seconds. Stop the machine and scrape down the side of the bowl with a rubber spatula. Increase the mixer speed to medium and beat the butter until smooth, 1½ to 2 minutes longer, scraping down the side of the bowl again if needed. Pour the batter into a 4-cup liquid measuring cup. You should have about 4 cups batter. Pour 1⅓ cups of batter into the prepared Bundt pan, smoothing the top with the rubber spatula, and sprinkle half of the streusel mixture over the top. Pour another 1⅓ cups batter over the top of the streusel, smoothing the top with the rubber spatula. Sprinkle the remaining streusel over the top. Then pour the remaining batter over the streusel, smoothing the top, and place the pan in the oven.

4. Bake the cake until it is golden brown and the top springs back when lightly pressed with a finger, 35 to 40 minutes. Transfer the Bundt pan to a wire rack and let the cake cool for 10 minutes. Run a long, sharp knife around the edge of the cake, shake the pan gently, and invert the cake onto a wire rack to cool completely, 15 to 20 minutes longer.

recipe reminders

Made for:

_____

_____

_____

_____

Prep Notes:

_____

_____

_____

_____

Don't Forget:

_____

_____

_____

_____

Special Touches:

_____

_____

_____

_____

5. Make the glaze: Place the confectioners' sugar, milk, and the dash of vanilla in a small mixing bowl and whisk until the glaze is smooth. Transfer the cake to a serving plate. Spoon the glaze over the top of the cake.

KEEP IT FRESH! Store the cake in a cake saver at room temperature for up to three days. Freeze the unglazed cake, wrapped in aluminum foil, for up to one month. Let the cake thaw overnight on the kitchen counter before glazing.

✦ ✦ ✦

The Cake Mix Doctor Says

Make muffins! Place a small scoop of batter into a paper-lined muffin tin, top with a teaspoon of streusel, followed by another small scoop of batter and another teaspoon of streusel. Repeat this to make about 18 muffins. Bake at 375°F for about 20 minutes.

Instant Pudding Mix

I use instant pudding mix more often in my kitchen as a baking add-in than for making puddings. In cakes that begin with a cake mix, the pudding mix adds moisture and helps to suspend such ingredients as chocolate chips, nuts, and raisins that would otherwise sink to the bottom. The instant pudding mixes made in the United States contain a starch from corn, so most brands are gluten-free. All-natural mixes, like those sold at Trader Joe's, are also gluten-free. To make sure, check the ingredient label or inquire on the company's website. With a 15-ounce gluten-free cake mix I tend to use half a package of the pudding mix, and this works out to be about ¼ cup. Seal the remaining pudding mix in the package and place it in a small plastic bag to use for your next cake recipe.

Caramel Melted Ice Cream Cake

✦ ✦ ✦

Melted ice cream cake was a legend when I first heard about it. You bake the cake using the melted ice cream as the fat and liquid. I have found that the better the ice cream, the better the cake. Choose your favorite premium ice cream; for this gluten-free recipe you need a whole pint. Sorry, no leftovers for noshing while you bake! *Dulce de leche* ice cream tastes like caramel. You can also make this cake with any gluten-free coffee, chocolate, or lemon ice cream, or whatever is your favorite flavor.

Vegetable oil spray, for misting the pan
1 tablespoon cinnamon sugar (see page 118)
  or rice flour, for dusting the pan
1 pint dulce de leche ice cream (see The Cake Mix Doctor Says,
  page 109), melted
1 package (15 ounces) yellow gluten-free cake mix
3 large eggs
Caramel Glaze (page 291)

1. Make the cake: Place a rack in the center of the oven and preheat the oven to 350°F. Lightly mist a 12-cup Bundt pan with vegetable oil spray. Dust the pan with the cinnamon sugar or rice flour. Shake out the excess. Set the pan aside.

serves: **10 to 12**

prep: **15 minutes**

bake: **38 to 42 minutes**

cool: **50 minutes to 1 hour**

DAIRY FREE

Sorry, it's not possible to make this cake dairy-free.

2. Place the ice cream in a glass bowl. Melt the ice cream in a microwave oven set to the defrost setting, 2 to 3 minutes.

3. Place the melted ice cream, cake mix, and eggs in a large mixing bowl and beat with an electric mixer on low speed until the ingredients are just incorporated, 30 seconds. Stop the machine and scrape down the side of the bowl with a rubber spatula. Increase the mixer speed to medium and beat the batter until smooth, 1½ to 2 minutes longer, scraping down the side of the bowl again if needed. Pour the batter into the prepared Bundt pan, smoothing the top with the rubber spatula, and place the pan in the oven.

4. Bake the cake until it is golden brown and the top springs back when lightly pressed with a finger, 38 to 42 minutes. Transfer the Bundt pan to a wire rack and let the cake cool for 10 minutes. Run a long, sharp knife around the edge of the cake, shake the pan gently, and invert the cake onto a wire rack to cool completely, 30 minutes longer.

5. Meanwhile, make the Caramel Glaze.

6. Transfer the cake to a serving plate. Pour the glaze over the cake and let the glaze set for 15 to 20 minutes longer, before slicing and serving the cake.

KEEP IT FRESH! Store the cake in a cake saver at room temperature for up to three days. Freeze the unglazed cake, wrapped in aluminum foil, for up to one month. Let the cake thaw overnight on the kitchen counter before glazing.

✦ ✦ ✦

The Cake Mix Doctor Says

Y ou must use a top-grade ice cream in this cake because you need ice cream with no filler and little air. Also check the label to make sure the ice cream you select is gluten-free. When a pint of good ice cream melts you will have about 1⅓ cups of melted ice cream.

Have Cake, Will Travel: 5 Cake-Taking Tips

1. Cool it: Make sure the cake and glaze are cool to the touch.

2. Wrap it up: Loosely wrapped with plastic wrap, place the cake in a cake saver or a basket with lid. Or just place the cake in a basket or box and drape it with plastic wrap.

3. Carry on: Invest in a sturdy plastic cake carrier with a handle and a locking lid. These cost between $10 and $50.

4. Come out on top: Carry messy toppings, like fresh fruit, sticky sauces, or more confectioners' sugar for dusting, with you and top the cake just before serving.

5. At your service: Slice the cake on site. Use the handy grooves on the Bundt cake to make even servings.

Susan's Lemon Cake

✦ ✦ ✦

serves: 10 to 12

prep: 20 minutes

bake: 35 to 40 minutes

cool: 25 to 30 minutes

My sister Susan's signature cake translates well to a gluten-free version and has a delicate texture not found in most gluten-free cakes. Flavored with lemon gelatin plus fresh lemon juice and zest, it's a simple and lemony cake, just right for slicing in the summertime. I call for half of a package of lemon gelatin, so save the rest for another cake. While the cake is still a little warm, you poke holes all over the top with a wooden skewer and spoon the glaze over the cake so that it soaks into it.

DAIRY FREE

No need to substitute. This is a dairy-free cake.

Vegetable oil spray,
    for misting the pan
1 tablespoon rice flour,
    for dusting the pan
1 large lemon
1 package (15 ounces) yellow
    gluten-free cake mix
¼ cup lemon gelatin (half of a of 3-ounce package)
½ cup vegetable oil
3 large eggs
¾ cup confectioners' sugar, sifted

1. Place a rack in the center of the oven and preheat the oven to 350°F. Lightly mist a 12-cup Bundt pan with vegetable oil spray, then dust it with the rice flour. Shake out the excess rice flour and set the pan aside.

2. Rinse and pat the lemon dry with a paper towel, then grate the yellow zest from the lemon onto a plate. Place all of the zest, about 2 teaspoons, in a large mixing bowl. Cut the lemon in half and squeeze the juice through a fine sieve, discarding the seeds. Set aside 1½ tablespoons of lemon juice in a small mixing bowl for the glaze. Pour the remaining juice into a measuring cup and add enough water to measure ½ cup. Pour the lemon juice and water mixture into the bowl with the lemon zest.

3. Add the cake mix, lemon gelatin, oil, and eggs to the bowl with the lemon juice mixture and zest and beat with an electric mixer on low speed until the ingredients are just incorporated, 30 seconds. Stop the machine and scrape down the side of the bowl with a rubber spatula. Increase the mixer speed to medium and beat the batter until smooth, 1½ to 2 minutes longer, scraping down the side of the bowl again if needed. Pour the batter into the prepared Bundt pan, smoothing the top with the rubber spatula, and place the pan in the oven.

4. Bake the cake until it is golden brown and the top springs back when lightly pressed with a finger, 35 to 40 minutes. Transfer the Bundt pan to a wire rack and let the cake cool for 10 minutes. Run a long, sharp knife around the edge of the cake, shake the pan gently, and invert the cake onto a wire rack. Using a wooden skewer, immediately poke a dozen holes in the top of the cake.

5. Add the confectioners' sugar to the bowl with the reserved lemon juice and whisk until the glaze is smooth. Transfer the cake to a serving plate. Slowly spoon the glaze over the top of the cake,

recipe reminders

Made for:

_____

_____

_____

_____

Prep Notes:

_____

_____

_____

_____

Don't Forget:

_____

_____

_____

_____

Special Touches:

_____

_____

_____

_____

letting it soak into the holes in the cake before adding more. Let the cake cool completely, 15 to 20 minutes longer, before slicing and serving.

KEEP IT FRESH! Store the cake in a cake saver at room temperature for up to three days. Freeze the unglazed cake, wrapped in aluminum foil, for up to one month. Let the cake thaw overnight on the kitchen counter before glazing.

✦ ✦ ✦

The Cake Mix Doctor Says

You can vary the size of the holes you poke into the cake. Use a toothpick and you have holes so small they won't be visible. Use a chopstick and you have large holes; they're more visible, but they let the cake soak up a lot of glaze. If you use a wooden skewer, you have holes somewhere in between.

If you wish, add a lemon Candied Citrus Garnish (see page 115).

Fresh Orange Bundt Cake

◆ ◆ ◆

What I love about this orange cake is that it is fresh and simple, yet buttery and rich. It's just the cake you want to serve with tea in the afternoon or for dessert after a meal of grilled fish or roasted chicken. And your gluten-eating friends will never, ever, believe this doesn't contain wheat flour! For a topping, make the easy orange juice glaze or simply sift confectioners' sugar over the cake.

serves: 10 to 12

prep: 15 minutes

bake: 35 to 40 minutes

cool: 25 to 30 minutes

For the cake

Vegetable oil spray, for misting the pan
1 tablespoon rice flour, for dusting the pan
1 medium-size orange
Orange juice (see The Cake Mix Doctor Says, page 116)
1 package (15 ounces) yellow gluten-free cake mix
¼ cup granulated sugar
8 tablespoons (1 stick) unsalted butter,
    at room temperature
3 large eggs
1 teaspoon pure vanilla extract

For the glaze (optional)

1 cup confectioners' sugar, sifted
3 tablespoons orange juice (fresh or from a carton)

DAIRY FREE

Substitute margarine for the butter in the cake batter.

recipe reminders

Made for:

_____

_____

_____

_____

Prep Notes:

_____

_____

_____

_____

Don't Forget:

_____

_____

_____

_____

Special Touches:

_____

_____

_____

_____

1. Make the cake: Place a rack in the center of the oven and preheat the oven to 350°F. Lightly mist a 12-cup Bundt pan with vegetable oil spray, then dust it with the rice flour. Shake out the excess rice flour and set the pan aside.

2. Rinse and pat the orange dry with paper towels, then grate enough orange zest to measure 2 teaspoons. Place the orange zest in a large mixing bowl. Cut the orange in half and squeeze the juice into a measuring cup. Add enough freshly squeezed orange juice or orange juice from a carton to measure ⅔ cup.

3. Add the orange juice, cake mix, granulated sugar, butter, eggs, and vanilla to the bowl with the orange zest and beat with an electric mixer on low speed until the ingredients are just incorporated, 30 seconds. Stop the machine and scrape down the side of the bowl with a rubber spatula. Increase the mixer speed to medium and beat the batter until smooth, 1½ to 2 minutes longer, scraping down the side of the bowl again if needed. Pour the batter into the prepared Bundt pan, smoothing the top with the rubber spatula, and place the pan in the oven.

4. Bake the cake until it is golden brown and the top springs back when lightly pressed with a finger, 35 to 40 minutes. Transfer the Bundt pan to a wire rack and let the cake cool for 10 minutes. Run a long, sharp knife around the edge of the cake, shake the pan gently, and invert the cake onto a wire rack.

How to Make a Candied Citrus Garnish

Whether the fruit is lemon, orange, or lime, and whether you are working with thin strips of citrus peel or slices of fruit, nothing is prettier than candied citrus atop a cake. It appears on several cakes in this book. Here is how to make candied citrus zest. You'll find instructions for making candied citrus slices on page 37.

Rinse two oranges or four lemons and pat them dry with paper towels. Using a zester, cut the zest into long strands. Or, run a sharp vegetable peeler around each orange or lemon, creating long 1 inch–wide strips. Slice these strips into ¼ inch–wide strands. Two medium-size oranges or four medium-size lemons will yield about one cup of loosely packed strands.

Place 2 cups of granulated sugar and 1¼ cups of water in a medium-size saucepan over medium heat and cook, stirring, until the sugar dissolves and the syrup comes to a simmer. Drop the zest into the pan and stir so that all of the strands are covered in syrup. Let the zest barely simmer until it is translucent, 1 to 1½ hours. If you let the zest simmer for the full 1½ hours, it will be crunchy; when simmered for only 1 hour the zest will be softer.

Using metal tongs, transfer the candied zest to a wire rack placed over paper towels and leave it to dry for several hours or overnight. Once the zest is cool enough to handle, but while it is still pliable, you can curl it, twist it, or tie it into knots. You can also coat the cooled zest in granulated sugar. One easy way to do this is to put the zest and some granulated sugar in a large plastic bag and shake it.

Once the candied zest has dried, store it in a tightly covered plastic container; it will keep for about two weeks. For a special treat, dip the candied zest into melted semisweet chocolate.

5. Meanwhile, make the glaze, if using: Place the confectioners' sugar and 3 tablespoons of orange juice in a small bowl and whisk until the glaze is smooth. Transfer the cake to a serving plate. Using a toothpick or wooden skewer, poke a dozen holes in the top of the cake. Slowly pour the glaze over the cake so that it soaks into the holes and dribbles down the sides of the cake. Or omit the glaze and sift some confectioners' sugar over the top of the cake. Let the cake cool completely, 15 to 20 minutes longer, before slicing and serving.

KEEP IT FRESH! Store the cake in a cake saver at room temperature for up to three days. Freeze the unglazed cake, wrapped in aluminum foil, for up to 1 month. Let the cake thaw overnight on the kitchen counter before glazing.

✦ ✦ ✦

The Cake Mix Doctor Says

To make the necessary ⅔ cup orange juice, you can either use orange juice from a carton on hand in the refrigerator or cut another orange or two and juice them for freshly squeezed juice. I always make orange cakes with orange juice from a carton.

Here's another cake that would look pretty with a citrus garnish (see page 115).

✦ ✦ ✦

Cran-Orange Muffins

If you love the Fresh Orange Bundt Cake, you will adore these breakfast muffins. My family can't resist their aroma or flavor. To make them, follow the orange cake directions but make these changes.

1. Omit the vegetable oil spray and rice flour for preparing the pan. Instead, line two 2½-inch cupcake pans with 18 paper liners.

2. Increase the granulated sugar to ⅓ cup.

3. Fold 2 cups fresh cranberries into the batter.

4. Spoon the batter into the cupcake cups, filling them about two-thirds full.

5. Bake the muffins at 375°F until they are golden brown and the top springs back when lightly pressed with a finger, 20 to 25 minutes.

Banana Bread Cake
with Caramel Glaze

♦ ◆ ♦

This yummy recipe was a lot harder to name than it was to polish off! Sort of a banana bread and sort of a cake, it's a little of both! And who ever thought you could indulge like this on a gluten-free diet? My kids have enjoyed the testing process and honestly, they cannot tell the difference between these cakes and one of my usual cakes. It's a real testament to the gluten-free mixes and their adaptability to fresh ingredients from the kitchen.

serves: **10 to 12**

prep: **20 minutes**

bake: **38 to 42 minutes**

cool: **50 minutes to 1 hour**

Vegetable oil spray, for misting
   the pan
1 tablespoon cinnamon sugar
   (see page 118), for dusting
   the pan
1 package (15 ounces) yellow gluten-
   free cake mix
¼ cup granulated sugar
1 heaping cup mashed bananas
   (from 3 small very ripe bananas)
8 tablespoons (1 stick) unsalted butter, melted
3 large eggs
2 teaspoons pure vanilla extract
1 teaspoon ground cinnamon
Caramel Glaze (page 291)

DAIRY FREE

Substitute ½ cup of vegetable oil for the butter in the cake batter. Omit the glaze and dust the cake with confectioners' sugar.

recipe reminders

Made for:

_____

_____

_____

_____

Prep Notes:

_____

_____

_____

_____

Don't Forget:

_____

_____

_____

_____

Special Touches:

_____

_____

_____

_____

Cinnamon Sugar

Y ou can buy cinnamon sugar; you'll find it in the baking aisle. Or, you can make your own: Stir 1 tablespoon of ground cinnamon into ¼ cup of granulated sugar. Spoon the mixture into a clean spice jar with a shaker lid and store it with your spices. My family shakes this on warm buttered toast, on top of oatmeal, atop a pie crust before it goes in the oven, on sautéed fresh apples—you name it.

1. Place a rack in the center of the oven and preheat the oven to 350°F. Lightly mist a 12-cup Bundt pan with vegetable oil spray, then dust it with the cinnamon sugar. Shake out the excess cinnamon sugar and set the pan aside.

2. Place the cake mix, sugar, mashed bananas, melted butter, eggs, vanilla, and cinnamon in a large mixing bowl and beat with an electric mixer on low speed until the ingredients are just incorporated, 30 seconds. Stop the machine and scrape down the side of the bowl with a rubber spatula. Increase the mixer speed to medium and beat the batter until smooth, 1½ to 2 minutes longer, scraping down the side of the bowl again if needed. Pour the batter into the prepared Bundt pan, smoothing the top with the rubber spatula, and place the pan in the oven.

3. Bake the cake until it is golden brown and the top springs back when lightly pressed with a finger, 38 to 42 minutes. Transfer the Bundt pan to a wire rack and let the cake cool for 10 minutes. Run a long, sharp knife around the edge of the cake, shake the pan gently, and invert the cake onto a wire rack to cool completely, 30 minutes longer.

4. Meanwhile, make the Caramel Glaze.

5. Transfer the cake to a serving plate. Pour the glaze over the cake and let the glaze set for 15 to 20 minutes before slicing and serving the cake.

KEEP IT FRESH! Store the cake in a cake saver at room temperature for up to three days. Freeze the unglazed cake, wrapped in aluminum foil, for up to one month. Let the cake thaw overnight on the kitchen counter before glazing.

✦ ✦ ✦

The Cake Mix Doctor Says

If you and your family eat nuts, scatter ⅓ cup finely chopped pecans in the Bundt pan after you dust it with the cinnamon sugar. The pecans will toast as the cake bakes and provide just the right topping for the moist banana cake. Or, after glazing scatter the top of the cake with chopped pecans or walnuts.

Applesauce Cake
with Apple Cider Glaze

✦ ✦ ✦

serves: 10 to 12

prep: 15 minutes

bake: 35 to 40 minutes

cool: 25 to 30 minutes

DAIRY FREE

No need to substitute. This cake is dairy-free.

No cake could be as simple or as delicious as this applesauce cake. The applesauce is what makes it moist and memorable. Use the best you can find—homemade if you have it. Just make sure it's chunky applesauce, the kind with pieces of apple in it. Adjust the seasoning as you like it, adding more cinnamon, nutmeg, even a dash of cloves for a spicier cake. But don't change the amount of applesauce or oil because that proportion is just right. When the glaze dribbles down the side of the cake and you fork into a slice, you'll wager it's got to be apple season no matter what the weather is outside.

For the cake

Vegetable oil spray, for misting the pan
1 tablespoon cinnamon sugar (see box, page 118),
   for dusting the pan
1 package (15 ounces) yellow gluten-free cake mix
¼ cup lightly packed light brown sugar
1 cup chunky applesauce (see The Cake Mix Doctor Says,
   page 122)
⅓ cup vegetable oil
3 large eggs
1 teaspoon ground cinnamon, or more to taste
Dash of ground nutmeg

Touchy-Feely: How to Tell When a Bundt Cake Is Done

Yellow cakes will turn golden brown when they are done, but chocolate cakes don't change color at all. That's why one of the best tests for whether a Bundt cake is done is simply to open the oven door and press gently on it. If the cake gives a little and springs back when you touch it, it's done. By touching the cake gently you don't disturb the baking, and if it is not done, you can carefully close the oven door and let it continue baking.

For the apple cider glaze

1 cup confectioners' sugar, sifted
2 tablespoons apple cider

1. Make the cake: Place a rack in the center of the oven and preheat the oven to 350°F. Lightly mist a 12-cup Bundt pan with vegetable oil spray, then dust it with the cinnamon sugar. Shake out the excess cinnamon sugar and set the pan aside.

2. Place the cake mix, brown sugar, applesauce, oil, eggs, cinnamon, and nutmeg in a large mixing bowl and beat with an electric mixer on low speed until the ingredients are just incorporated, 30 seconds. Stop the machine and scrape down the side of the bowl with a rubber spatula. Increase the mixer speed to medium and beat the batter for 1½ to 2 minutes longer, scraping down the side of the bowl again if needed. Pour the batter into the prepared Bundt pan, smoothing the top with the rubber spatula, and place the pan in the oven.

Made for:

Prep Notes:

Don't Forget:

Special Touches:

3. Bake the cake until it is golden brown and the top springs back when lightly pressed with a finger, 35 to 40 minutes. Transfer the Bundt pan to a wire rack and let the cake cool for 10 minutes. Run a long, sharp knife around the edge of the cake, shake the pan gently, and invert the cake onto a wire rack.

4. Meanwhile, make the glaze: Place the confectioners' sugar and cider in a small saucepan over low heat. Heat, stirring until the glaze is smooth, 2 to 3 minutes. Transfer the cake to a serving plate. Pour the glaze over the cake and let the cake cool completely, 15 to 20 minutes longer before slicing and serving. If desired, press chopped dried apples or apple chips into the glaze.

KEEP IT FRESH! Store the cake in a cake saver at room temperature for up to three days. Freeze the unglazed cake, wrapped in aluminum foil, for up to one month. Let the cake thaw overnight on the kitchen counter before glazing.

✦ ✦ ✦

The Cake Mix Doctor Says

The two best and most "appley" applesauces I have tasted are homemade applesauce made when good tart apples are in season and Trader Joe's "chunky spiced apples." You can use either sweetened or unsweetened applesauce. Just be sure it's the highest quality you can find because the applesauce makes a real difference in this cake.

Toasted Coconut Pound Cake
with Coconut Drizzle

◆ ✦ ◆

I challenge anyone to tell in a blind taste test that this cake is gluten-free. And I also challenge you to find a better coconut pound cake—period. With shredded coconut pressed into the bottom of the Bundt pan and then both coconut milk and coconut extract in the batter, the cake is three times coconut. And if you drizzle on the glaze I offer at the end of the recipe, your cake will be four times coconut. Just about right!

serves: 10 to 12

prep: 15 minutes

bake: 38 to 42 minutes

cool: 25 to 30 minutes

For the cake

Vegetable oil spray, for misting the pan
⅓ cup lightly packed sweetened flaked coconut
1 package (15 ounces) yellow gluten-free cake mix
¼ cup (half of a 3.4-ounce package) vanilla instant pudding mix
1 cup light coconut milk (see Notes)
½ cup vegetable oil
3 large eggs
1 teaspoon gluten-free coconut extract (see Notes)
1 teaspoon pure vanilla extract

For the coconut drizzle glaze (optional)

½ cup confectioners' sugar, sifted
4½ teaspoons light coconut milk
1 teaspoon rum (optional)

DAIRY FREE

No need to substitute. This cake is dairy-free.

1. Make the cake: Place a rack in the center of the oven and preheat the oven to 350°F. Lightly mist a 12-cup Bundt pan with vegetable oil spray. Scatter the coconut evenly in the bottom of the Bundt pan; it will toast as the cake bakes. Set the pan aside.

2. Place the cake mix, pudding mix, 1 cup of coconut milk, and the oil, eggs, coconut extract, and vanilla in a large mixing bowl and beat with an electric mixer on low speed until the ingredients are just incorporated, 30 seconds. Stop the machine and scrape down the side of the bowl with a rubber spatula. Increase the mixer speed to medium and beat the batter until smooth, 1½ to 2 minutes longer, scraping down the side of the bowl again if needed. Pour the batter over the coconut in the prepared Bundt pan, smoothing the top with the rubber spatula, and place the pan in the oven.

3. Bake the cake until it is golden brown and the top springs back when lightly pressed with a finger, 38 to 42 minutes. Transfer the Bundt pan to a wire rack and let the cake cool for 10 minutes. Run a long, sharp knife around the edges of the cake, shake the pan gently, and invert the cake onto a wire rack to cool completely, 15 to 20 minutes.

4. Meanwhile, make the coconut drizzle glaze, if using: Place the confectioners' sugar, 4½ teaspoons of coconut milk, and the rum, if using, in a small mixing bowl and whisk until smooth. Transfer the cake to a serving plate. Using the end of the whisk, drizzle the glaze over the cake. Let the cake rest 5 minutes before slicing and serving.

NOTES: Light coconut milk is lower in fat and calories than regular coconut milk. You can find canned light coconut milk on the supermarket aisle where Thai ingredients are sold. It frequently comes in 13½-ounce cans. Save the leftover coconut milk for another cake recipe or use it in curries or sauces. It can be refrigerated in a glass jar or plastic container for up to 10 days.

Be sure to read the label on the coconut extract. Some is imitation coconut flavoring and some is pure coconut extract, which is more expensive. Either should be gluten-free, but read the label to make sure.

KEEP IT FRESH! Store the cake in a cake saver at room temperature for up to three days. Freeze the unglazed cake, wrapped in aluminum foil, for up to one month. Let the cake thaw overnight on the kitchen counter before glazing.

◆ ◆ ◆

The Cake Mix Doctor Says

Turn this into a banana-coconut pound cake by substituting one mashed, small, very ripe banana for part of the oil. Measure the mashed banana and add up to ½ cup to the batter. If you have less than ½ cup of banana, add enough oil to measure ½ cup. If you are adding ½ cup of banana, omit the oil.

recipe reminders

Made for:

Prep Notes:

Don't Forget:

Special Touches:

Pumpkin Party Cake

✦ ✦ ✦

serves: 10 to 12

prep: 20 minutes

bake: 35 to 40 minutes

cool: 25 to 30 minutes

DAIRY FREE

Use apple juice, orange juice, or water in the cake batter and orange juice in the glaze.

I n the middle of a cool, crisp October or at a potluck party on a hot July day, there is nothing better than a slice of spiced pumpkin cake. It's a do-ahead cake that appeals to everyone. If you want to create a showier cake, bake the variation on page 128, which looks like a real pumpkin.

For the cake

Vegetable oil spray, for misting the pan
1 tablespoon cinnamon sugar (see box, page 118),
    for dusting the pan
1 package (15 ounces) yellow gluten-free cake mix
¼ cup granulated sugar
1 cup canned pumpkin
½ cup vegetable oil
3 tablespoons buttermilk, apple juice, orange juice, or water
3 large eggs
2 teaspoons pure vanilla extract
2 teaspoons ground cinnamon
¼ teaspoon ground ginger
¼ teaspoon ground cloves

For the glaze

1 cup confectioners' sugar
2 tablespoons milk or orange juice
Orange food color, if desired
Mint leaves, or other edible leaves (optional),
    for garnish

1. Make the cake: Place a rack in the center of the oven and preheat the oven to 350°F. Lightly mist a 12-cup Bundt pan with vegetable oil spray, then dust it with the cinnamon sugar. Shake out the excess cinnamon sugar and set the pan aside.

2. Place the cake mix, granulated sugar, pumpkin, oil, buttermilk, eggs, vanilla, cinnamon, ginger, and cloves in a large mixing bowl and beat with an electric mixer on low speed until the ingredients are just incorporated, 30 seconds. Stop the machine and scrape down the side of the bowl with a rubber spatula. Increase the mixer speed to medium and beat the batter until smooth, 1½ to 2 minutes longer, scraping down the side of the bowl again if needed. Pour the batter into the prepared Bundt pan, smoothing the top with the rubber spatula, and place the pan in the oven.

3. Bake the cake until the top springs back when lightly pressed with a finger, 35 to 40 minutes. Transfer the Bundt pan to a wire rack and let the cake cool for 10 minutes. Run a long, sharp knife around the edges of the cake, shake the pan gently, and invert the cake onto a wire rack to cool completely, 15 to 20 minutes longer.

4. Meanwhile, make the glaze: Place the confectioners' sugar and milk in a small mixing bowl and whisk until smooth. Add enough food color, if using, to achieve the desired shade of orange. Transfer the cake to a serving plate. Spoon the glaze over the top of the cake, allowing it to dribble down the side. Garnish the cake with mint leaves, if desired.

recipe reminders

Made for:

_____

_____

_____

_____

Prep Notes:

_____

_____

_____

_____

Don't Forget:

_____

_____

_____

_____

Special Touches:

_____

_____

_____

_____

_____

KEEP IT FRESH! Store the cake in a cake saver at room temperature for up to three days. Freeze the unglazed cake, wrapped in aluminum foil, for up to one month. Let the cake thaw overnight on the kitchen counter before glazing.

✦ ✦ ✦

The Cake Mix Doctor Says

Add whatever spices you like to this batter. I chose cinnamon, ginger, and cloves, but you might like nutmeg better, so add it instead of the ginger or cloves. It does help to have other spices to complement cinnamon when baking. It makes the flavor of the cake more interesting than just cinnamon alone.

✦ ✦ ✦

Whole Pumpkin Party Cake

Want a cake that looks more like a pumpkin? Bake two Pumpkin Party Cakes. Make three recipes of glaze. Slice ¼ inch off the bottom of each cake, to make them flatter. Sandwich the two cakes together with about ½ cup of glaze. Place the pumpkin cake on a serving plate. Spoon the remaining glaze over the top and let it dribble down the side, then decorate the cake with fresh edible leaves, such as mint, lemon verbena, or chocolate geranium.

Southern Sweet Potato Pound Cake

✦ ✦ ✦

Iloved sweet potatoes even before I was told they were good for me! It might be a stretch to say this cake is healthy because of the sweet potatoes inside, so I can't go that far, but why not add something healthy and delicious to your cakes? Sweet potatoes are a perfect ingredient because they are moist and keep the cake fresh for days. And, they are naturally brightly colored, so they turn this cake into the most beautiful melon color. To glaze or not to glaze? I opt for nothing at all. If you must, dust the cake with confectioners' sugar or place tiny marshmallows on top of the cake and run it under the broiler.

serves: **10 to 12**

prep: **25 minutes**

bake: **35 to 40 minutes**

cool: **25 to 30 minutes**

Vegetable oil spray, for misting the pan

1 tablespoon cinnamon sugar (see box, page 118),
for dusting the pan

1 medium-size or 2 small sweet potatoes

1 package (15 ounces) yellow gluten-free cake mix

¼ cup lightly packed light brown sugar

½ cup vegetable oil

3 tablespoons buttermilk, apple juice, orange juice,
or water

3 large eggs

2 teaspoons pure vanilla extract

2 teaspoons ground cinnamon

½ teaspoon ground nutmeg

½ cup dried currants (optional)

DAIRY FREE

Use apple juice, orange juice, or water in the cake batter.

1. Place a rack in the center of the oven and preheat the oven to 350°F. Lightly mist a 12-cup Bundt pan with vegetable oil spray, then dust it with the cinnamon sugar. Shake out the excess cinnamon sugar and set the pan aside.

2. Peel and quarter the sweet potatoes. Place them in a medium-size saucepan and add enough cold water to cover. Bring to a boil over medium-high heat, then reduce the heat to low and cover the pan. Let the sweet potatoes simmer until tender, about 20 minutes. Drain the potatoes, let them cool, and then mash them; you should have 1 cup. Place the mashed sweet potatoes in a large mixing bowl.

3. Add the cake mix, brown sugar, oil, buttermilk, eggs, vanilla, cinnamon, and nutmeg to the bowl, and beat with an electric mixer on low speed until the ingredients are just incorporated, 30 seconds. Stop the machine and scrape down the side of the bowl with a rubber spatula. Increase the mixer speed to medium and beat the batter until smooth, for 1½ to 2 minutes longer, scraping down the side of the bowl again if needed. Fold in the currants, if using. Pour the batter into the prepared Bundt pan, smoothing the top with the rubber spatula, and place the pan in the oven.

4. Bake the cake until the top springs back when lightly pressed with a finger, 35 to 40 minutes. Transfer the Bundt pan to a wire rack and let the cake cool completely, for 10 minutes. Run a long, sharp knife around the edge of the cake, shake the pan gently, and invert the cake onto a wire rack to cool completely, 15 to 20 minutes longer, before slicing and serving.

KEEP IT FRESH! Store the cake in a cake saver at room temperature for up to three days. Freeze the unglazed cake, wrapped in aluminum foil, for up to one month. Let the cake thaw overnight on the kitchen counter.

✦ ✦ ✦

The Cake Mix Doctor Says

By adding orange juice instead of buttermilk to the batter and melting marshmallows on top you can turn this into a sweet potato casserole cake. Scatter small marshmallows over the top of the cake, pressing them gently into the cake to stick. How many you add is up to you—I add about ¼ cup. Place the cake on a baking sheet about 6 inches away from the broiler. Let the marshmallows broil until they puff up and are golden, about 1 minute. Most marshmallows are gluten-free, but read the ingredient list to be sure.

Sweet Potatoes: Not Just for Cake

Boil and mash some extra sweet potatoes to turn into a delicious dinner side dish. Fold in pats of softened butter, some honey, and salt and pepper to taste. Or, add a little orange juice, maple syrup, and salt and pepper to taste.

Chocolate Chip Cake

✦ ✦ ✦

serves: 10 to 12

prep: 15 minutes

bake: 40 to 45 minutes

cool: 25 to 30 minutes

DAIRY FREE

Substitute water or brewed coffee for the milk and use dairy-free chocolate chips. You may only be able to find the regular-size chips, but that is okay.

Many of you know my love of the chocolate chip cake, and one of my favorites from my books is a Bundt recipe from Stacy Ross of Nashville. That cake contains both semisweet chocolate chips and grated German's sweet chocolate. This gluten-free recipe is much the same, but without the German's chocolate. I find that miniature chocolate chips suspend the best in this cake batter, so use mini chips if you can find them.

Vegetable oil spray, for misting the pan
1 tablespoon rice flour or unsweetened cocoa powder,
    for dusting the pan
1 package (15 ounces) yellow gluten-free cake mix
¼ cup (half of a 3.4-ounce package) vanilla instant
    pudding mix
½ cup vegetable oil
½ cup plus 2 tablespoons milk
3 large eggs
1 tablespoon pure vanilla extract
1 cup miniature semisweet chocolate chips
    (see Note on page 142)
2 teaspoons confectioners' sugar, for dusting the cake

1. Place a rack in the center of the oven and preheat the oven to 350°F. Lightly mist a 12-cup Bundt pan with vegetable oil spray. Dust the pan with the rice flour or cocoa and shake out the excess. Set the pan aside.

2. Place the cake mix, pudding mix, oil, milk, eggs, and vanilla in a large mixing bowl and beat with an electric mixer on low speed until the ingredients are just incorporated, 30 seconds. Stop the machine and scrape down the side of the bowl with a rubber spatula. Increase the mixer speed to medium and beat the batter until smooth, 1½ to 2 minutes longer, scraping down the side of the bowl again if needed. Fold in the chocolate chips. Pour the batter into the prepared Bundt pan, smoothing the top with the rubber spatula, and place the pan in the oven.

3. Bake the cake until it is golden brown and the top springs back when lightly pressed with a finger, 40 to 45 minutes. Transfer the Bundt pan to a wire rack and let the cake cool for 10 minutes. Run a long, sharp knife around the edge of the cake, shake the pan gently, and invert the cake onto a wire rack to cool completely, 15 to 20 minutes longer.

4. Transfer the cake to a serving plate. Sift the confectioners' sugar over the top of the cake before slicing and serving.

KEEP IT FRESH! Store the cake in a cake saver at room temperature for up to three days. Freeze the unglazed cake, wrapped in aluminum foil, for up to one month. Let the cake thaw overnight on the kitchen counter before adding a dusting of confectioners' sugar.

✦ ✦ ✦

The Cake Mix Doctor Says

Turn this cake into Stacy's Chocolate Chip Cake by folding in 2 ounces of grated German's sweet chocolate (half of a package).

---

recipe reminders

Made for:

_____

_____

_____

_____

Prep Notes:

_____

_____

_____

_____

_____

Don't Forget:

_____

_____

_____

_____

Special Touches:

_____

_____

_____

_____

Old-Fashioned Chocolate Pound Cake
with Peppermint Drizzle

✦ ✦ ✦

serves: 10 to 12

prep: 15 minutes

bake: 40 to 45 minutes

cool: 45 to 50 minutes

DAIRY FREE

Omit the Andes mints and use dairy-free chocolate in the cake batter. Use water instead of milk in the glaze.

I absolutely love this cake—it's chocolatey without being overpowering, just like the chocolate pound cakes that were such a fixture on picnic and potluck tables when I was growing up. You make it by beginning with a yellow cake mix and adding half a package of chocolate pudding mix and two ounces of bittersweet chocolate. As the cake bakes the chopped Andes mint candies melt into pockets of mint-chocolate wonderfulness. On top is a brightly flavored confectioners' sugar glaze made with peppermint extract.

For the cake

Vegetable oil spray, for misting the pan

1 tablespoon rice flour or unsweetened cocoa powder, for dusting the pan

1 package (15 ounces) yellow gluten-free cake mix

¼ cup (half of a 3.9-ounce package) chocolate instant pudding mix

1 cup milk

½ cup vegetable oil

3 large eggs

2 teaspoons pure vanilla extract

2 ounces bittersweet chocolate, melted (see The Cake Mix Doctor Says, page 136)

3 ounces Andes mints, chopped (18 mints, ⅔ cup chopped)

For the peppermint drizzle and garnish

- 1 cup confectioners' sugar, sifted
- 3 tablespoons milk
- ¼ teaspoon pure peppermint extract
- 2 or 3 gluten-free peppermint hard candies, coarsely crushed

1. Make the cake: Place a rack in the center of the oven and preheat the oven to 350°F. Lightly mist a 12-cup Bundt pan with vegetable oil spray. Dust the pan with the rice flour or cocoa and shake out the excess. Set the pan aside.

2. Place the cake mix, pudding mix, milk, oil, eggs, vanilla, and melted chocolate in a large mixing bowl and beat with an electric mixer on low speed until the ingredients are just incorporated, 30 seconds. Stop the machine and scrape down the side of the bowl with a rubber spatula. Increase the mixer speed to medium and beat the batter until smooth, 1½ to 2 minutes longer, scraping down the side of the bowl again if needed. Fold in the chopped Andes mints. Pour the batter into the prepared Bundt pan, smoothing the top with the rubber spatula, and place the pan in the oven.

Gluten-Free Extracts

Most pure vanilla extract is gluten-free, but to be sure, read the label. Extracts are the concentrated flavors distilled from beans, nut oils, fruit, spices, and plants such as peppermint, that are then dissolved in an alcohol base. A small quantity adds a lot of flavor, and extracts are invaluable in jazzing up gluten-free cakes. Some flavorings are not from the actual plant but man-made. It's up to you whether you want to use these in your baking, and you can find gluten-free versions. Because extracts and flavorings are expensive, you want to take care when storing them. Close the bottle tightly after each use so it doesn't evaporate. And store them in a dark, cool place. If you use a lot of vanilla extract like I do, buy it in bulk from a warehouse store. Costco's Kirkland brand of vanilla is gluten-free.

3. Bake the cake until the top springs back when lightly pressed with a finger, 40 to 45 minutes. Transfer the Bundt pan to a wire rack and let the cake cool for 10 minutes. Run a long, sharp knife around the edge of the cake, shake the pan gently, and invert the cake onto a wire rack to cool completely, 15 to 20 minutes longer.

4. Meanwhile, make the peppermint drizzle: Place the confectioners' sugar in a small bowl and whisk in the milk and peppermint extract until smooth. Transfer the cake to a serving plate. Spoon the glaze over the cooled cake and, while the glaze is still wet sprinkle the crushed peppermints over the top. Let the drizzle set for 20 minutes, before slicing and serving.

KEEP IT FRESH! Store the cake in a cake saver at room temperature for up to three days. Freeze the unglazed cake, wrapped in aluminum foil, for up to one month. Let the cake thaw overnight on the kitchen counter before glazing.

✦ ◆ ✦

The Cake Mix Doctor Says

Use whatever good semisweet or bittersweet chocolate you have for the cake. Melt it in a saucepan over low heat for 2 to 3 minutes, stirring. Or, break the chocolate into 1-inch pieces and place these in a glass bowl. Melt the chocolate in the microwave on high power for 45 seconds, then remove it and stir. Return the chocolate to the microwave and run it at 15-second intervals, stirring in between, until the chocolate is smooth.

Chocolate Marbled Cappuccino Cake

✦ ✦ ✦

Favorite flavor alert! I love all the tastes in this cake, whether they are alone or piled together. And they remind me of some exotic morning coffee you might order with a hint of cinnamon, some cream, and perhaps shaved chocolate on top. The fun comes when you marble a mocha batter into the coffee-flavored batter. It's just a little trouble, but it provides glitz and glamour. Take this cake to the next bake sale and it will be gone in no time!

serves: 10 to 12

prep: 25 minutes

bake: 38 to 42 minutes

cool: 25 to 30 minutes

Vegetable oil spray, for misting the pan
1 tablespoon cinnamon sugar (see box, page 118),
    for dusting the pan
1 package (15 ounces) yellow gluten-free cake mix
¼ cup lightly packed light brown sugar
2 tablespoons vanilla instant pudding mix, almond flour,
    or potato starch
1 cup reduced-fat sour cream
⅓ cup vegetable oil
3 large eggs
1 to 2 teaspoons espresso powder (see Note)
1 teaspoon pure vanilla extract
2 tablespoons unsweetened cocoa powder
Half recipe Chocolate Pan Frosting (page 290)

DAIRY FREE

Substitute soy yogurt for the sour cream.

1. Place a rack in the center of the oven and preheat the oven to 350°F. Lightly mist a 12-cup Bundt pan with vegetable oil spray, then dust it with the cinnamon sugar. Shake out the excess cinnamon sugar and set the pan aside.

2. Place the cake mix, brown sugar, pudding mix, sour cream, oil, eggs, espresso powder, and vanilla in a large mixing bowl and beat with an electric mixer on low speed until the ingredients are just incorporated, 30 seconds. Stop the machine and scrape down the side of the bowl with a rubber spatula. Increase the mixer speed to medium and beat the batter until smooth, 1½ to 2 minutes longer, scraping down the side of the bowl again if needed. Measure 1 cup of the batter and place it in a small mixing bowl. Stir in the cocoa and set the mocha batter aside. Pour the remaining batter into the prepared Bundt pan, smoothing the top with the rubber spatula. Drop the mocha batter onto the top by tablespoonful. Using a dinner knife, swirl the mocha batter through the cake batter. Smooth the top again with the rubber spatula and place the pan in the oven.

3. Bake the cake until the top springs back when lightly pressed with a finger, 38 to 42 minutes. Transfer the Bundt pan to a wire

rack and let the cake cool for 10 minutes. Run a long, sharp knife around the edge of the cake, shake the pan gently, and invert the cake onto a wire rack.

4. Meanwhile, make the half recipe of Chocolate Pan Frosting.

5. Transfer the cake to a serving plate. Spoon the glaze over the cake, then let the cake cool completely, 15 to 20 minutes longer, before slicing and serving.

NOTE: Espresso powder is spray-dried espresso, and you can order it from baking supply stores, such as King Arthur. It is very fine and dissolves quickly. A less expensive alternative is to use freeze-dried coffee granules, which don't dissolve in the batter as quickly but still give a nice coffee flavor.

KEEP IT FRESH! Store the cake in a cake saver at room temperature for up to three days. Freeze the unglazed cake, wrapped in aluminum foil, for up to one month. Let the cake thaw overnight on the kitchen counter before glazing.

✦ ✦ ✦

The Cake Mix Doctor Says

I added a little instant pudding mix to this batter to make it less gritty in texture. Rice flour is the main ingredient in gluten-free mixes, and it is gritty. You can use some almond flour or potato starch in much the same way as the pudding mix should you have them on hand.

recipe reminders

Made for:

_____

_____

_____

_____

Prep Notes:

_____

_____

_____

_____

_____

Don't Forget:

_____

_____

_____

_____

Special Touches:

_____

_____

_____

_____

Darn Good Chocolate Cake

✦ ◆ ✦

serves: **10 to 12**

prep: **30 minutes**

bake: **45 to 50 minutes**

cool: **25 minutes**

DAIRY FREE
Use soy yogurt instead of sour cream and use dairy-free chocolate chips.

Here is a gluten-free version of my most beloved chocolate cake. But how to adapt this family favorite into a gluten-free cake was a bit of a challenge. Without gluten, the heavy chocolate chips didn't suspend in the batter. So I switched to mini chips. And I thought the cake lacked a decided chocolate punch, so I added a bit of cocoa. Now I love this cake, and I know you will, too! I serve it at room temperature or zap slices in the microwave oven for ten seconds so the chocolate chips are warm and gooey.

Vegetable oil spray, for misting the pan
1 tablespoon rice flour or unsweetened cocoa powder, for dusting the pan
1 package (15 ounces) chocolate gluten-free cake mix
2 tablespoons unsweetened cocoa powder
1 cup sour cream
½ cup vegetable oil
3 large eggs
2 teaspoons pure vanilla extract
1 cup miniature semisweet chocolate chips (see Note)
1 teaspoon confectioners' sugar, for dusting the cake

Bundt or Tube Pan . . . That Is the Question

And my answer is use either. All of the recipes in this chapter call for a 12-cup Bundt pan but can also be successfully baked in a 10-inch tube pan. Allow a little extra baking time—up to 5 minutes—for the tube pan and, when you remove the cake from the pan, invert it twice onto a cooling rack so that the larger side of the cake is up.

1. Place a rack in the center of the oven and preheat the oven to 350°F. Lightly mist a 12-cup Bundt pan with vegetable oil spray. Dust the pan with the rice flour or cocoa and shake out the excess. Set the pan aside.

2. Place the cake mix, cocoa, sour cream, oil, eggs, and vanilla in a large mixing bowl and beat with an electric mixer on low speed until the ingredients are just incorporated, 30 seconds. Stop the machine and scrape down the side of the bowl with a rubber spatula. Increase the mixer speed to medium and beat the batter until smooth, 1½ to 2 minutes longer, scraping down the side of the bowl again if needed. Fold in the chocolate chips. Pour the batter into the prepared Bundt pan, smoothing the top with the rubber spatula, and place the pan in the oven.

3. Bake the cake until the top springs back when lightly pressed with a finger, 45 to 50 minutes. Transfer the Bundt pan to a wire rack and let the cake cool for 10 minutes. Run a long, sharp knife around the edge of the cake, shake the pan gently, and invert the cake onto a wire rack to cool completely 15 to 20 minutes longer.

recipe reminders

Made for:

_____

_____

_____

_____

Prep Notes:

_____

_____

_____

_____

Don't Forget:

_____

_____

_____

_____

Special Touches:

_____

_____

_____

_____

_____

4. Transfer the cake onto a serving plate. Sift the confectioners' sugar over the top of the cake before slicing and serving.

NOTE: If you don't have miniature chocolate chips, you can use 6 ounces of semisweet or bittersweet chocolate. Take a heavy, sharp knife and, beginning at one end of the bar, cut the bar into shavings. Use all of the shavings in the cake. If you have an extra bar on hand, use it to make shavings for the top of the cake.

KEEP IT FRESH! Store the cake in a cake saver at room temperature for up to three days. Freeze the plain cake, wrapped in aluminum foil, for up to one month. Let the cake thaw overnight on the kitchen counter before adding a dusting of confectioners' sugar.

✦ ◆ ✦

The Cake Mix Doctor Says

If you love this cake, you'll love Chocolate Espresso Muffins. Prepare the batter as directed, adding 1 teaspoon of espresso powder or instant coffee granules and ½ teaspoon of ground cinnamon. Line cupcake cups with paper liners or mist them with vegetable oil spray. Fill the pans two-thirds full; you'll have 18 to 20 muffins. Bake the muffins in a 350°F oven for 20 to 25 minutes.

Chocolate Chip Amaretto Cake

✦ ✦ ✦

Many years ago my friend and media escort in the Tampa–St. Pete area, Libbie Jae, shared her famous chocolate amaretto cake recipe with me. I love this almond and chocolate cake, which uses the almond liqueur. I wanted to create a gluten-free version so I streamlined Libbie's recipe and came up with a fabulous cake that really needs no garnish other than a dusting of confectioners' sugar. However, if you want to dress the cake up, see The Cake Mix Doctor Says (page 145) for a quick almond glaze.

serves: **10 to 12**

prep: **15 minutes**

bake: **40 to 45 minutes**

cool: **25 to 30 minutes**

Vegetable oil spray, for misting the pan
1 tablespoon rice flour or unsweetened cocoa powder, for dusting the pan
1 package (15 ounces) chocolate gluten-free cake mix
¼ cup (half of a 3.9-ounce package) chocolate instant pudding mix
½ cup vegetable oil
½ cup reduced-fat sour cream
¼ cup amaretto or dark rum
3 large eggs
½ teaspoon pure almond extract
1 cup miniature semisweet chocolate chips (see the Note on page 142)
2 teaspoons confectioners' sugar, for dusting the cake
Sliced almonds, for garnish (optional)

DAIRY FREE

Substitute soy yogurt for the sour cream and use dairy-free chocolate chips.

1. Place a rack in the center of the oven and preheat the oven to 350°F. Lightly mist a 12-cup Bundt pan with vegetable oil spray. Dust the pan with the rice flour or cocoa. Shake out the excess and set the pan aside.

2. Place the cake mix, pudding mix, oil, sour cream, amaretto, eggs, and almond extract in a large mixing bowl and beat with an electric mixer on low speed until the ingredients are just incorporated, 30 seconds. Stop the machine and scrape down the side of the bowl with a rubber spatula. Increase the mixer speed to medium and beat the batter until smooth, 1½ to 2 minutes longer, scraping down the side of the bowl again if needed. Fold in the chocolate chips. Pour the batter into the prepared Bundt pan, smoothing the top with the rubber spatula, and place the pan in the oven.

3. Bake the cake until the top springs back when lightly pressed with a finger, 40 to 45 minutes. Transfer the Bundt pan to a wire rack and let the cake cool for 10 minutes. Run a long, sharp knife around the edge of the cake, shake the pan gently, and invert the cake onto a wire rack to cool completely, 15 to 20 minutes longer.

4. Transfer the cake to a serving plate. Sift the confectioners' sugar over the top of the cake and garnish with the sliced almonds, if desired, before slicing and serving.

KEEP IT FRESH! Store the cake in a cake saver at room temperature for up to three days. Freeze the plain cake, wrapped in aluminum foil, for up to one month. Let the cake thaw overnight on the kitchen counter before adding a dusting of confectioners' sugar.

✦ ✦ ✦

The Cake Mix Doctor Says

Here is how to make an easy almond glaze to drizzle over the cake after it has cooled. Place 1 cup of confectioners' sugar, sifted, 2 tablespoons of milk, and ½ teaspoon of almond extract in a small mixing bowl and whisk until smooth. Pour the glaze over the cake and press toasted sliced almonds into the top, if desired, while the glaze is still sticky.

recipe reminders

Made for:

Prep Notes:

Don't Forget:

Special Touches:

Bacardi Rum Cake
with Buttered Rum Glaze

✦ ✦ ✦

serves: 10 to 12

prep: 20 minutes

bake: 40 to 45 minutes

cool: 35 to 40 minutes

There is nothing better than a good rum Bundt cake, and the classic Bacardi cake is the best of them all. This recipe is much like the original Bacardi cake from my first Cake Mix Doctor book, but made with a gluten-free cake mix, of course. The difference is the glaze, a better glaze with some brown sugar in it. The glaze seeps into the cake, keeping it moist, and full of good rum flavor. The pecans in the bottom of the pan are totally optional, but I love how they get crunchy as the cake bakes.

For the cake

Vegetable oil spray, for misting the pan
½ cup finely chopped pecans (optional, see Note)
1 package (15 ounces) yellow gluten-free cake mix
¼ cup (half of a 3.4-ounce package) vanilla instant
   pudding mix
½ cup sour cream
½ cup vegetable oil
⅓ cup Bacardi dark rum (see The Cake Mix Doctor Says,
   page 149)
¼ cup water
3 large eggs
2 teaspoons pure vanilla extract

For the buttered rum glaze

4 tablespoons (½ stick) unsalted butter
½ cup lightly packed light brown sugar
3 tablespoons Bacardi dark rum

1. Make the cake: Place a rack in the center of the oven and preheat the oven to 350°F. Lightly mist a 12-cup Bundt pan with vegetable oil spray. Scatter the pecans evenly in the bottom of the Bundt pan. Set the pan aside.

2. Place the cake mix, pudding mix, sour cream, oil, ⅓ cup of rum, and the water, eggs, and vanilla in a large mixing bowl and beat with an electric mixer on low speed until the ingredients are just incorporated, 30 seconds. Stop the machine and scrape down the side of the bowl with a rubber spatula. Increase the mixer speed to medium and beat the batter until smooth, 1½ to 2 minutes longer, scraping down the side of the bowl again if needed. Pour the batter over the pecans in the prepared Bundt pan, smoothing the top with the rubber spatula, and place the pan in the oven.

3. Bake the cake until it is golden brown and the top springs back when lightly pressed with a finger, 40 to 45 minutes.

4. Meanwhile, make the buttered rum glaze: Place the butter in a small saucepan over low heat and stir until melted. Add the brown sugar and 3 tablespoons of rum, and stir to combine over low heat until the sugar dissolves and the mixture boils and thickens, 3 minutes. Remove from the heat and let the glaze cool.

5. Transfer the Bundt pan to a wire rack and let the cake cool for 10 minutes. Run a long, sharp knife around the edges of the cake, shake the pan gently, and invert the cake onto a wire rack to cool completely, 5 to 10 minutes longer.

6. Using a wooden skewer, poke a dozen holes in the top of the cake, being careful not to loosen the pecans. Very slowly spoon the cooled glaze over the warm cake letting it soak into the holes in the cake before adding more. Let the cake cool to room temperature, 20 minutes longer before slicing and serving.

NOTE: If you have a nut allergy, omit the pecans and dust the pan with cinnamon sugar (see box, page 118). The cake will be just as delicious.

KEEP IT FRESH! Store the cake in a cake saver at room temperature for up to three days. Freeze the unglazed cake, wrapped in aluminum foil, for up to one month. Let the cake thaw overnight on the kitchen counter before glazing.

✦ ✦ ✦

The Cake Mix Doctor Says

The rich flavor of dark rum is perfect with this cake, but if you just have light rum go ahead and use it. And add a few chopped walnuts or pecans as a final flourish. This cake not only tastes rummy freshly baked, but it tastes great the next day and the day after that!

STRAIGHT FROM THE PAN

✦ ✦ ✦ ✦

The perfect kitchen, I think, comes with someone to shop for you, someone to prep recipes for you, and someone to wash the dishes. So mine is obviously an imperfect kitchen because I wind up doing all three.

Chocolate Espresso
Buttermilk Cake (page 193)

How to Turn a Yellow Cake Mix into a Chocolate Mix

Yellow gluten-free cake mixes are often easier to find than chocolate ones, so be industrious and make your own chocolate mix from a yellow one. You can:

✦ Add half of a package (¼ cup) of chocolate instant pudding mix and 2 ounces of melted bittersweet chocolate to the batter, or

✦ Add 3 tablespoons of unsweetened cocoa powder to the batter, or

✦ Marble the cake batter in the pan with gluten-free chocolate syrup just before baking. Squirt 3 tablespoons of the syrup in a zigzag pattern over an 8-inch pan filled with yellow cake batter or squirt 5 to 6 tablespoons of syrup over a 13 by 9–inch pan. Using a dinner knife, swirl the chocolate syrup into the batter to create a marbled effect.

Therefore, when I bake, I look for cakes that streamline the process and make cooking more fun and less work. This chapter is all about baking cakes in a pan, frosting them in that pan, and then serving them right from the pan. Love it! These might be what some people call snack cakes, others call sheet cakes, or they are simply the only cakes many people know. My grandmother always made her cakes in small eight-inch pans, and she carefully cut us tiny pieces, right from those pans.

In this chapter I revisit the nostalgic quality of these warm and friendly cakes and also their timeliness in today's busy world. Bake them as an eight-inch square or pour them into a larger thirteen by nine–inch pan, depending upon what the recipe directs.

Cover the cakes with plastic wrap or aluminum foil and take them to a picnic or to the office or just bake them for the folks at home and keep them on the counter for a few days. You can also freeze the cakes, then thaw them first before frosting or glazing them, and you will have that same great freshly baked taste.

The recipes in this chapter range from gingerbread to Lemon Gooey Butter, pumpkin to Pineapple Upside-Down, Honey Bun to Holy Cow, and Orange Cheesecake to Chocolate Zucchini. They're an eclectic assortment of cakes I love, and they will be cakes you'll love, too, because they're baked with gluten-free mixes. They're also easy on you, perfect for your kitchen. You can bake, take, share, eat, and then clean just one pan.

✦ ✦ ✦

Kitchen Sink Gingerbread

✦ ✦ ✦

Whoever thought a simple yellow cake mix could be doctored with spices, cocoa, and molasses to turn it into a rich and moist gingerbread, perfect fare for snowed-in afternoons and wintry weekend dinner parties? I didn't. And I felt a bit guilty adding so many spices and other ingredients, thus the name "kitchen sink." But I found out this is one easy and lovable cake you can assemble in about fifteen minutes. Serve it straight from the pan with a dollop of whipped cream or just a dusting of confectioners' sugar.

serves: **8 to 12**

prep: **15 minutes**

bake: **52 to 57 minutes**

cool: **15 to 20 minutes**

Vegetable oil spray, for misting the pan
1 package (15 ounces) yellow gluten-free cake mix
1 tablespoon unsweetened cocoa powder
1 teaspoon ground ginger
1 teaspoon ground cinnamon
½ teaspoon ground nutmeg
¼ teaspoon ground cloves
8 tablespoons (1 stick) unsalted butter, at room temperature
3 large eggs
⅔ cup apple cider or water
2 tablespoons molasses
1 teaspoon pure vanilla extract, or 1 teaspoon grated
    orange zest
1 medium-size apple or pear, peeled, cored, and finely
    chopped (¾ cup, optional)
Whipped cream or vanilla ice cream (optional), for serving
Chopped toasted walnuts (optional, see page 172), for garnish
Confectioners' sugar (optional), for dusting the cake

DAIRY FREE

Use margarine instead of butter in the cake and serve the cake with a dusting of confectioners' sugar.

1. Place a rack in the center of the oven and preheat the oven to 350°F. Lightly mist an 8-inch square pan with vegetable oil spray and set the pan aside.

2. Place the cake mix, cocoa, ginger, cinnamon, nutmeg, and cloves in a large mixing bowl and whisk to combine. Cut the butter into tablespoons, then add it and the eggs, apple cider or water, molasses, and vanilla and beat with an electric mixer on low speed until the ingredients are just incorporated, 30 seconds. Stop the machine and scrape down the side of the bowl with a rubber spatula. Increase the mixer speed to medium and beat the batter until smooth, 1½ to 2 minutes longer, scraping down the side of the bowl again if needed. Fold in the chopped apple or pear, if using. Pour the batter into the prepared pan, smoothing the top with the rubber spatula, and place the pan in the oven.

3. Bake the cake until the top springs back when lightly pressed with a finger, 52 to 57 minutes. Transfer the pan to a wire rack and let the cake cool completely, 15 to 20 minutes. Serve the cake with any of the suggested garnishes, if desired.

KEEP IT FRESH! Store the cake in the pan, covered with plastic wrap, at room temperature for up to three days. Freeze the cake, wrapped in aluminum foil, for up to one month. To serve the cake warm, reheat it, partially covered with aluminum foil, in a 300°F oven until warmed through, 30 minutes.

✦ ✦ ✦

The Cake Mix Doctor Says

I'm always experimenting on varying all my cakes and urge you to do the same. I had particular fun with my gingerbread recipe, so I included the special doctoring that follows.

Pear and Blueberry Gingerbread Upside-Down Cake

I f you love this gingerbread, try a variation with pear and blueberries on the bottom of the cake.

1. Preheat the oven to 350°F. Spread ¼ cup lightly packed dark brown sugar in a thin layer on the bottom of an 8-inch square baking pan.

2. Melt 3 tablespoons of unsalted butter and pour the butter evenly over the brown sugar. Peel, core, and thinly slice one pear and arrange the pear slices side by side on top of the brown sugar and butter. Scatter ½ cup of fresh blueberries on top of the pear slices.

3. Prepare the Kitchen Sink Gingerbread cake batter as directed but omit the finely chopped apple or pear. Pour the batter over the pear slices and blueberries and place the pan in the oven.

4. Bake the cake until the top springs back when lightly pressed with a finger, 55 to 60 minutes.

5. Remove the pan from the oven and carefully run a knife around the edges of the cake. Invert the pan onto a serving plate and let it cool for 10 minutes before serving it while still warm. Or, leave the cake in the pan and cut it into serving pieces, making sure to slide underneath each slice with a spatula to get the brown sugar and fruit on the bottom. Serve the warm cake with vanilla ice cream.

recipe reminders

Made for:

Prep Notes:

Don't Forget:

Special Touches:

Easy One-Pan Caramel Cake

✦ ✦ ✦

serves: 8 to 12

prep: 15 minutes

bake: 48 to 52 minutes

cool: 40 minutes

DAIRY FREE

Substitute 4 ounces (half of an 8-ounce package) of a dairy-free cream cheese, such as Better Than Cream Cheese made by Tofutti, in place of the 8 ounces of whipped cream cheese. When making the caramel frosting, use margarine instead of butter and soy milk instead of the regular milk.

For all the times I spread chocolate frosting over a yellow cake there are those rare exceptions when I think, no, not chocolate this time. Why not caramel? And then I wonder why I don't make caramel cake more often. You, too, should make caramel cake often with a gluten-free cake mix and my simple but luscious frosting.

Vegetable oil spray, for misting the pan
1 package (15 ounces) yellow gluten-free cake mix
2 tablespoons lightly packed light brown sugar
1 container (8 ounces) whipped cream cheese
½ cup vegetable oil
3 large eggs
3 tablespoons warm water
1 tablespoon pure vanilla extract
1 teaspoon pure almond extract or maple flavoring
Half recipe Quick Caramel Frosting (page 286)

1. Place a rack in the center of the oven and preheat the oven to 350°F. Lightly mist an 8-inch square baking pan with vegetable oil spray and set the pan aside.

2. Place the cake mix, brown sugar, cream cheese, oil, eggs, water, vanilla, and almond extract or maple flavoring in a large mixing bowl and beat with an electric mixer on low speed until the ingredients are just incorporated, 30 seconds. Stop the machine and scrape down the side of the bowl with a rubber spatula. Increase the mixer speed to medium and beat the batter until smooth, 1½ to 2 minutes longer, scraping down the side of the bowl again if needed. Pour the batter into the prepared pan, smoothing the top with the rubber spatula, and place the pan in the oven.

3. Bake the cake until it is golden brown and the top springs back when lightly pressed with a finger, 48 to 52 minutes. Transfer the pan to a wire rack and let the cake cool completely, 20 minutes.

4. Meanwhile, make the Quick Caramel Frosting.

5. Ladle the warm frosting over the cooled cake in the pan and smooth the top with a metal spatula. Let the frosting set 20 minutes before slicing and serving the cake.

KEEP IT FRESH! Store the cake in the pan, covered with plastic wrap, at room temperature for up to three days. Freeze the unfrosted cake, wrapped in aluminum foil, for up to one month. Let the cake thaw overnight on the kitchen counter before frosting.

✦ ✦ ✦

The Cake Mix Doctor Says

Turn the cake orange by using fresh orange juice instead of the water in the cake batter. Omit the almond extract or maple flavoring and fold in 1 teaspoon of grated orange zest. Frost the cake with the Quick Caramel Frosting or opt for the Orange Cream Cheese Frosting (page 278).

recipe reminders

Made for:

Prep Notes:

Don't Forget:

Special Touches:

Honey Bun Cake

✦ ✦ ✦

serves: 12 to 16

prep: 20 minutes

bake: 35 to 40 minutes

cool: 20 to 25 minutes

DAIRY FREE

Use soy yogurt or coconut milk instead of sour cream and water instead of milk in the cake.

Anyone who loves cinnamon will love this coffee cake. Named for the gooey sweet roll called a honey bun, the cake is perfect for breakfasts and brunches. The original recipe called for a glaze of confectioners' sugar over the top, but with this gluten-free version I've decided there is plenty of sugar in the cake and filling without it. Enjoy!

For the cake

Vegetable oil spray, for misting the pan
1 package (15 ounces) yellow gluten-free cake mix
¼ cup (half of a 3.4-ounce package) vanilla instant pudding mix
1 cup sour cream
½ cup vegetable oil
3 large eggs
2 tablespoons milk
1 tablespoon pure vanilla extract

For the filling

¼ cup honey
⅓ cup lightly packed light brown sugar
2 teaspoons ground cinnamon
⅓ cup finely chopped pecans (optional)

1. Make the cake: Place a rack in the center of the oven and preheat the oven to 350°F. Lightly mist a 13 by 9–inch metal baking pan with vegetable oil spray and set the pan aside.

2. Place the cake mix, pudding mix, sour cream, oil, eggs, milk, and vanilla in a large mixing bowl and beat with an electric mixer on low speed until the ingredients are just incorporated, 30 seconds. Stop the machine and scrape down the side of the bowl with a rubber spatula. Increase the mixer speed to medium and beat the batter until smooth, 1½ to 2 minutes longer, scraping down the side of the bowl again if needed. Pour the batter into the prepared pan, smoothing the top with the rubber spatula.

3. Make the filling: Drizzle the honey evenly over the top of the batter. Place the brown sugar, cinnamon, and pecans, if using, in a small mixing bowl and stir to combine. Spoon the filling over the top of the cake. Using a dinner knife, swirl the brown sugar mixture into the cake batter to marble it.

4. Place the pan in the oven and bake the cake until it is golden brown and the top springs back when lightly pressed with a finger, 35 to 40 minutes. Transfer the pan to a wire rack and let the cake cool completely, 20 minutes, before slicing and serving.

NOTE: Okay, if you've got to have the glaze, whisk 2 to 3 tablespoons of milk into 1 cup of confectioners' sugar and pour it over the warm cake.

recipe reminders

Made for:

Prep Notes:

Don't Forget:

Special Touches:

KEEP IT FRESH! Store the cake in the pan, covered with plastic wrap, at room temperature for up to three days. Freeze the cake, wrapped in aluminum foil, for up to one month. Let the cake thaw overnight on the kitchen counter before frosting.

✦ ◆ ✦

The Cake Mix Doctor Says

Lightly mist the measuring cup with vegetable oil spray before pouring in the honey. The honey will slip right out and not stick to the cup.

Pan Switcheroo

✦ If a recipe in this chapter calls for an 8-inch square pan but you want to bake the cake in a 13 by 9–inch metal baking pan, reduce the baking time to 28 to 32 minutes and double the amount of frosting or glaze.

✦ If a recipe in this chapter calls for a 13 by 9–inch pan but you want to bake an 8-inch square cake, increase the baking time to about 50 minutes and reduce the amount of frosting by half.

Tres Leches Cake
with Whipped Cream and Summer Berries

✦ ✦ ✦

Creamy and flavorful, the *tres leches* cake originated in Nicaragua but can be found on U.S. restaurant menus coast to coast. It's simple to make at home, using a springform pan. The secret is baking a sturdy cake that can soak up all the flavorful milk syrup you pour over it. But I wondered whether without gluten the cake would be able to soak up the syrup or would it just fall apart? To make the cake batter more stable I added a package of instant pudding mix. To give it pizzazz, I added Kahlúa. The cake turned out to be a huge success. It really begs for fresh fruit of all kinds—berries or summer peaches or tropical fruits such as mango, pineapple, or banana.

serves: 10 to 12

prep: 30 minutes

bake: 42 to 46 minutes

cool: 45 minutes

soaking time:
At least 3 hours

DAIRY FREE

Since this cake is all about the milk syrup poured over it, it's not possible to make a dairy-free version unless you forgo the syrup, bake the cake with water or fresh orange juice instead of milk, and then serve the cake with fresh berries and a dusting of confectioners' sugar.

For the cake

Vegetable oil spray, for misting the pan
2 teaspoons rice flour, for dusting the pan
1 package (15 ounces) yellow gluten-free cake mix
1 package (3.4 ounces) vanilla instant pudding mix
¾ cup milk
½ cup vegetable oil
3 large eggs
2 teaspoons pure vanilla extract

For the milk syrup and topping

1 pint (2 cups) heavy (whipping) cream
⅔ cup sweetened condensed milk
(about half of a 14-ounce can)
1 can (5 ounces) evaporated milk, shaken well
3 tablespoons Kahlúa
1 teaspoon pure vanilla extract
1 teaspoon confectioners' sugar
1 to 2 cups fresh berries (strawberries, blueberries, blackberries, and/or raspberries, lightly sweetened) or sliced fresh peaches or nectarines

1. Make the cake: Place a rack in the center of the oven and preheat the oven to 350°F. Lightly mist a 9-inch springform pan with vegetable oil spray, then dust it with the rice flour. Shake out the excess rice flour and set the pan aside.

2. Place the cake mix and pudding mix in a large bowl and stir to combine. Add the milk, oil, eggs, and 2 teaspoons of vanilla and beat with an electric mixer on low speed until the ingredients are just incorporated, 30 seconds. Stop the machine and scrape down the side of the bowl with a rubber spatula. Increase the mixer speed to medium and beat the batter until smooth, 1 to 1½ minutes longer, scraping down the side of the bowl again if needed. Pour the batter into the prepared pan and place the pan in the oven.

3. Bake the cake until it is golden brown and the top springs back when lightly pressed with a finger, 42 to 46 minutes. Transfer the cake pan to a wire rack and let the cake cool in the pan on the rack until it comes to room temperature, about 45 minutes.

4. Meanwhile, make the milk syrup: Set aside 1½ cups of the cream for the topping. Pour the remaining ½ cup of cream and the sweetened condensed milk, evaporated milk, Kahlúa, and 1 teaspoon of vanilla in a small bowl or a quart-size canning jar with a lid. Whisk or shake the ingredients until well combined. You can make the milk syrup up to a day ahead and store it in the refrigerator. Shake the milk syrup again before using.

5. Run a sharp knife around the edge of the cooled cake. Place the cake still in the springform pan on top of a baking sheet with rims. Using a wooden skewer, poke 20 holes in the top of the cake. Slowly ladle the milk syrup over the top of the cake letting it soak into the holes in the cake before adding more. This will take 4 to 5 minutes and there will still be some milk syrup on top of the cake. Cover the springform pan with plastic wrap and place

recipe reminders

Made for:

_____

_____

_____

_____

Prep Notes:

_____

_____

_____

_____

Don't Forget:

_____

_____

_____

_____

Special Touches:

_____

_____

_____

_____

Tres Leches with a Twist?

Jazz up the milk syrup. Here are three more ways to make fun milk syrup for your cake.

1. Use coconut milk instead of cream.

2. Use canned dulce de leche instead of sweetened condensed milk.

3. Add ½ teaspoon ground cinnamon to the syrup. Omit the Kahlúa.

it, while still on top of the baking sheet, in the refrigerator for at least 3 hours, preferably for 6 hours.

6. Make the topping: Place a large bowl and the beaters of an electric mixer in the refrigerator to chill for at least 20 minutes. Pour the remaining 1½ cups of heavy cream into the bowl, add the confectioners' sugar, and beat with the electric mixer on high speed until stiff peaks form, 3 minutes. Cover the bowl with plastic wrap and place it in the refrigerator until you are ready to serve.

7. To assemble, unfasten the side of the springform pan and transfer the cake on the springform pan insert to a serving plate. Spoon the whipped cream on the center of the cake, spread it evenly over the top, and garnish with the fruit. Or cut the cake into slices and dollop each with whipped cream and fresh fruit.

KEEP IT FRESH! Store the cake, lightly wrapped or in a cake saver, in the refrigerator for three to five days. Freeze the unsoaked cake, wrapped in aluminum foil, for up to one month. Let the cake thaw overnight on the kitchen counter, then soak it in the milk syrup.

✦ ✦ ✦

The Cake Mix Doctor Says

For a fun banana pudding version of this *tres leches* cake, garnish it with sliced bananas, whipped cream, and a generous drizzle of Kahlúa.

Easy Fruit Crisp

✦ ◆ ✦

Don't think cake mixes are just for making cakes! You can turn gluten-free yellow mix into the crumble topping for a fruit crisp. Rely on the ease of frozen berries, or substitute pears and cranberries in the fall or four cups of your favorite summer fruit when it comes in season. There is no need to sweeten the fruit as the crumble has plenty of sugar.

serves: 12 to 16

prep: 15 to 20 minutes

bake: 30 to 35 minutes

cool: 5 minutes

2 packages (about 16 ounces each) frozen unsweetened
   berry medley (strawberries, raspberries, blueberries,
   and blackberries), or see The Cake Mix Doctor Says
   (page 166)
1 package (15 ounces) yellow gluten-free cake mix
½ teaspoon ground cinnamon
⅓ cup lightly packed light brown sugar
12 tablespoons (1½ sticks) unsalted
   butter, melted
1 large egg (see Note)
1 teaspoon pure vanilla extract
Vanilla ice cream (optional),
   for serving

DAIRY FREE

Use margarine instead of butter in the cinnamon crumble.

recipe reminders

Made for: _____

_____

_____

_____

_____

Prep Notes: _____

_____

_____

_____

_____

Don't Forget: _____

_____

_____

_____

_____

Special Touches: _____

_____

_____

_____

_____

1. Place a rack in the center of the oven and preheat the oven to 375°F.

2. Place the frozen berries in a 13 by 9–inch glass baking dish and set the pan aside.

3. Place the cake mix, cinnamon, and brown sugar in a large mixing bowl and stir with a fork to combine. Add the melted butter, egg, and vanilla and stir with the fork until the mixture is well combined, 1 to 2 minutes. Scatter 1-inch pieces of the crumble over the top of the fruit, leaving spaces so that the fruit is not completely covered. Place the pan in the oven.

4. Bake the crisp until the crumble topping is golden brown and the fruit bubbles up around it, 30 to 35 minutes. Transfer the pan to a wire rack and let the crisp cool for 5 minutes, then serve it warm with vanilla ice cream, if desired.

NOTE: You can omit the egg for a crunchier crust.

KEEP IT FRESH! Store the crisp in the pan, covered with plastic wrap, at room temperature for up to three days. The crisp does not freeze well.

✦ ✦ ✦

The Cake Mix Doctor Says

You can use fresh or frozen fruit in this easy crisp. For an autumn crumble, scatter 1 cup of fresh cranberries and 2 to 3 cups of sliced fresh pears (2 large pears) on the bottom of the pan before adding the crumble. For a springtime crumble, use 4 cups of fresh blueberries.

Fresh Apple and Pear Skillet Cake

✦ ✦ ✦

Cast-iron skillets are a kitchen staple in many parts of the United States, and down South we are known for baking our cornbread in them. But cakes, too, can be baked in those simple skillets, especially cakes with fruit on the bottom such as this one. The cast-iron skillet creates a crisp buttery fruit layer on the bottom and the cake bakes quickly and evenly. My skillet is ten inches in diameter; see the Note if you will be using a pan of a different size. Spoon this cake warm from the pan and serve it with vanilla ice cream or fresh whipped cream, or turn it out of the skillet, slice it into wedges, and dust them with confectioners' sugar.

serves: **10 to 12**

prep: **20 minutes**

bake: **25 to 30 minutes**

cool: **5 minutes**

DAIRY FREE

Substitute margarine for the butter in the cake batter.

6 tablespoons (¾ stick) unsalted butter,
    at room temperature
2 tablespoons lightly packed light brown sugar
1 large apple, peeled, cored, and cut into
    ¼-inch slices
1 large pear, peeled, cored, and cut into
    ¼-inch slices
1 package (15 ounces) yellow gluten-free cake mix
¼ cup (half of a 3.4-ounce package) vanilla instant
    pudding mix
¾ cup apple cider or apple juice
3 large eggs
1 teaspoon ground cinnamon
¼ teaspoon ground cloves

1. Place a rack in the center of the oven and preheat the oven to 350°F. Place 2 tablespoons of the butter in a 10-inch cast-iron skillet and melt the butter over low heat. Remove the skillet from the heat and stir in the brown sugar. Using a spatula, press the butter and brown sugar mixture evenly over the bottom of the skillet. Arrange the apple and pear slices on top of the brown sugar mixture, pressing them into it. Set the skillet aside.

2. Place the cake mix, pudding mix, cider, eggs, cinnamon, cloves, and the remaining 4 tablespoons of butter in a large mixing bowl and beat with an electric mixer on low speed until the ingredients are just incorporated, 30 seconds. Stop the machine and scrape down the side of the bowl with a rubber spatula. Increase the mixer speed to medium and beat the batter until smooth, 1½ to 2 minutes longer, scraping down the side of the bowl again if needed. Pour the batter into the skillet over the apples and pears, smoothing the top with the rubber spatula, and place the skillet in the oven.

3. Bake the cake until it is golden brown and the top springs back when lightly pressed with a finger, 25 to 30 minutes. Transfer the skillet to a wire rack and let the cake cool for 5 minutes. Run a sharp knife around the edge of the cake and invert it onto a serving plate. Serve the cake warm.

NOTE: Skillet sizes differ. If your pan is larger than 10 inches across, decrease the baking time. If it is smaller, you will need to increase the baking time.

KEEP IT FRESH! Store the cake on a serving plate, covered with plastic wrap, at room temperature for up to three days. Freeze the cake, wrapped in aluminum foil, for up to one month. Let the cake thaw overnight on the kitchen counter before serving.

✦ ✦ ✦

The Cake Mix Doctor Says

Use the ripest pear you have and the most flavorful baking apple you can find. Tart apples are best for baking, and sweet apples are best for eating. You can bake this cake using two pears or two apples if you like. It's even good made with 1½ to 2 cups of chunky applesauce instead of the fresh fruit. Spoon the applesauce over the brown sugar mixture in the bottom of the skillet before adding the cake batter.

recipe reminders

Made for: _____

_____

_____

_____

_____

Prep Notes: _____

_____

_____

_____

Don't Forget: _____

_____

_____

_____

_____

Special Touches: _____

_____

_____

_____

_____

Lunchbox Applesauce Cake

✦ ✦ ✦

serves: **12 to 16**

prep: **20 minutes**

bake: **35 to 40 minutes**

cool: **40 minutes**

Sturdy and substantial, this cake is just the sort you want to cut into squares and tuck in a lunchbox or lunch bag or pile on a plate to share with your office mates. There are so many wonderful things going on here— the spices, the raisins, the applesauce—and on top is my favorite caramel frosting. Want a healthier option? Omit the frosting. The cake is good just on its own.

DAIRY FREE

The cake itself is dairy-free! Omit the Quick Caramel Frosting.

Vegetable oil spray, for misting the pan
1 package (15 ounces) yellow gluten-free cake mix
1 teaspoon ground cinnamon
¼ teaspoon ground nutmeg
¼ teaspoon ground cloves
1⅓ cups unsweetened applesauce
⅓ cup vegetable oil
3 large eggs
2 teaspoons pure vanilla extract
½ cup golden raisins (see Note)
½ teaspoon rice flour
Quick Caramel Frosting (page 285)
½ cup chopped toasted walnuts (optional; see box,
    page 172), for garnish

1. Place a rack in the center of the oven and preheat the oven to 350°F. Lightly mist a 13 by 9–inch metal baking pan with vegetable oil spray and set the pan aside.

2. Place the cake mix, cinnamon, nutmeg, and cloves in a large mixing bowl and, holding the beaters of an electric mixer in your hand, whisk with them to combine. Add the applesauce, oil, eggs, and vanilla, attach the beaters to the mixer, and beat the batter on low speed until the ingredients are just incorporated, 30 seconds. Stop the machine and scrape down the side of the bowl with a rubber spatula. Increase the mixer speed to medium and beat the batter until smooth, 1½ to 2 minutes longer, scraping down the side of the bowl again if needed. Toss the raisins with the rice flour, then fold them into the batter. Pour the batter into the prepared pan, smoothing the top with the rubber spatula, and place the pan in the oven.

3. Bake the cake until it is golden brown and the top springs back when lightly pressed with a finger, 35 to 40 minutes. Transfer the pan to a wire rack and let the cake cool completely, 20 minutes.

4. Meanwhile, make the Quick Caramel Frosting.

5. Ladle the warm frosting over the cooled cake in the pan and smooth the top with a metal spatula. Scatter the walnuts, if using, on top of the cake while the frosting is still warm. Let the frosting set for 20 minutes before slicing and serving the cake.

NOTE: No golden raisins? Use ½ cup of currants, dark raisins, or dried sweetened cranberries or cherries. To prevent the dried fruit from sinking in the batter, toss them with a little rice flour before you add them.

KEEP IT FRESH! Store the cake in the pan, covered with plastic wrap, at room temperature for up to three days. Freeze the unfrosted cake, wrapped in aluminum foil, for up to one month. Let the cake thaw overnight on the kitchen counter before frosting.

✦ ✦ ✦

recipe reminders

Made for:

Prep Notes:

Don't Forget:

Special Touches:

recipe reminders

Made for:

_____

_____

_____

_____

Prep Notes:

_____

_____

_____

_____

Don't Forget:

_____

_____

_____

_____

Special Touches:

_____

_____

_____

_____

The Cake Mix Doctor Says

Ideally, unsweetened applesauce is what you need to use in this cake. But as a cook who does not like to waste ingredients or run to the store unnecessarily, I'd say you can use whatever applesauce you have on hand—sweetened, chunky, or seasoned with cinnamon. But you might want to go easy on the cinnamon if you use an applesauce that is already seasoned.

A Toast to Nuts

Toasting brings out the flavor of nuts. To do this, preheat the oven to 350°F. Arrange the nuts in a single layer on a rimmed baking sheet. Here is how long to toast some nuts until they are fragrant.

Almonds: whole—10 minutes; when toasted they will be light brown; slivered—2 to 3 minutes

Hazelnuts: 20 minutes; rub off the skins before using the hazelnuts

Macadamia nuts: whole—7 to 8 minutes; chopped—3 to 4 minutes

Pecans: halves—4 to 5 minutes; chopped—2 to 3 minutes

Walnuts: halves—7 to 8 minutes; chopped—3 to 4 minutes

Pineapple Upside-Down Cake

✦ ✦ ✦

A favorite American dessert, pineapple upside-down cake knows no single region of the country because everyone everywhere seems to love it.

Vegetable oil spray, for misting the pan
Parchment paper, for lining the pan
6 tablespoons (¾ stick) unsalted butter
¾ cup lightly packed light brown sugar
12 to 16 whole maraschino cherries (optional)
1 can (20 ounces) crushed pineapple, drained,
    reserving ¼ cup juice
1 package (15 ounces) yellow gluten-free cake mix
¼ cup (half package) vanilla instant pudding mix
½ cup sour cream
½ cup vegetable oil
1 tablespoon pure vanilla extract

serves: 12 to 16

prep: 20 minutes

bake: 38 to 42 minutes

cool: 22 to 23 minutes

1. Place a rack in the center of the oven and preheat the oven to 350°F. Lightly mist a 13 by 9–inch glass baking dish. Trace the bottom of the baking dish on a piece of parchment paper, then cut along the trace marks. Place the piece of parchment paper in the bottom of the baking dish and set the pan aside.

2. Melt the butter in a small saucepan over low heat. Remove the pan from the heat and stir in the brown sugar until blended. Pour the brown sugar mixture onto the parchment paper, spreading it

DAIRY FREE

Use soy yogurt instead of sour cream in the cake batter and use margarine instead of butter in the topping.

evenly. Arrange the maraschino cherries, if using, at intervals in the brown sugar. Spoon the drained pineapple on top of the brown sugar and cherries. Set the baking dish aside.

3. Place the cake mix, pudding mix, sour cream, oil, reserved ¼ cup of pineapple juice, and the vanilla in a large mixing bowl and beat with an electric mixer on low speed until the ingredients are just incorporated, 30 seconds. Stop the machine and scrape down the side of the bowl with a rubber spatula. Increase the mixer speed to medium and beat the batter until smooth, 1½ to 2 minutes longer, scraping down the side of the bowl again if needed. The batter will be thick. Scoop the batter carefully on top of the pineapple, smoothing it out with the rubber spatula. Place the pan in the oven.

4. Bake the cake until it is golden brown and the top springs back when lightly pressed with a finger, 38 to 42 minutes. If the cake starts to brown too quickly, shield it by draping a piece of aluminum foil over the top of the cake. Transfer the pan to a wire rack and let the cake cool for 2 to 3 minutes.

5. Run a sharp knife around the edges of the pan and invert the cake onto a serving plate or tray. Peel off and discard the parchment paper and let the cake cool for 20 minutes. Serve warm.

KEEP IT FRESH! Store the cake in the pan, covered with plastic wrap, at room temperature for up to three days. The cake does not freeze well.

✦ ✦ ✦

The Cake Mix Doctor Says

Scatter ½ cup of finely chopped pecans on top of the butter and brown sugar mixture before topping it with the pineapple.

Hot Lemon Poke Cake

✦ ✦ ✦

This has to be one of the yummiest cakes in this book. Whether or not you serve it "hot" is up to you. But once you pour the lemon glaze over the cake, right out of the oven, the cake is ready for slicing. I like it as is, but you might serve it with strawberries when they are in season or with a spoonful of vanilla ice cream. There is something about the lemon gelatin, lemon juice, and orange juice that just takes this cake to a higher level!

serves: **8 to 12**

prep: **10 minutes**

bake: **45 to 50 minutes**

cool: **5 minutes**

DAIRY FREE

No need to substitute. This recipe is dairy-free!

For the cake

Vegetable oil spray, for misting the pan
1 package (15 ounces) yellow gluten-free cake mix
¼ cup lemon gelatin (half of a 3-ounce package)
⅔ cup orange juice (fresh or from a carton)
½ cup vegetable oil
3 large eggs

For the lemon glaze

1 cup confectioners' sugar, sifted
1 medium-size lemon

recipe reminders

Made for:

_____

_____

_____

_____

Prep Notes:

_____

_____

_____

_____

Don't Forget:

_____

_____

_____

_____

Special Touches:

_____

_____

_____

_____

1. Make the cake: Place a rack in the center of the oven and preheat the oven to 350°F. Lightly mist an 8-inch square baking pan with vegetable oil spray and set the pan aside.

2. Place the cake mix, lemon gelatin, orange juice, oil, and eggs in a large mixing bowl and beat with an electric mixer on low speed until the ingredients are just incorporated, 30 seconds. Stop the machine and scrape down the side of the bowl with a rubber spatula. Increase the mixer speed to medium and beat the batter until smooth, 1½ to 2 minutes longer, scraping down the side of the bowl again if needed. Pour the batter into the prepared pan, smoothing the top with the rubber spatula, and place the pan in the oven.

3. Bake the cake until it is golden brown and the top springs back when lightly pressed with a finger, 45 to 50 minutes. Transfer the pan to a wire rack.

4. Make the glaze: Place the confectioners' sugar in a small bowl. Rinse the lemon and pat it dry with a paper towel, then grate the yellow zest from the lemon into the bowl with the confectioners' sugar. You should have about 2 teaspoons. Cut the lemon in half and squeeze the juice through a fine sieve into the bowl, discarding the seeds. You will get about 2 tablespoons of juice. Whisk the lemon juice and confectioners' sugar together until the glaze is smooth. If there is not enough lemon juice, add 1 to 2 teaspoons of water to thin the glaze to a pouring consistency.

5. Using a wooden skewer, poke about 15 holes in the top of the cake. Slowly spoon the glaze over the cake, letting it soak into the holes before adding more. Slice and serve the cake while it is still warm or wait until it cools.

KEEP IT FRESH! Store the cake in the pan, covered with plastic wrap, at room temperature for up to three days. Freeze the unglazed cake, wrapped in aluminum foil, for up to one month. Let the cake thaw overnight on the kitchen counter before glazing.

✦ ✦ ✦

The Cake Mix Doctor Says

How about a hot key lime cake? Use lime gelatin instead of lemon gelatin and, for the liquid, half key lime juice and half orange juice—⅓ cup of each—to make a warm key lime cake. Substitute 2 tablespoons of key lime juice for the lemon juice and zest. You can buy bottles of key lime juice in most supermarkets. Definitely serve this cake with whipped cream.

Glaze 1, 2, 3

It really is as easy as one, two, three to whip up a glaze to top the snack cakes in this chapter. Begin with 1 cup of confectioners' sugar and add 2 tablespoons of the liquid of your choice, such as milk, orange juice, or water. Then as the third step add whatever flavoring you like, such as 1 teaspoon of grated citrus zest, 1 teaspoon of vanilla extract, or a smidgen of espresso powder. Whisk to blend, then pour the glaze over the cake in the pan and let it set for 10 to 15 minutes before slicing the cake.

Lemon Gooey Butter Cake

✦ ✦ ✦

serves: **16 to 24**

prep: **20 minutes**

bake: **38 to 42 minutes**

cool: **30 minutes**

A perennial favorite, Gooey Butter Cake has a deep and rich history with the folks of St. Louis where it originated. But we love it, too, in the South and in the East, the West—all over. I knew I wanted to make a gluten-free Gooey Butter Cake but wondered how. So as a starting point, I tried making my regular recipe with a gluten-free mix. It worked with a few changes. You will love the fresh lemon flavor and the almost cheesecake-like filling. Garnish with fresh lemon slices, if desired. For chocolate chip fans, don't miss my new chocolate chip version that follows.

For the cake

1 package (15 ounces) yellow gluten-free cake mix
8 tablespoons (1 stick) unsalted butter, melted
2 large eggs
1 teaspoon pure vanilla extract

For the filling

2 large lemons
1 package (8 ounces) cream cheese, at room temperature
2 large eggs
1 teaspoon pure vanilla extract
3¾ cups confectioners' sugar, sifted

1. Place a rack in the center of the oven and preheat the oven to 350°F. Set aside an ungreased 13 by 9–inch metal baking pan.

2. Make the cake: Place the cake mix, butter, 2 eggs, and 1 teaspoon of vanilla in a large mixing bowl and beat with an electric mixer on low speed until the ingredients are well combined, 1½ to 2 minutes. Stop the machine and scrape down the side of the bowl with a rubber spatula. The batter will be wet and pourable. Pour the batter into the baking pan, pushing it up the sides ½ to ¾ inch using the spatula. Set the pan aside.

3. Make the filling: Rinse and pat dry the lemons with paper towels, then grate enough yellow zest onto a plate to measure about 2 teaspoons. Cut the lemons in half and squeeze the juice through a fine sieve into a small bowl, discarding the seeds. You will have about 6 tablespoons.

4. Place the cream cheese in the same mixing bowl that was used to make the cake and, using the same beaters (no need to clean), beat with an electric mixer on low speed until fluffy, 30 seconds. Stop the machine and add the lemon juice and lemon zest and the 2 eggs and 1 teaspoon of vanilla and beat on medium speed for 1 minute. Stop the machine and add the confectioners' sugar. Beat on medium speed until the sugar is well incorporated, 1 minute. Stop the machine and scrape down the side of the bowl with a rubber spatula. Pour the filling into the baking pan with the cake and spread it with the rubber spatula so that it completely covers the bottom and reaches the sides of the pan. Carefully place the pan in the oven.

5. Bake the cake until it is well browned but the center still jiggles when you shake the pan, 38 to 42 minutes. Transfer the pan to a wire rack and let the cake cool for 30 minutes before cutting and serving.

recipe reminders

Made for:

_____

_____

_____

_____

Prep Notes:

_____

_____

_____

_____

Don't Forget:

_____

_____

_____

_____

Special Touches:

_____

_____

_____

_____

Freezer Fashion: How to Wrap a Cake for the Freezer

You wouldn't go out in the snow with just a sweater on, so don't send your cakes to the freezer with only a thin wrap of plastic. Double wrap cakes before freezing. Begin by wrapping the cooled cakes in regular or heavy-duty aluminum foil. Then place them in a resealable freezer bag and freeze them. Gluten-free cakes keep for up to one month in the freezer.

KEEP IT FRESH! Store the cake in the pan, covered with plastic wrap, at room temperature for up to three days. Freeze the cake, wrapped in aluminum foil, for up to one month. Let the cake thaw overnight on the kitchen counter before serving.

✦ ✦ ✦

The Cake Mix Doctor Says

Add 2 teaspoons of grated orange zest and 6 tablespoons of orange juice in place of the lemon and you have a gooey orange cake!

✦ ✦ ✦

Chocolate Chip Gooey Butter Cake

For a gooey butter cake with chocolate chips, follow the Lemon Gooey Butter Cake recipe, but make these changes.

1. Increase the vanilla in the crust to 2 teaspoons.

2. Scatter 1½ cups of semisweet chocolate chips over the cake after you have pressed it into the pan.

3. If you like nuts, scatter 1 cup of toasted finely chopped walnuts over the chocolate chips. To toast the walnuts, place them on a rimmed baking sheet and bake them for 3 to 4 minutes in a 350°F oven.

4. Omit the lemon zest and juice in the filling and then bake the cake as the recipe directs.

Pumpkin Spice Cake

with Orange Cream Cheese Frosting

✦ ✦ ✦

There is nothing better than a pumpkin cake in the fall. Its aroma puts you in that autumn spirit, whether you are home from a football game or have just finished raking leaves. But I'm also partial to pumpkin cake in winter around the holidays, especially when the cake has a festive orange-flavored cream cheese frosting. And in the warmer months, too, it's a quick dessert to follow barbecued ribs on the grill. Top the cake with fresh orange sections for a finishing touch, if desired.

serves: **8 to 12**

prep: **15 minutes**

bake: **40 to 45 minutes**

cool: **20 minutes**

DAIRY FREE

The cake itself is dairy-free! Omit the Orange Cream Cheese Frosting and dust the cake with confectioners' sugar. Or glaze the cake: Place 1 cup of confectioners' sugar in a small bowl and whisk in 2 tablespoons of orange juice until smooth. Pour the glaze over the cooled cake, then let the glaze set for 10 to 15 minutes before slicing and serving the cake.

Vegetable oil spray, for misting the pan
1 package (15 ounces) yellow gluten-free cake mix
2 teaspoons ground cinnamon
½ teaspoon ground ginger
¼ teaspoon ground cloves
1 cup canned pumpkin
½ cup vegetable oil
3 large eggs
2 teaspoons pure vanilla extract
Orange Cream Cheese Frosting (page 278)

1. Place a rack in the center of the oven and preheat the oven to 350°F. Lightly mist an 8-inch square pan with vegetable oil spray and set the pan aside.

2. Place the cake mix, cinnamon, ginger, and cloves in a large mixing bowl and, holding the beaters of an electric mixer in your hand, whisk them to combine. Add the pumpkin, oil, eggs, and vanilla, attach the beaters to the mixer, and beat on low speed until the ingredients are just incorporated, 30 seconds. Stop the machine and scrape down the side of the bowl with a rubber spatula. Increase the mixer speed to medium and beat the batter until smooth, 1½ to 2 minutes longer, scraping down the side of the bowl again if needed. Pour the batter into the prepared pan, smoothing the top with the rubber spatula, and place the pan in the oven.

3. Bake the cake until the top springs back when lightly pressed with a finger, 40 to 45 minutes. Transfer the pan to a wire rack and let the cake cool completely, 20 minutes.

4. Meanwhile, make the Orange Cream Cheese Frosting.

5. Spoon the frosting onto the cooled cake in the pan and, using a metal spatula, spread it smoothly over the cake.

KEEP IT FRESH! Store the cake in the pan, loosely covered with plastic wrap, in the refrigerator for up to three days. Freeze the unfrosted cake, wrapped in aluminum foil, for up to one month. Let the cake thaw overnight on the kitchen counter before frosting or glazing.

✦ ◆ ✦

The Cake Mix Doctor Says

If you are feeding a crowd, bake this cake in a 13 by 9–inch metal baking pan for about 35 to 40 minutes. There will be plenty of frosting to smooth over the larger cake. Chill the frosted cake in the pan before cutting it into squares.

recipe reminders

Made for:

_____

_____

_____

_____

Prep Notes:

_____

_____

_____

_____

Don't Forget:

_____

_____

_____

_____

Special Touches:

_____

_____

_____

_____

Orange Cheesecake Squares

✦ ✦ ✦

serves: **16 to 24**

prep: **35 minutes**

bake: **40 to 45 minutes**

cool: **90 minutes**

DAIRY FREE

Sᴇᴇ the dairy-free cheesecake recipes on page 186.

It's fun how a basic cake mix can jump-start a cheesecake. For this one you use the mix in the ginger crust, then whip up a quick cream cheese filling.

For the ginger crust

1 package (15 ounces) yellow gluten-free cake mix
¼ cup (half of a 3.4-ounce package) vanilla instant
   pudding mix
8 tablespoons (1 stick) unsalted butter, melted
1 large egg
¾ teaspoon ground ginger

For the orange filling

2 packages (8 ounces each) reduced-fat cream cheese,
   at room temperature
½ cup reduced-fat sour cream
   ½ cup granulated sugar (see Note)
      2 teaspoons grated fresh orange zest
      (from 1 medium-size orange)
   2 large eggs
2 teaspoons pure vanilla extract
Sweetened Whipped Cream (optional; page 292), for serving

1. Place a rack in the center of the oven and preheat the oven to 325°F. Set aside an ungreased 13 by 9–inch metal baking pan.

2. Make the crust: Place the cake mix, pudding mix, melted butter, 1 egg, and the ginger in a large mixing bowl and beat with an electric mixer on medium speed until the ingredients come together, 1 minute. Transfer the crust mixture to the baking pan and, using your fingers, press it evenly on the bottom and about 1 inch up the sides of the pan. Set the pan aside.

3. Make the filling: Place the cream cheese, sour cream, sugar, and orange zest in the same mixing bowl that was used to make the crust and, using the same beaters (no need to wash either), beat with the electric mixer on low speed until creamy, 1 to 1½ minutes. Stop the machine and scrape down the side of the bowl with a rubber spatula. Add the 2 eggs and the vanilla, increase the speed to medium, and beat the batter until smooth, 1 to 1½ minutes. Pour the filling over the crust, spreading the top evenly with the rubber spatula. Place the pan in the oven.

4. Bake the cheesecake until it is golden brown around the edges but still a little jiggly in the center, 40 to 45 minutes. Transfer the pan to a wire rack and let the cheesecake cool completely, about 1 hour. Cover the pan with plastic wrap and refrigerate cheesecake for 30 minutes. Serve with Sweetened Whipped Cream, if desired.

NOTE: For a sweeter cheesecake, increase the sugar to ¾ cup.

KEEP IT FRESH! Store the cheesecake in the pan, covered with plastic wrap, in the refrigerator for up to three days. The cheesecake does not freeze well.

✦ ✦ ✦

The Cake Mix Doctor Says

For a basic cheesecake, omit the ginger in the crust and add a pinch of cinnamon. Omit the orange zest in the filling.

recipe reminders

Made for:

Prep Notes:

Don't Forget:

Special Touches:

Dairy-Free Cheesecake Squares Two Ways

It's easy to make dairy-free cheesecake squares. Here are a lemon cheesecake and a chocolate swirl version.

For the crust

1 package (15 ounces) yellow gluten-free
    cake mix
¼ cup (half of a 3.4-ounce package)
    vanilla instant pudding mix
8 tablespoons (1 stick) margarine,
    melted
1 large egg
½ teaspoon ground cinnamon,
    for the chocolate swirl variation

For the filling

2 packages (8 ounces each) dairy-free cream
    cheese, such as Better Than Cream Cheese
½ cup granulated sugar
2 teaspoons grated lemon zest, for the
    lemon variation
2 large eggs
¼ cup soy yogurt
1 tablespoon pure vanilla extract
⅔ cup Hershey's chocolate syrup,
    for the chocolate swirl variation

1. Place a rack in the center of the oven and preheat the oven to 325°F. Set aside an ungreased 13 by 9–inch metal baking pan.

2. Make the crust: Place the cake mix, pudding mix, melted margarine, 1 egg, and the cinnamon, if using, in a large mixing bowl and beat with an electric mixer on medium speed until the ingredients come together, 1 minute. Transfer the crust mixture to the baking pan and, using your fingers, press it evenly on the bottom and about 1 inch up the sides of the pan. Set the pan aside.

3. Make the filling: Place the cream cheese substitute, sugar, and lemon zest, if making the lemon variation, in the same mixing bowl that was used to make the crust and, using the same beaters (no need to wash), beat with the electric mixer on low speed until creamy, 1 minute. Stop the machine and scrape down the side of the bowl with a rubber spatula. Add the eggs and the soy yogurt and vanilla, increase the speed to medium, and beat the batter until smooth, 1 to 1½ minutes. Pour the filling over the crust, spreading the top evenly with the rubber spatula.

If making the chocolate swirl variation, dribble the chocolate syrup in rows across the top and, using a dinner knife, swirl the syrup into the filling to create a marbled effect. Place the pan in the oven.

4. Bake the cheesecake until it is golden brown around the edges but still a little jiggly in the center, 42 to 45 minutes. Transfer the pan to a wire rack and let the cheesecake cool completely, about 1 hour. Cover the pan with plastic wrap and refrigerate the cheesecake for 30 minutes to make slicing easier.

Chocolate Zucchini Snack Cake

✦ ✦ ✦

If you have never combined chocolate and zucchini, you must. They are natural partners because the flavorless zucchini allows the taste of chocolate to shine through. When you add a pinch of cinnamon to this easy snack cake the result is sort of a spice cake, sort of a chocolate cake. And what I love best is that you can use a modest cake mix to turn out a fabulous cake that will serve nearly sixteen. For dinner parties spoon a dollop of Sweetened Whipped Cream onto each serving.

serves: 12 to 16

prep: 20 minutes

bake: 35 to 40 minutes

cool: 20 to 25 minutes

Vegetable oil spray, for misting the pan
1 package (4 ounces) German's sweet chocolate
1 package (15 ounces) yellow gluten-free cake mix
⅔ cup buttermilk
½ cup vegetable oil
3 large eggs
1 tablespoon pure vanilla extract
½ teaspoon ground cinnamon
1½ cups lightly packed shredded zucchini
    (1 small zucchini)
½ cup raisins, chopped (see Note)
½ cup finely chopped pecans
2 teaspoons confectioners' sugar, for dusting the cake
Sweetened Whipped Cream (optional; page 292),
    for serving
Chocolate curls (optional; page 69), for garnish

DAIRY FREE

Use soy milk instead of buttermilk in the cake batter. Omit the Sweetened Whipped Cream.

recipe reminders

Made for:

_____

_____

_____

_____

Prep Notes:

_____

_____

_____

_____

Don't Forget:

_____

_____

_____

_____

Special Touches:

_____

_____

_____

_____

1. Place a rack in the center of the oven and preheat the oven to 350°F. Lightly mist a 13 by 9–inch metal baking pan with vegetable oil spray and set the pan aside.

2. Cut the chocolate into quarters. Place the chocolate in a small saucepan over very low heat and stir constantly until the chocolate melts, 3 to 4 minutes. Remove the pan from the heat and let the chocolate cool slightly.

3. Place the cake mix, melted chocolate, buttermilk, oil, eggs, vanilla, and cinnamon in a large mixing bowl and beat with an electric mixer on low speed until the ingredients are just incorporated, 30 seconds. Stop the machine and scrape down the side of the bowl with a rubber spatula. Increase the mixer speed to medium and beat the batter until smooth, 1½ to 2 minutes longer, scraping down the side of the bowl again if needed. Fold in the zucchini, raisins, and pecans. Pour the batter into the prepared pan, smoothing the top with the rubber spatula, and place the pan in the oven.

4. Bake the cake until the top springs back when lightly pressed with a finger, 35 to 40 minutes. Transfer the pan to a wire rack and let the cake cool completely, 20 minutes. Sift the confectioners' sugar over the cake and, if desired, serve it with dollops of whipped cream or chocolate curls.

NOTE: To prevent the raisins from sinking in the batter, you can toss them with a little (½ teaspoon) rice flour before adding them.

KEEP IT FRESH! Store the cake in the pan, covered with plastic wrap, at room temperature for up to three days. Freeze the unfrosted cake, wrapped in aluminum foil, for up to one month. Let the cake thaw overnight on the kitchen counter before adding a dusting of confectioners' sugar.

✦ ✦ ✦

The Cake Mix Doctor Says

Zucchini contributes absolutely no flavor to this cake, but the cake is a great way to use up a summertime garden bounty of zucchini. If you like, substitute shredded carrots for the zucchini.

5 Fun Fold-Ins

Want to add pizzazz to a simple cake batter? Try these fold-ins.

1. Miniature semisweet chocolate chips: Fold ½ to 1 cup of chips into the batter before baking.

2. Finely chopped nuts: Add ½ cup of pecans, walnuts, or almonds to the batter or to the bottom of the baking pan before you pour in the batter.

3. Fresh blueberries: You cannot beat this fresh addition to lemon or yellow cake batters. Fold 1 to 2 cups of fresh berries into the batter before baking.

4. Candy bars: Add ½ cup of chopped gluten-free candy bars such as Butterfinger or Snickers.

5. Citrus zest: A little goes a long way, so add just 1 to 2 teaspoons of grated orange, lemon, or lime zest to the batter before baking.

Chocolate Sheet Cake
with Chocolate Pan Frosting

✦ ✦ ✦

serves: **12 to 16**

prep: **20 minutes**

bake: **28 to 32 minutes**

cool: **40 minutes**

O ne day I was shopping for gluten-free cake mixes and I also had a long list of other things to do. So when the supermarket didn't have any chocolate mixes in stock, I bought a few yellow mixes and thought in the car how, in a pinch, I could turn a yellow mix to chocolate. After adding melted chocolate plus a half package of chocolate instant pudding mix, I am happy to say I love this new concoction. It is old-fashioned in flavor and reminds me of the subtle but decadent chocolate cakes my mom used to bake.

DAIRY FREE

U se rice or almond milk instead of regular milk in the cake. Use a dairy-free chocolate and omit the semisweet chocolate chips. When making the Chocolate Pan Frosting use margarine instead of butter and use rice or almond milk instead of milk.

Vegetable oil spray, for misting the pan

2 ounces bittersweet chocolate (see Note), coarsely chopped

1 package (15 ounces) yellow gluten-free cake mix

¼ cup (half of a 3.9-ounce package) chocolate instant
pudding mix

¾ cup milk

½ cup vegetable oil

3 large eggs

1 teaspoon pure vanilla extract

½ cup miniature semisweet chocolate chips

Chocolate Pan Frosting (page 289)

½ cup finely chopped toasted pecans or walnuts or
mini chocolate chips (optional; see box, page 172)

1. Place a rack in the center of the oven and preheat the oven to 350°F. Lightly mist a 13 by 9–inch metal baking pan with vegetable oil spray and set the pan aside.

2. Place the chocolate chunks in a small glass bowl in the microwave oven and melt on high power for 45 seconds, stirring. Let the chocolate cool slightly.

3. Place the cake mix, pudding mix, milk, oil, eggs, vanilla, and the melted chocolate in a large mixing bowl and beat with an electric mixer on low speed until the ingredients are just incorporated, 30 seconds. Stop the machine and scrape down the side of the bowl with a rubber spatula. Increase the mixer speed to medium and beat the batter until smooth, 1½ to 2 minutes longer, scraping down the side of the bowl again if needed. Pour the batter into the prepared pan, smoothing the top with the rubber spatula. Scatter the chocolate chips over the top of the batter and place the pan in the oven.

4. Bake the cake until the top springs back when lightly pressed with a finger, 28 to 32 minutes. Transfer the pan to a wire rack and let the cake cool completely, 20 minutes.

recipe reminders

Made for:

Prep Notes:

Don't Forget:

Special Touches:

5. Meanwhile, make the Chocolate Pan Frosting.

6. Ladle the warm frosting over the cooled cake in the pan and smooth the top with a metal spatula. If desired, scatter pecans or walnuts or more mini chips on top while the frosting is warm. Let the frosting set for 20 minutes before slicing and serving the cake.

NOTE: Whole Foods 365 Everyday Value Dark Chocolate Mini Chunks are perfect for this recipe. Measure out 2 ounces, which is a generous ⅓ cup. Melt the chocolate in the microwave oven on high power for about 45 seconds to 1 minute, stirring. Or use whatever bittersweet or semisweet baking chocolate you have.

KEEP IT FRESH! Store the cake in the pan, covered with plastic wrap, at room temperature for up to three days. Freeze the unfrosted cake, wrapped in aluminum foil, for up to one month. Let the cake thaw overnight on the kitchen counter before frosting.

✦ ✦ ✦

The Cake Mix Doctor Says

Turn this recipe into a Mississippi mud cake, so named because these gooey chocolate cakes resemble the gooey mud of the Mississippi River: Bake the chocolate sheet cake as directed. After removing the pan from the oven, let the cake cool for 5 minutes, then carefully spread 1 cup of marshmallow creme over the top. The heat of the cake will melt the marshmallow creme slightly. Make the Chocolate Pan Frosting and pour it over the marshmallow creme. While the frosting is still warm, scatter chopped toasted pecans on top. Let the cake rest for 20 minutes before slicing and serving.

Chocolate Espresso Buttermilk Cake

✦ ✦ ✦

Cakes don't get much simpler or much more enjoyable than this chocolate snack cake. Bake it for your family to enjoy over the weekend or for your friends at work. The little bit of espresso powder adds a kick and marries well with the chocolate, but if you are serving the cake to kids, I'd recommend omitting the espresso. If you like, top the cake with chocolate-covered coffee beans.

serves: 8 to 12

prep: 10 minutes

bake: 48 to 52 minutes

cool: 20 to 25 minutes

Vegetable oil spray, for misting the pan
1 package (15 ounces) chocolate gluten-free cake mix
1 tablespoon unsweetened cocoa powder
½ teaspoon espresso powder (see Note)
¾ cup buttermilk
½ cup vegetable oil
3 large eggs
1 tablespoon pure vanilla extract
Chocolate Buttercream Frosting (page 287)

DAIRY FREE

Use coconut milk instead of buttermilk in the cake. For the Chocolate Buttercream Frosting, use margarine instead of the butter and almond or rice milk instead of milk.

1. Place a rack in the center of the oven and preheat the oven to 350°F. Lightly mist an 8-inch square baking pan with vegetable oil spray and set the pan aside.

2. Place the cake mix, cocoa, espresso powder, buttermilk, oil, eggs, and vanilla in a large mixing

recipe reminders

Made for:

_____

_____

_____

_____

Prep Notes:

_____

_____

_____

_____

Don't Forget:

_____

_____

_____

_____

Special Touches:

_____

_____

_____

_____

bowl and beat with an electric mixer on low speed until the ingredients are just incorporated, 30 seconds. Stop the machine and scrape down the side of the bowl with a rubber spatula. Increase the mixer speed to medium and beat the batter until smooth, 1½ to 2 minutes longer, scraping down the side of the bowl again if needed. Pour the batter into the prepared pan, smoothing the top with the rubber spatula and place the pan in the oven.

3. Bake the cake until the top springs back when lightly pressed with a finger, 48 to 52 minutes. Transfer the pan to a wire rack and let the cake cool completely, 20 to 25 minutes.

4. Meanwhile, make the Chocolate Buttercream Frosting. Spread a thick layer of frosting over the cooled cake, then slice it and serve.

NOTE: Espresso powder adds a little kick to this recipe, something you definitely want if you are baking for your office friends. You can add up to 1 teaspoon of espresso powder. If you don't have espresso powder, just use a ½ teaspoon of instant coffee granules.

KEEP IT FRESH! Store the cake in the pan, covered with plastic wrap, at room temperature for up to three days. Freeze the unfrosted cake, wrapped in aluminum foil, for up to one month. Let the cake thaw overnight on the kitchen counter before frosting.

✦ ✦ ✦

The Cake Mix Doctor Says

This cake keeps best at room temperature, as do most of the gluten-free cakes. The refrigerator can dry out cakes, especially gluten-free ones, so use the fridge for storage only if the recipe suggests this.

Holy Cow Cake

✦ ✦ ✦

One of the crazy-good recipes from my first Cake Mix Doctor book, this cake is so ooey-gooey people say "Holy cow!" when they take a bite. It has been a favorite of readers through the years, and I was eager to try it with a gluten-free mix once I learned that a key ingredient—Butterfinger candy bars—is gluten-free. In testing this recipe, I streamlined and slimmed down the original recipe. I hope you like this version just as much, and I hope it's so good you say "Holy cow!"

serves: 12 to 16

prep: 15 minutes

bake: 30 to 35 minutes

cool: 25 to 30 minutes

For the cake

Vegetable oil spray, for misting the pan
1 package (15 ounces) chocolate gluten-free cake mix
1 tablespoon unsweetened cocoa powder
¾ cup milk
½ cup vegetable oil
3 large eggs
1 teaspoon pure vanilla extract

For the topping

8 ounces Butterfinger candy bars, crushed
    (about 1½ cups, see Notes)
2 cups Sweetened Whipped Cream (page 292), or
    2 cups real whipped cream topping
1 cup caramel gluten-free ice cream topping
    (see Notes)

DAIRY FREE

Because of the candy and the whipped cream, it's not possible to make a dairy-free version of this cake.

recipe reminders

Made for: _____

_____

_____

_____

_____

Prep Notes: _____

_____

_____

_____

Don't Forget: _____

_____

_____

_____

_____

Special Touches: _____

_____

_____

_____

_____

1. Make the cake: Place a rack in the center of the oven and preheat the oven to 350°F. Lightly mist a 13 by 9–inch metal baking pan with vegetable oil spray and set the pan aside.

2. Place the cake mix, cocoa, milk, oil, eggs, and vanilla in a large mixing bowl and beat with an electric mixer on low speed until the ingredients are just incorporated, 30 seconds. Stop the machine and scrape down the side of the bowl with a rubber spatula. Increase the mixer speed to medium and beat the batter until smooth, 1½ to 2 minutes longer, scraping down the side of the bowl again if needed. Pour the batter into the prepared pan, smoothing the top with the rubber spatula, and place the pan in the oven.

3. Bake the cake until the top springs back when lightly pressed with a finger, 30 to 35 minutes. Transfer the pan to a wire rack and let the cake cool completely, 25 to 30 minutes.

4. Meanwhile, make the topping: Crush the candy bars and prepare the Sweetened Whipped Cream, if using.

5. Using a wooden skewer, poke holes all over the top of the cake. Slowly spoon the caramel topping over the top of the cake, letting it soak into the holes in the cake before adding more. Scatter half of the crushed candy evenly over the top. Spread the whipped cream carefully over the candy, then scatter the remaining crushed candy over the top. Drape plastic wrap over the top of the cake and refrigerate the cake until it is time to serve.

NOTES: Because candy bars are sold in so many different sizes, I am calling for 8 ounces. You can use about 4 standard-size candy bars or about 24 miniature bars. Unwrap the candy, place it in a plastic bag, and seal the bag, pressing out all the air. Place the bag on a cutting board and tap the bag with a rolling pin to crush the candy into pieces.

As for the ice cream topping, Smucker's caramel topping is gluten-free.

KEEP IT FRESH! Store the cake in the pan, covered with plastic wrap, in the refrigerator for up to three days. Or, slice the cake, transfer the slices to a plastic container with a lid, and store them in the refrigerator for up to three days. The cake does not freeze well.

How About a Frozen Holy Cow?

Bake the cake as directed and let it cool completely. Poke holes all over the top of the cake and slowly spoon caramel or hot fudge sauce over the top of the cake. Spread softened vanilla ice cream over the topping, then scatter crushed candy pieces or crumbled gluten-free Oreos on top. Cover and freeze until time to serve.

✦ ✦ ✦

The Cake Mix Doctor Says

This cake improves in flavor after it has been chilled for three or four hours. The caramel has a chance to soak into the cake and the cream mingles with the peanut butter flavor of the Butterfinger candy. Delicious!

CUPCAKES & MUFFINS

◆ ◆ ◆ ◆ ◆

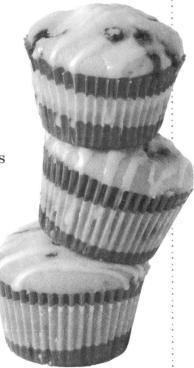

I'm crazy about cupcakes. And if they don't contain gluten, it does not matter to me a bit; this chapter of gluten-free cupcakes is utterly tempting. The batters are inviting and varied—from strawberry to peach to peanut butter to chocolate. And the frostings are the same fabulous ones I slather on cakes.

I'm mad about muffins, too. Baked in the same pans as the cupcakes, these darlings don't need frosting, so they save time and have fewer calories. Sure, you can glaze them with a little

Fresh Blueberry Muffins
(page 225)

confectioners' sugar and orange juice whisked together. Or you can top them with a creative crumble of walnuts, banana chips, and brown sugar. And you can make them interesting by folding in fresh blueberries, raspberries, or raisins. But you certainly don't have to go to the trouble.

For the baker's dozen of recipes here you need just two muffin pans because the recipes yield somewhere between twelve and twenty cupcakes or muffins of a nice generous size. And just as important as good pans are for baking a layer cake, an ice cream scoop is invaluable for making top-notch cupcakes. One scoop fills a cupcake cup two-thirds full and doesn't dribble batter onto the pan, making cleanup a snap. Use a smaller scoop and you will make up to twenty-four cupcakes to feed the class or the girlfriends at the bridal shower.

Cupcake liners make cleanup even easier, no matter whether the recipe is for cupcakes or muffins. The only exception is the lone corn muffin recipe in this chapter, which is best baked in a lightly oiled pan so that the sides of the maple-flavored muffins get crisp and crunchy, making biting into one all pleasure.

Have fun with these cupcake and muffin recipes. Substitute the ingredients your family prefers. Bake them to share with others or freeze them for the days ahead. You will never buy baked gluten-free cupcakes or muffins again when you can bake your own this simply, inexpensively, and deliciously.

✦ ✦ ✦

Favorite Yellow Birthday Cupcakes

✦ ✦ ✦

These are the cupcakes for the birthdays in your life. Top them with a chocolate buttercream or a caramel or strawberry cream cheese frosting, but just be sure to bake these cupcakes. They are moist and rich and plain and simple, just as yellow cupcakes should be. Yet they have just a bit of orange juice, which adds a little natural color to the batter and works well for a dairy-free diet, too. To turn these into confetti cupcakes, see the directions on page 203.

makes: **16 to 18 cupcakes (2½ inches in diameter)**

prep: **20 minutes**

bake: **18 to 21 minutes**

cool: **25 minutes**

18 paper liners for cupcake pans (2½-inch size)
1 package (15 ounces) yellow gluten-free cake mix
¼ cup (half of a 3.4-ounce package) vanilla instant
    pudding mix
¼ cup granulated sugar
½ cup sour cream
½ cup vegetable oil
3 tablespoons orange juice (fresh or from a carton)
3 large eggs
1 tablespoon pure vanilla extract
Chocolate Buttercream Frosting (page 287) or
    Quick Caramel Frosting (page 285)
Gluten-free sugar sprinkles (optional), for garnish

DAIRY FREE

Substitute coconut milk for the sour cream in the cupcake batter.

1. Place a rack in the center of the oven and preheat the oven to 350°F. Line 18 cupcake cups with paper liners and set the pans aside.

recipe reminders

Made for: _____

_____

_____

_____

Prep Notes: _____

_____

_____

_____

Don't Forget: _____

_____

_____

_____

Special Touches: _____

_____

_____

_____

_____

2. Place the cake mix, pudding mix, sugar, sour cream, oil, orange juice, eggs, and vanilla in a large mixing bowl and beat with an electric mixer on low speed until the ingredients are just incorporated, 30 seconds. Stop the machine and scrape down the side of the bowl with a rubber spatula. Increase the mixer speed to medium and beat the batter until smooth, 1 to 1½ minutes longer, scraping down the side of the bowl again if needed. Spoon or scoop the batter into the lined cupcake cups, filling each two-thirds full. Remove any unfilled paper liners.

3. Place the pans in the oven side by side and bake the cupcakes until the tops spring back when lightly pressed with a finger, 18 to 21 minutes. Transfer the pans to wire racks and let the cupcakes cool for 5 minutes. Run a dinner knife around the edge of the cupcake cups and transfer the cupcakes to wire racks to cool completely before frosting, 20 minutes longer.

4. Meanwhile, make the frosting.

5. Spoon a tablespoon of frosting on top of each cupcake and, using a small metal icing spatula, spread it in a swirl, covering all of the top. Garnish the cupcakes with sprinkles, if desired. Place the frosted cupcakes on a serving plate.

KEEP IT FRESH! Store the cupcakes in a cake saver at room temperature for up to three days. Freeze the unfrosted cupcakes, wrapped in aluminum foil or in a plastic storage box, for up to one month. Let the cupcakes thaw overnight on the kitchen counter before frosting them.

✦ ✦ ✦

The Cake Mix Doctor Says

Grate a teaspoon of orange zest and fold it into the cupcake batter. Make the Orange Cream Cheese Frosting (page 278) and you will have the most delicious fresh orange cupcakes you have ever tasted.

✦ ◆ ✦

Confetti Cupcakes: Easy as 1, 2, 3

Kids love confetti cupcakes, but making sure they are gluten-free is another matter. Here is a way to take my basic birthday cupcake recipe and fancy it up for parties.

1. Measure 3 tablespoons of gluten-free decorating sprinkles.

2. Prepare the Favorite Yellow Birthday Cupcakes batter. Fill a cupcake liner one third full, add ½ teaspoon of sprinkles, then top them with enough batter to make the liner two thirds full.

3. Bake the cupcakes as directed, let them cool, then frost them with Vanilla Buttercream Frosting (page 271). When you bite into a cupcake you will see the colored sprinkles inside.

Don't Hold the Sprinkles

Believe it or not, there is gluten in some decorating sprinkles. But never fear, gluten-free sprinkles are here! Look for the brand called Let's Do . . . Sprinkelz that makes three types of decorating sprinkles that are gluten- and dairy-free: confetti (pastel dots), chocolate, and carnival (pastel jimmies). These all-natural sprinkles are sold in natural food stores, Whole Foods, and online at websites that sell gluten-free ingredients.

Think Big Cupcake

Blythe Clippinger of Nashville suggested one recipe for this book, a gluten-free cake she could bake in her Big Top Cupcake pans. Blythe is seven, and her older brother Brian has Down syndrome and is on a gluten-free diet. So I turned the basic but wonderful Favorite Yellow Birthday Cupcakes recipe into a big cupcake for Blythe and everyone who needs to bake gluten-free. You can make this with the Big Top Cupcake pans, which have a pan for the top of the cupcake and one for the bottom, or with the Williams-Sonoma Great Cupcake Pan or the Wilton giant cupcake pan, which are two sided. Please follow the manufacturer's directions for preparing the pans. Here is how I made the cake in my Williams-Sonoma pan.

Prepare the Favorite Yellow Birthday Cupcakes recipe as directed on page 201. Mist the big cupcake pan with vegetable oil spray and dust it with rice flour. The recipe makes about 3½ cups of batter. Spoon 2¼ cups of batter in the part of the pan that will be the bottom of the cupcake and 1¼ cups of batter in the top part. Place the pan in a 325°F oven.

Bake the cakes until they are lightly golden and the tops spring back when lightly pressed with a finger, 40 to 45 minutes. Transfer the pan to a wire rack and let the cakes cool for 20 minutes. Run a sharp knife around the edge of each half of the cake, shake the pan, and unmold the top and bottom portions of the cupcake onto the wire rack. Flip the cupcake bottom over carefully with your fingers so it cools right side up. Let the cakes cool for 30 minutes longer.

When cool, level the top of the cupcake bottom and the bottom of the cupcake top by slicing off ¼ inch of cake.

Make the Chocolate Buttercream Frosting following the directions on page 287. For the right amount of frosting for a big cupcake, use 4 tablespoons of butter, ⅓ cup of unsweetened cocoa powder, 1½ to 1¾ cups of confectioners' sugar, 3 tablespoons of milk, and 1 teaspoon of vanilla.

To assemble the cake, place the cupcake bottom on a cake stand and spread the top of it evenly with ⅓ to ½ cup of the frosting, leaving the side bare. Place the cupcake top on top. Cover the top with the remaining frosting, taking care to swirl it along the indentations of the cake. Do not frost the bottom half of the cupcake. Sprinkle gluten-free decorating sprinkles over the top of the cake (see Don't Hold the Sprinkles on page 203). This cake will serve 8 to 10.

What cake to bake as a big cupcake? The yellow cake is the one Blythe and I think is perfect for this pan. But should you want to adapt your favorite gluten-free recipe to the pan, choose a cake with at least 3½ cups of batter. If your recipe makes more batter, you will need to bake the cake halves longer.

Pretty in Pink Strawberry Cupcakes

✦ ✦ ✦

Present a pink cupcake to a girl—at any age—and you will receive a smile in return. Pink cupcakes just make little girls smile on their birthdays, and they make big girls happy, too, especially if they love the flavor of fresh strawberries. For an added touch of pink, turn the frosted cupcakes upside down and dredge them in gluten-free pink sprinkles so they cover the top.

18 paper liners for cupcake pans (2½-inch size)
1 package (16 ounces, 2 cups) fresh strawberries
1 package (15 ounces) yellow gluten-free cake mix
3 tablespoons strawberry gelatin (half of a 3-ounce package)
¼ cup unsweetened applesauce
¼ cup vegetable oil
3 large eggs
Strawberry Cream Cheese Frosting (page 276)
Gluten-free pink sugar sprinkles (optional, see Note)

1. Place a rack in the center of the oven and preheat the oven to 350°F. Line 18 cupcake cups with paper liners and set the pans aside.

2. Rinse and drain the strawberries and pat them dry on paper towels. Set aside 5 of the largest strawberries for garnish, if desired. Select one large strawberry to use in the Strawberry Cream Cheese Frosting and set it aside. Cut the green caps off

makes: 16 to 18 cupcakes (2½ inches in diameter)

prep: 25 minutes

bake: 18 to 21 minutes

cool: 25 minutes

DAIRY FREE

These cupcakes are dairy-free. Substitute a dairy-free cream cheese, such as Better Than Cream Cheese made by Tofutti, for the cream cheese and margarine for the butter in the Strawberry Cream Cheese Frosting. Or, forgo the frosting, dust the tops of the cupcakes with confectioners' sugar.

recipe reminders

Made for:

Prep Notes:

Don't Forget:

Special Touches:

the remaining berries and mash the berries with a fork or place them in a food processor and pulse until you have a smooth puree, about 10 pulses. You need ¾ cup of pureed strawberries. Set it aside.

3. Place the cake mix and strawberry gelatin in a large mixing bowl and stir to combine. Add the reserved strawberry puree and the applesauce, oil, and eggs and beat with an electric mixer on low speed until the ingredients are just incorporated, 30 seconds. Stop the machine and scrape down the side of the bowl with a rubber spatula. Increase the mixer speed to medium and beat the batter until smooth, 1 to 1½ minutes longer, scraping down the side of the bowl again if needed. Spoon or scoop the batter into the lined cupcake cups, filling each two-thirds full. Remove any unfilled paper liners.

4. Place the pans in the oven side by side and bake the cupcakes until the tops spring back when lightly pressed with a finger, 18 to 21 minutes. Transfer the pans to wire racks and let the cupcakes cool for 5 minutes. Run a dinner knife around the edge of the cupcake cups and transfer the cupcakes to wire racks to cool completely before frosting, 20 minutes longer.

5. Meanwhile, make the Strawberry Cream Cheese Frosting and refrigerate it until you are ready to frost the cupcakes.

6. Spoon a tablespoon of frosting on top of each cupcake and, using a small metal icing spatula, spread it in a swirl, covering all of the top. Place the frosted cupcakes on a serving plate and, if a garnish is desired, cut the reserved strawberries into quarters and arrange one strawberry quarter on each cupcake. Or place pink sugar sprinkles in a shallow plate and dredge the tops of the cupcakes in them to cover.

NOTE: Cake Mate and some Betty Crocker sprinkles are gluten-free. Whole Foods stores carry gluten-free sprinkles and other cake decorations.

KEEP IT FRESH! If your kitchen is cool, store the cupcakes in a cake saver on the counter for twenty-four hours. Or, store them in the refrigerator for three days. Freeze the unfrosted cupcakes, wrapped in aluminum foil or in a plastic storage box, for up to one month. Let the cupcakes thaw on the kitchen counter overnight before frosting them.

✦ ◆ ✦

The Cake Mix Doctor Says

Frost these yummy strawberry cupcakes with the Chocolate Pan Frosting (page 289) or the Chocolate Buttercream Frosting (page 287) and you will have chocolate-covered strawberry cupcakes.

Hartley's Coconut Cupcakes

with Pineapple Frosting

✦ ✦ ✦

makes: 12 to 14 cupcakes (2½ inches in diameter)

prep: 15 minutes

bake: 18 to 22 minutes

cool: 25 minutes

DAIRY FREE

No need to substitute. These cupcakes are dairy-free.

Hartley Steiner is an avid cake baker, writer, and mother of three boys who lives in Bothell, Washington, in the Seattle area. She had baked from my chocolate Cake Mix Doctor book for years until her oldest son was diagnosed with high functioning autism and placed on a gluten- and casein-free diet. Feeling her love of baking might be stifled, Hartley started experimenting with gluten-free cake mixes. She sent me this coconut cupcake recipe, which is brilliant. The secret is coconut milk—she calls it her "lifesaver." Hartley's philosophy is to bake cupcakes so good her children's friends won't notice that they are gluten-free.

For the cupcakes

> 14 paper liners for cupcake pans (2½-inch size)
> 1 package (15 ounces) yellow gluten-free cake mix
> ⅔ cup coconut milk (see Notes)
> ½ cup butter-flavored vegetable shortening sticks (see Notes)
> 3 large eggs
> 1 teaspoon gluten-free coconut extract

For the frosting

> 1 container (8 ounces) frozen whipped nondairy topping, thawed
> 1 cup finely chopped fresh pineapple

1. Make the cupcakes: Place a rack in the center of the oven and preheat the oven to 350°F. Line 14 cupcake cups with paper liners and set the pans aside.

2. Place the cake mix, coconut milk, vegetable shortening, eggs, and coconut extract in a large mixing bowl and beat with an electric mixer on low speed until the ingredients are just incorporated, 30 seconds. Stop the machine and scrape down the side of the bowl with a rubber spatula. Increase the mixer speed to medium and beat the batter until smooth, 1 to 1½ minutes longer, scraping down the side of the bowl again if needed. Spoon or scoop the batter into the lined cupcake cups, filling each two-thirds full. Remove any unfilled paper liners.

3. Place the pans in the oven side by side and bake the cupcakes until the tops spring back when lightly pressed with a finger, 18 to 22 minutes. Transfer the pans to wire racks and let the cupcakes cool for 5 minutes. Run a dinner knife around the edge of the cupcake cups and transfer the cupcakes to wire racks to cool completely before frosting, 20 minutes longer.

4. Meanwhile, make the frosting: Spoon the thawed topping into a medium-size mixing bowl and fold in the pineapple until incorporated. Keep the frosting chilled until you are ready to frost the cupcakes.

5. Spoon a generous tablespoon of frosting on top of each cupcake. Serve any remaining frosting on the side.

NOTES: Do not use light coconut milk. Use the regular, full-fat coconut milk found in most supermarkets. The vegetable shortening sticks Hartley recommends are made by Crisco.

recipe reminders

Made for:

Prep Notes:

Don't Forget:

Special Touches:

KEEP IT FRESH! Store the cupcakes in a cake saver in the refrigerator for three days. Freeze the unfrosted cupcakes, wrapped in aluminum foil or in a plastic storage box, for up to one month. Let the cupcakes thaw on the kitchen counter overnight before frosting them.

✦ ✦ ✦

The Cake Mix Doctor Says

Hartley either spreads these moist and yummy cupcakes with the pineapple frosting, dips them in a dairy-free chocolate glaze and dredges them in toasted coconut, or tops them with a dairy-free buttercream frosting, using coconut milk as the liquid.

Here's the Scoop

I remember the day in my kitchen when I first used a scoop to measure out cupcake batter and get it from bowl to pan perfectly. It was a revelation! What had taken me so long? Why had I continued to use two large spoons, scraping spoon on spoon, waiting for the batter to drop into the cupcake liner, then furiously wiping off the batter that spilled onto the top of the pan? Restaurant chefs have long used scoops for making muffins, portioning cookie dough, or scooping chicken or potato salad onto plates. For them it is all about portion control. But for me, scooping batter into a cupcake pan is all about sanity! I have happily regained mine because I have a half dozen scoops of various sizes in my cupcake baking arsenal. My cupcakes and muffins are now uniform in size, they bake for the same amount of time, and best of all, there is no bickering about who gets the largest cupcake! All of the cupcakes look the same. For regular-size cupcakes, use an ice cream scoop that holds ¼ cup of batter. For minis, use a 1½- or 2-tablespoon scoop.

Georgia Peach Cupcakes

✦ ✦ ✦

I'm partial to peaches, especially Georgia peaches, having spent nearly twenty years in the Peach State. But I know in summertime that peaches from South Carolina and Alabama are also drip-down-your-arm good. Choose the ripest peaches from your area to use in this easy fruit cupcake recipe. If you don't have peaches, you can use nectarines or apricots. All you need is a cup of pureed fresh fruit and you have simple and delicious summer cupcakes.

makes: 16 to 18 cupcakes (2½ inches in diameter)

prep: 25 minutes

bake: 19 to 22 minutes

cool: 25 minutes

DAIRY FREE

These cupcakes are dairy-free. Substitute margarine or butter-flavored vegetable shortening sticks for the butter in the frosting and orange juice for the milk. You may need to add a little more liquid to make up for the butter.

18 paper liners for cupcake pans (2½-inch size)

1 cup sliced peaches, packed (1 large or 2 small peaches, see Notes), plus 1 thinly sliced peach for garnish (optional)

1 package (15 ounces) yellow gluten-free cake mix

¼ cup (half of a 3.4-ounce package) vanilla instant pudding mix

½ cup vegetable oil

3 large eggs

1 teaspoon pure vanilla extract

½ teaspoon pure almond extract (see Notes)

Vanilla Buttercream Frosting (page 271)

1. Place a rack in the center of the oven and preheat the oven to 350°F. Line 18 cupcake cups with paper liners and set the pans aside.

2. Place the 1 cup of peach slices in a food processor and puree until smooth, 15 to 20 pulses. You need 1 cup of puree. Place the peach puree in a large mixing bowl. Add the cake mix, pudding mix, oil, eggs, and vanilla and almond extracts and beat with an electric mixer on low speed until the ingredients are just incorporated, 30 seconds. Stop the machine and scrape down the side of the bowl with a rubber spatula. Increase the mixer speed to medium and beat the batter until smooth, 1 to 1½ minutes longer, scraping down the side of the bowl again if needed. Spoon or scoop the batter into the lined cupcake cups, filling each two-thirds full. Remove any unfilled paper liners.

3. Place the pans in the oven side by side and bake the cupcakes until the tops spring back when lightly pressed with a finger, 19 to 22 minutes. Transfer the pans to wire racks and let the cupcakes cool for 5 minutes. Run a dinner knife around the edge of the cupcake cups and transfer the cupcakes to wire racks to cool completely before frosting, 20 minutes longer.

4. Meanwhile, make the Vanilla Buttercream Frosting and keep it refrigerated until you are ready to frost the cupcakes.

5. Spoon a tablespoon of frosting on top of each cupcake and, using a small metal icing spatula, spread it in a swirl, covering all of the top. Place the frosted cupcakes on a serving plate and, if desired, garnish each with a slice of fresh peach.

NOTES: For the most peach flavor use the ripest summer peaches you can find. Peel and pit them, then slice them and pack the slices into a measuring cup. If you prefer, you can add a pinch of nutmeg instead of the almond extract.

KEEP IT FRESH! Store the cupcakes in a cake saver at room temperature for up to three days. Freeze the unfrosted cupcakes, wrapped in aluminum foil or in a plastic storage box, for up to one month. Let the cupcakes thaw on the kitchen counter overnight before frosting them.

✦ ✦ ✦

The Cake Mix Doctor Says

Instead of using peaches, be creative and rely on other summer fruit such as nectarines, apricots, or plums. Just peel, pit, and slice them, then measure a packed cup of slices and puree them; you'll need one cup of puree. Use the ripest fruit you can find.

Bake for Success Tips

Here are five tips for best-ever cupcakes.

1. Make sure the paper cupcake liners fit snugly in the pans.

2. Use an ice cream scoop to fill the liners two-thirds full with batter.

3. Bake the cupcakes until the tops spring back when you lightly touch the center.

4. Let the cupcakes cool in the pans for no more than five minutes, then transfer them to a wire rack.

5. When they are completely cool, use a small icing spatula to frost the cupcakes or spoon the frosting into a pastry bag and pipe the frosting in a swirl on top of each cupcake.

Hawaiian Cupcakes
with Cream Cheese Frosting

✦ ◆ ✦

makes: 16 to 18 cupcakes (2½ inches in diameter)

prep: 20 minutes

bake: 18 to 22 minutes

cool: 25 minutes

C upcakes and cakes with these flavor combinations go by all sorts of names, but regardless of what you call them, you know you've got a winner when you put mashed bananas with crushed pineapple and a little cinnamon. And you know you've really got a winner when you spread the cupcakes with a cream cheese frosting and top them with toasted macadamia nuts. Yes, it's over the top, but for special days these cupcakes truly take the cake!

18 paper liners for cupcake pans (2½-inch size)

1 package (15 ounces) yellow gluten-free cake mix

1 cup mashed banana (from 2 medium-size very ripe
   bananas)

½ cup well-drained canned crushed pineapple
   (see Dairy-Free sidebar)

½ cup vegetable oil

3 large eggs

1 teaspoon pure vanilla extract

1 teaspoon ground cinnamon

Cream Cheese Frosting (page 273)

½ cup toasted chopped macadamia nuts
   (see box, page 172), or 16 to 18 banana chips

1. Place a rack in the center of the oven and preheat the oven to 350°F. Line 18 cupcake cups with paper liners and set the pans aside.

2. Place the cake mix, banana, pineapple, oil, eggs, vanilla, and cinnamon in a large mixing bowl and beat with an electric mixer on low speed until the ingredients are just incorporated, 30 seconds. Stop the machine and scrape down the side of the bowl with a rubber spatula. Increase the mixer speed to medium and beat the batter until smooth, 1 to 1½ minutes longer, scraping down the side of the bowl again if needed. Spoon or scoop the batter into the lined cupcake cups, filling each two-thirds full. Remove any unfilled paper liners.

3. Place the pans in the oven side by side and bake the cupcakes until the tops spring back when lightly pressed with a finger, 18 to 22 minutes. Transfer the pans to wire racks and let the cupcakes cool for 5 minutes. Run a dinner knife around the edge of the cupcake cups and transfer the cupcakes to wire racks to cool completely before frosting, 20 minutes longer.

DAIRY FREE

These cupcakes are dairy-free. To make a simple pineapple glaze instead of the cream cheese frosting set aside 2 tablespoons of the liquid from the crushed pineapple when you drain it. Whisk the pineapple liquid into 1 cup of confectioners' sugar until smooth and spoon the glaze over the cupcakes. Let the glaze set for 10 minutes.

recipe reminders

Made for:

_____

_____

_____

_____

Prep Notes:

_____

_____

_____

_____

Don't Forget:

_____

_____

_____

_____

Special Touches:

_____

_____

_____

_____

4. Meanwhile, make the Cream Cheese Frosting. Finely chop the macadamia nuts, if using.

5. Spoon a tablespoon of frosting on top of each cupcake and, using a small metal icing spatula, spread it in a swirl, covering all of the top. Place the frosted cupcakes on a serving plate and garnish each with a sprinkling of macadamia nuts or a banana chip.

KEEP IT FRESH! If your kitchen is cool, store the cupcakes in a cake saver on the counter for twenty-four hours. Or, store them in the refrigerator for three days. Freeze the unfrosted cupcakes, wrapped in aluminum foil or in a plastic storage box, for up to one month. Let the cupcakes thaw on the kitchen counter overnight before frosting them.

✦ ✦ ✦

The Cake Mix Doctor Says

Don't have ripe bananas? Substitute 1 cup of unsweetened applesauce.

Peanut Butter Cupcakes
with Chocolate Pan Frosting

✦ ◆ ✦

You don't have to be a child to love peanut butter. It is a staple ingredient in our house, and it's as common for my kids to say "Mom, we're about out of peanut butter." as it is to say we are running low on milk or eggs. Peanut butter has been one of my favorite add-ins throughout my books because it makes cakes richer and adds flavor. Plus, it is a natural partner for chocolate. Take a bite and see for yourself.

makes: 16 to 18 cupcakes (2½ inches in diameter)

prep: 20 minutes

bake: 18 to 22 minutes

cool: 25 minutes

18 paper liners for cupcake pans (2½-inch size)
1 package (15 ounces) yellow gluten-free cake mix
¼ cup (half of a 3.4-ounce package) vanilla instant pudding mix
½ cup creamy peanut butter
½ cup water
¼ cup vegetable oil
3 large eggs
1 teaspoon pure vanilla extract
Chocolate Pan Frosting (page 289)
Chopped dry-roasted peanuts (optional), for garnish

DAIRY FREE

These cupcakes are dairy-free. In place of the frosting, just before baking press 6 or 7 dairy-free chocolate chips into the top of the batter of each cupcake for that irresistible chocolate and peanut butter combination.

recipe reminders

Made for: _____

_____

_____

_____

_____

Prep Notes: _____

_____

_____

_____

_____

Don't Forget: _____

_____

_____

_____

_____

Special Touches: _____

_____

_____

_____

_____

1. Place a rack in the center of the oven and preheat the oven to 350°F. Line 18 cupcake cups with paper liners and set the pans aside.

2. Place the cake mix, pudding mix, peanut butter, water, oil, eggs, and vanilla in a large mixing bowl and beat with an electric mixer on low speed until the ingredients are just incorporated, 30 seconds. Stop the machine and scrape down the side of the bowl with a rubber spatula. Increase the mixer speed to medium and beat the batter until smooth, 1 to 1½ minutes longer, scraping down the side of the bowl again if needed. Spoon or scoop the batter into the lined cupcake cups, filling each two-thirds full. Remove any unfilled paper liners.

3. Place the pans in the oven side by side and bake the cupcakes until the tops spring back when lightly pressed with a finger, 18 to 22 minutes. Transfer the pans to wire racks and let the cupcakes cool for 5 minutes. Run a dinner knife around the edge of the cupcake cups and transfer the cupcakes to wire racks to cool completely before frosting, 20 minutes longer.

4. Meanwhile, make the Chocolate Pan Frosting.

5. Spoon a tablespoon of frosting on top of each cupcake and, using a small metal icing spatula, spread it in a swirl, covering all of the top. Sprinkle the cupcakes with chopped peanuts, if desired. Place the frosted cupcakes on a serving plate.

KEEP IT FRESH! Store the cupcakes in a cake saver at room temperature for up to three days. Freeze the unfrosted cupcakes, wrapped in aluminum foil or in a plastic storage box, for up to one month. Let the cupcakes thaw on the kitchen counter overnight before frosting.

✦ ✦ ✦

The Cake Mix Doctor Says

Add a fun garnish of chopped Reese's peanut butter cups to the top of each frosted cupcake before the frosting sets.

What Can I Bring? Cupcakes!

Unless your family is a large one, when you bake cupcakes, it's probably for a party or to share with friends. Here are some tips for transporting cupcakes so they'll look picture-perfect when you arrive.

✦ Bake and take muffins. Or, choose cupcakes that travel well. These would be cupcakes that don't have to stay refrigerated and ones that are glazed or frosted with a caramel or chocolate frosting that sets once it cools.

✦ Pack cupcakes and muffins in shirt boxes with lids that have been lined with waxed paper.

✦ Or, pack them in rectangular cake savers with locking lids.

✦ In a pinch, pack cupcakes in a 13 by 9-inch baking pan, and drape plastic wrap over the top of the pan.

✦ If you're toting just one cupcake, place it in a small plastic cup with a lid. Or look for the Cup-a-Cake, a sturdy locking plastic container that holds one cupcake firmly in place. I recently carried a chocolate cupcake in a Cup-a-Cake on a flight from Nashville to Seattle, and the cupcake was flawless on arrival. You'll find Cup-a-Cake at www.cupacake.com.

Chocolate Sour Cream Cupcakes

✦ ✦ ✦

makes: 16 to 18 cupcakes (2½ inches in diameter)

prep: 20 minutes

bake: 19 to 23 minutes

cool: 25 minutes

The chocolate counterpart to the Favorite Yellow Birthday Cupcakes, these cupcakes are for the chocolate lover. You begin with a chocolate mix, add a smidgen of cocoa and a healthy dose of sour cream, then slather the cupcakes with your choice of frosting—either the vanilla or chocolate buttercream. I am a little more partial to the vanilla, as the visual contrast of light frosting and dark cake is too much for me to resist. I read somewhere that the most frequently requested cake is dark chocolate with a white frosting. Here it is, but in cupcake form.

18 paper liners for cupcake pans (2½-inch size)
1 package (15 ounces) chocolate gluten-free cake mix
1 tablespoon unsweetened cocoa powder
¾ cup sour cream
½ cup vegetable oil
3 large eggs
1 tablespoon pure vanilla extract
Vanilla Buttercream Frosting (page 271) or
    Chocolate Buttercream Frosting (page 287)
Chocolate curls (see page 69), for garnish

1. Place a rack in the center of the oven and preheat the oven to 350°F. Line 18 cupcake cups with paper liners and set the pans aside.

2. Place the cake mix, cocoa, sour cream, oil, eggs, and vanilla in a large mixing bowl and beat with an electric mixer on low speed until the ingredients are just incorporated, 30 seconds. Stop the machine and scrape down the side of the bowl with a rubber spatula. Increase the mixer speed to medium and beat the batter until smooth, 1 to 1½ minutes longer, scraping down the side of the bowl again if needed. Spoon or scoop the batter into the lined cupcake cups, filling each two-thirds full. Remove any unfilled paper liners.

3. Place the pans in the oven side by side and bake the cupcakes until the tops spring back when lightly pressed with a finger, 19 to 23 minutes. Transfer the pans to wire racks and let the cupcakes cool for 5 minutes. Run a dinner knife around the edge of the cupcake cups and transfer the cupcakes to wire racks to cool completely before frosting, 20 minutes longer.

4. Meanwhile, make the buttercream frosting.

recipe reminders

Made for:

_____

_____

_____

_____

Prep Notes:

_____

_____

_____

_____

Don't Forget:

_____

_____

_____

_____

Special Touches:

_____

_____

_____

_____

Turning Cupcakes into Bundts

It seems that once I write a recipe for cupcakes, I wonder how they would taste as a cake. So if you're like me and want to bake a cake from one of these cupcake recipes, here's how to do it: Prepare the batter as the recipe directs, then pour it into a 12-cup Bundt pan that has been misted with vegetable oil spray and dusted with rice flour. Bake the cake until it tests done—the top will spring back when lightly pressed with the tip of your finger—40 to 45 minutes. Either glaze the cake or just dust it with confectioners' sugar.

5. Spoon a tablespoon of frosting on top of each cupcake and, using a small metal icing spatula, spread it in a swirl, covering all of the top. Place a chocolate curl in the center of each cupcake, if desired. Place the frosted cupcakes on a serving plate.

KEEP IT FRESH! Store the cupcakes in a cake saver at room temperature for up to three days. Freeze the unfrosted cupcakes, wrapped in aluminum foil or in a plastic storage box, for up to one month. Let the cupcakes thaw on the kitchen counter overnight before frosting.

✦ ✦ ✦

The Cake Mix Doctor Says

Add 1 teaspoon of cinnamon to turn these into Mexican chocolate cupcakes or add 1 teaspoon of espresso powder for a decided coffee kick.

Chocolate Chip Muffins

✦ ✦ ✦

Warm from the oven, these muffins are hard to resist. They will remind you of chocolate chip pancakes, and they need no more adornment than a dusting of confectioners' sugar. Serve the muffins at brunch or on a dessert tray at a party, especially when kids of all ages are present.

18 paper liners for muffin pans (2½-inch size)
1 package (15 ounces) yellow gluten-free cake mix
½ cup reduced-fat sour cream
½ cup vegetable oil
3 tablespoons water
3 large eggs
1 tablespoon pure vanilla extract
1 cup miniature semisweet chocolate chips
½ cup finely chopped pecans (optional)
1 tablespoon confectioners' sugar,
    for dusting
    the muffins

makes: 16 to 18 muffins (2½ inches in diameter)

prep: 10 minutes

bake: 18 to 21 minutes

cool: 5 minutes

DAIRY FREE

Use ½ cup of coconut milk instead of the sour cream. It will not impart a coconut flavor to the muffins. And use dairy-free chocolate chips.

recipe reminders

Made for:

_____

_____

_____

_____

Prep Notes:

_____

_____

_____

_____

Don't Forget:

_____

_____

_____

_____

Special Touches:

_____

_____

_____

_____

1. Place a rack in the center of the oven and preheat the oven to 350°F. Line 18 cupcake cups with paper liners and set the pans aside.

2. Place the cake mix, sour cream, oil, water, eggs, and vanilla in a large mixing bowl and beat with an electric mixer on low speed until the ingredients are just combined, 30 seconds. Fold the chocolate chips and pecans, if using, into the muffin batter. Spoon or scoop the batter into the lined cupcake cups, filling each two-thirds full. Remove any unfilled paper liners.

3. Place the pans in the oven side by side and bake the muffins until they are golden brown and the tops spring back when lightly pressed with a finger, 18 to 21 minutes. Transfer the pans to wire racks and let the muffins cool for 5 minutes. Run a dinner knife around the edge of the muffins and transfer them to wire racks to cool completely or to a serving plate to serve at once. Sift the confectioners' sugar over the tops of the cooled muffins.

KEEP IT FRESH! Store the muffins in a plastic bag or in a cake saver at room temperature for up to three days. Freeze the muffins, in a plastic bag or wrapped in heavy-duty aluminum foil, for up to two months. Let the muffins thaw on the kitchen counter overnight before serving.

✦ ✦ ✦

The Cake Mix Doctor Says

These muffins taste like chocolate chip cookies. With that in mind, you can add whatever other ingredients you like best in cookies: pecans or walnuts, raisins, coconut—you name it!

Fresh Blueberry Muffins

✦ ✦ ✦

If you've got a cake mix, some fresh blueberries, a little orange juice, some eggs, and a stick of butter, you can create your own blueberry muffins in no time. You won't find a fresher flavor or a lower price than by making your own. Take these into the office to share with your friends. You'll only have to mention they're gluten-free if someone who is gluten sensitive thinks he or she can't eat one. The orange juice not only gives the muffins a nice tang, but it seems to improve the texture of the mix.

makes: 18 to 20 muffins (2½ inches in diameter)

prep: 10 minutes

bake: 19 to 22 minutes

cool: 5 minutes

For the muffins

20 paper liners for muffin pans (2½-inch size)
1 package (15 ounces) yellow gluten-free cake mix
¼ cup granulated sugar
¾ cup orange juice (fresh or from a carton)
8 tablespoons (1 stick) unsalted butter, melted
3 large eggs
1 tablespoon pure vanilla extract
1½ cups fresh blueberries, rinsed and patted dry

For the glaze

1 cup confectioners' sugar, sifted
2 tablespoons orange juice (fresh or from a carton)

DAIRY FREE

Use ½ cup of vegetable oil instead of the melted butter in the muffin batter.

1. Make the muffins: Place a rack in the center of the oven and preheat the oven to 350°F. Line 20 cupcake cups with paper liners and set the pans aside.

2. Measure 1 tablespoon of the cake mix, place it in a small bowl, and set it aside. Place the remaining cake mix and the sugar, ¾ cup of orange juice, melted butter, eggs, and vanilla in a large mixing bowl and beat with an electric mixer on low speed until the ingredients are just combined, 30 seconds. Toss the blueberries with the reserved tablespoon of cake mix and fold the coated blueberries into the muffin batter. Spoon or scoop the batter into the lined cupcake cups, filling each two-thirds full. Remove any unfilled paper liners.

3. Place the pans in the oven side by side and bake the muffins until they are golden brown and the tops spring back when lightly pressed with a finger, 19 to 22 minutes. Transfer the pans to wire racks and let the muffins cool for 5 minutes. Run a dinner knife around the edge of the muffins and transfer them to wire racks to cool completely before glazing, 20 minutes longer.

4. Meanwhile, make the glaze: Place the confectioners' sugar in a small bowl and whisk in the 2 tablespoons of orange juice. Spoon the glaze over the cooled muffins and serve.

KEEP IT FRESH! Store the muffins in a plastic bag or in a cake saver at room temperature for up to three days. Freeze the muffins in a plastic bag or wrapped in heavy-duty aluminum foil for up to two months. Let the muffins thaw on the kitchen counter overnight before serving.

✦ ✦ ✦

The Cake Mix Doctor Says

If you love these muffins with blueberries, you will adore them made with fresh raspberries.

Pumpkin Raisin Muffins
with an Orange Drizzle

✦ ◆ ✦

They smell like Thanksgiving, taste like Thanksgiving, and they look like Thanksgiving piled into a basket. But bake these warm, fragrant, spice-filled pumpkin and raisin muffins any time of the year. Purchase canned pumpkin when you see it at the supermarket and you can store it on your pantry shelf for up to one year. If you can't find canned pumpkin, you can substitute pureed cooked fresh pumpkin or butternut squash.

makes: 16 to 18 muffins (2½ inches in diameter)

prep: 15 minutes

bake: 19 to 22 minutes

cool: 5 minutes

For the muffins

18 paper liners for muffin pans (2½-inch size)
1 package (15 ounces) yellow gluten-free cake mix
1 cup canned pumpkin
½ cup vegetable oil
3 large eggs
1 tablespoon pure vanilla extract
1½ teaspoons ground cinnamon
¾ cup baking raisins (see The Cake Mix Doctor Says, page 229)

For the orange drizzle

1 cup confectioners' sugar, sifted
2 tablespoons orange juice
¼ cup finely chopped pecans, toasted (optional, see Notes)

DAIRY FREE

No need to substitute. These muffins are dairy-free!

1. Make the muffins: Place a rack in the center of the oven and preheat the oven to 350°F. Line 18 cupcake cups with paper liners and set the pans aside.

2. Place the cake mix, pumpkin, oil, eggs, vanilla, and cinnamon in a large mixing bowl and beat with an electric mixer on low speed until the ingredients are just combined, 30 seconds. Fold the raisins into the muffin batter. Spoon or scoop the batter into the lined cupcake cups, filling each two-thirds full. Remove any unfilled paper liners.

3. Place the pans in the oven side by side and bake the muffins until the tops spring back when lightly pressed with a finger, 19 to 22 minutes. Transfer the pans to wire racks and let the muffins cool for 5 minutes. Run a dinner knife around the edge of the muffins, and transfer them to wire racks to completely cool.

4. Meanwhile, make the orange drizzle: Place the confectioners' sugar in a small mixing bowl and whisk in the orange juice until smooth. Spoon the glaze over the muffins and immediately sprinkle the pecans, if using, on top.

NOTES: If desired, you can add a pinch of ground cloves or nutmeg to the muffin batter.

To toast the pecans, leave the oven on after removing the baked muffins. Place the pecans on a rimmed cookie sheet and bake them until toasted, 2 to 3 minutes.

KEEP IT FRESH! Store the muffins in a plastic bag or in a cake saver at room temperature for up to three days. Freeze the muffins in a plastic bag or wrapped in heavy-duty aluminum foil for up to two months. Let the muffins thaw on the kitchen counter overnight before serving.

✦ ✦ ✦

The Cake Mix Doctor Says

Baking raisins are sold on the same supermarket aisle as regular raisins. More moist than regular raisins, they are perfect to add to muffins, cakes, and coffee cakes. To make your own baking raisins, add 2 tablespoons of a liquid such as water or orange juice to a cup of regular raisins and microwave them on high power until the liquid is hot, 30 to 40 seconds. Remove the raisins from the microwave and let them sit on the counter until they absorb all of the liquid.

recipe reminders

Made for:

Prep Notes:

Don't Forget:

Special Touches:

New-Fashioned Banana Muffins

◆ ◆ ◆

makes: 16 to 18 muffins (2½ inches in diameter)

prep: 15 minutes

bake: 16 to 20 minutes

cool: 10 minutes

DAIRY FREE

Omit the cinnamon chips and the muffins will be dairy-free.

There's absolutely nothing old-fashioned about these bright-flavored banana muffins made with mashed bananas and tiny cinnamon chips. And there is nothing old about the topping, a brown sugar, banana chip, and walnut combination. Make the muffins for brunch or for weekend guests or just to stash in the freezer and have on hand for a midweek breakfast when you need to dash out the door.

For the muffins

18 paper liners for muffin pans (2½-inch size)
1 package (15 ounces) yellow gluten-free cake mix
1 heaping cup mashed very ripe banana
   (from 3 small or 2 medium-size bananas)
½ cup vegetable oil
3 large eggs
2 teaspoons pure vanilla extract
½ cup miniature cinnamon chips
   (optional, see Notes)

For the topping

½ cup lightly packed light brown sugar
½ cup finely chopped walnuts (optional)
½ cup chopped banana chips
   (about ⅔ cup whole banana chips, see Notes)

1. Make the muffins: Place a rack in the center of the oven and preheat the oven to 350°F. Line 18 cupcake cups with paper liners and set the pans aside.

2. Place the cake mix, mashed banana, oil, eggs, and vanilla in a large mixing bowl and beat with an electric mixer on low speed until the ingredients are just combined, 30 seconds. Fold the cinnamon chips, if using, into the muffin batter. Spoon or scoop the batter into the lined cupcake cups, filling each two-thirds full. Remove any unfilled paper liners.

3. Make the topping: Place the brown sugar, walnuts, if using, and banana chips in a small bowl; stir to combine. Sprinkle about 1 tablespoon of the mixture on top of each muffin, using your fingers, and press the topping into the batter slightly.

4. Place the pans in the oven side by side and bake the muffins until they are golden brown and the tops spring back when lightly pressed with a finger, 16 to 20 minutes. Transfer the pans to wire racks and let the muffins cool for 5 minutes. Run a dinner knife around the edge of the muffins and transfer them to wire racks to cool for another 5 minutes, then serve.

recipe reminders

Made for: _____

_____

_____

_____

_____

Prep Notes: _____

_____

_____

_____

_____

Don't Forget: _____

_____

_____

_____

_____

Special Touches: _____

_____

_____

_____

_____

Out with the New, In with the Old...

Let's say you are more old-fashioned than new-fashioned. Bake these muffins without the cinnamon chips and without the topping. And don't even think of adding mini chocolate chips to the batter because that would be new!

NOTES: You can find cinnamon chips where you find specialty baking items or you can order them from the King Arthur Flour website. Store any leftover cinnamon chips in a cool, dry place. They will keep for up to 6 months. You can use them the way you would chocolate chips—in cookies, brownies, bars, pancakes—you name it.

Banana chips are sold in the produce section of most supermarkets or where you find nuts and dried fruit.

KEEP IT FRESH! Store the muffins in a plastic bag or in a cake saver at room temperature for up to three days. Freeze the muffins in a plastic bag or wrapped in heavy-duty aluminum foil for up to two months. Let the muffins thaw on the kitchen counter overnight before serving.

✦ ✦ ✦

The Cake Mix Doctor Says

Banana chips are a fun substitute for nuts as a topping, but if you have a nut allergy read the label before buying them. Many banana chips are processed on equipment that also processes tree nuts. The chips are easy to chop and will be crisp and crunchy when the muffins are warm from the oven. They will get a little softer the next day.

Lemon Buttermilk Poppy Seed Muffins

♦ ♦ ♦

Buttermilk, poppy seeds, and fresh lemon were popular in a Cake Mix Doctor Bundt cake, so I wanted to recreate that yummy trilogy in muffins for you gluten-free bakers. You will need at least one large lemon for this recipe, and if you have another lemon, great, because its extra juice can be used in the glaze that's spooned over the muffins after they have cooled. If you don't have a second lemon, that's okay; just use milk or water in the tangy glaze.

makes: 16 to 18 muffins (2½ inches in diameter)

prep: 10 minutes

bake: 19 to 22 minutes

cool: 15 minutes

18 paper liners for muffin pans (2½-inch size)
1 large lemon
1 package (15 ounces) yellow gluten-free cake mix
⅔ cup buttermilk
½ cup vegetable oil
3 large eggs
2 teaspoons pure vanilla extract
1 tablespoon poppy seeds
1 cup confectioners' sugar, sifted
Candied lemon zest (optional, see page 115),
    for garnish

DAIRY FREE

Use coconut milk instead of the buttermilk. It will not impart a coconut flavor to the muffins.

1. Place a rack in the center of the oven and preheat the oven to 350°F. Line 18 cupcake cups with paper liners and set the pans aside.

recipe reminders

Made for:

_____

_____

_____

_____

Prep Notes:

_____

_____

_____

_____

Don't Forget:

_____

_____

_____

_____

Special Touches:

_____

_____

_____

_____

2. Rinse and pat the lemon dry with a paper towel, then grate the yellow zest from the lemon onto a plate; it should measure about 2 teaspoons. Place 1 teaspoon of zest in a large mixing bowl for the cake and place the remaining teaspoon in a small bowl for the glaze. Cut the lemon in half and squeeze the juice through a fine-mesh sieve, to yield at least 3 tablespoons, discarding the seeds and pulp. Place 3 tablespoons of lemon juice in the large bowl. If there is any extra juice, measure it and place it in the small bowl. Set the small bowl aside.

3. Place the cake mix, buttermilk, oil, eggs, and vanilla in the large mixing bowl with the lemon zest and juice and beat with an electric mixer on low speed until the ingredients are just combined, 30 seconds. Fold the poppy seeds into the muffin batter. Spoon or scoop the batter into the lined cupcake cups, filling each two-thirds full. Remove any unfilled paper liners.

4. Place the pans in the oven side by side and bake the muffins until they are golden brown and the tops spring back when lightly pressed with a finger, 19 to 22 minutes. Transfer the pans to wire racks and let the muffins cool for 5 minutes. Run a dinner knife around the edge of the muffins, and transfer them to wire racks to cool 10 minutes before glazing them.

5. Meanwhile, make the glaze: If you have less than 2 tablespoons of lemon juice, measure enough water or milk to make a total of 2 tablespoons of liquid and place this in the small bowl with the lemon juice and zest. Add the confectioners' sugar and whisk until smooth. Spoon the glaze over the cooled muffins and serve. Garnish with the candied lemon zest, if desired.

KEEP IT FRESH! Store the muffins in a plastic bag or in a cake saver at room temperature for up to three days. Freeze the muffins in a plastic bag or wrapped in heavy-duty aluminum foil, for up to two months. Let the muffins thaw on the kitchen counter overnight before serving.

✦ ✦ ✦

The Cake Mix Doctor Says

Hungry for a lemon buttermilk poppy seed cake? Beat the batter until smooth, then pour it into a 12-cup Bundt pan that has been misted with vegetable oil spray and dusted with rice flour. Bake the cake until it tests done—the top will spring back when lightly pressed with a finger, about 40 minutes. Let the cake cool on a rack, for 30 minutes, before pouring the glaze over the top.

Making Minis

Most of the cupcake and muffin recipes in this chapter make between 16 to 18 generous cupcakes or muffins. That said, if you choose to make minis you will get about 28 miniature cupcakes measuring 2 inches across. There are mini paper liners you can fit into miniature cupcake pans, or forgo liners and just mist the mini pans with vegetable oil spray before adding the batter. These smaller cupcakes need less time in the oven—14 to 18 minutes—and they freeze well in plastic containers with lids.

Maple Corn Muffins

✦ ◆ ✦

makes: 18 to 20 muffins (2½ inches in diameter)

prep: 10 minutes

bake: 17 to 20 minutes

cool: 10 minutes

DAIRY FREE

Use coconut milk instead of sour cream. It will not impart a coconut flavor.

From the moment I tasted the first gluten-free cake made from a mix I knew it would make a great corn muffin. There was something about the coarse texture, the fact that the mixes are not overly sweet, and the blank canvas they afford that made me want to turn them into corn muffins. When I added yellow corn meal, sour cream, and maple flavoring and split and served the muffins warm with butter, they reminded my friend Martha Bowden of the corn meal pancakes her mother made and served with maple syrup. Serve these for breakfast or brunch or pack them into a lunchbox for an afternoon snack.

Vegetable oil spray, for misting the pans or 20 paper liners
    for muffin pans
1 package (15 ounces) yellow gluten-free cake mix
1⅓ cups yellow corn meal (see Note)
1 cup reduced-fat sour cream
½ cup vegetable oil
⅓ cup water
3 large eggs
1½ teaspoons maple flavoring
¾ cup finely chopped pecans (optional)
¼ cup lightly packed light brown sugar
Butter (optional), for serving

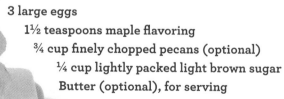

1. Place a rack in the center of the oven and preheat the oven to 350°F. Lightly mist 20 cupcake cups with vegetable oil spray or line with paper liners and set the pans aside.

2. Place the cake mix and corn meal in a large mixing bowl and stir to combine. Add the sour cream, oil, water, eggs, and maple flavoring and beat with an electric mixer on low speed until the ingredients are just combined, 30 seconds. Fold in the pecans, if using. Spoon or scoop the batter into the prepared cupcake cups, filling each two-thirds full. Sprinkle the tops with a little of the brown sugar.

3. Place the pans in the oven side by side and bake the muffins until they are golden brown and the tops spring back when lightly pressed with a finger, 17 to 20 minutes. Transfer the pans to wire racks and let the muffins cool for 5 minutes. Run a dinner knife around the edge of the muffins, and transfer them to wire racks to cool for another 5 minutes. Then serve with butter, if desired.

NOTE: Do not use corn meal mix. It contains flour.

KEEP IT FRESH! Store the muffins in a plastic bag or in a cake saver at room temperature for up to three days. Freeze the muffins in a plastic bag or wrapped in heavy-duty aluminum foil, for up to two months. Let the muffins thaw on the kitchen counter overnight before serving.

✦ ◆ ✦

The Cake Mix Doctor Says

Not keen about maple? Omit the maple flavoring. Fold in 1 cup of fresh blueberries before baking. And you don't have to make muffins at all! Pour the batter onto a lightly greased griddle over medium heat and make corn cakes.

recipe reminders

Made for:

_____

_____

_____

_____

Prep Notes:

_____

_____

_____

_____

Don't Forget:

_____

_____

_____

_____

Special Touches:

_____

_____

_____

_____

BROWNIES, BARS & COOKIES

✦ ✦ ✦ ✦ ✦

Baking cookies with my mother and sisters was as much a part of my childhood as riding a bike and learning to read. I don't want anyone to go without this joyful rite of passage, so I am happy to say these gluten-free recipes will make the process easier and also deliciously memorable.

Peanut Butter Cookies
(page 260)

The cookies are proof you can take the gluten-free mix, vary the flavoring, the number of eggs, and the amount of liquid and come up with crisp, home-baked cookies that no one would ever guess came from a mix, much less a gluten-free one. Wait till you try the Snickerdoodle, Peanut Butter, and Almond Sugar Cookies, the Chocolate Clouds, and the Gingerbread Boys and Girls.

After cookies I created bars—a classic Lemon Bar, the old-fashioned Magic Bars, and a few brownies. For the brownies, I began with a gluten-free brownie mix and added flavorings and toppings that gave simple brownies new life.

"Saving the best things for last" rings true in this book. I never expected some of my favorite recipes to be in a chapter so near the end, but they most definitely are.

Cookie Chatter: You Heard It Here

The more you bake the better you get, so it should come as no surprise that the best cookie bakers have made plenty of mistakes in the kitchen and learned from them. Here are some of my favorite cookie baking tips.

✦ Don't grease the baking sheets.

✦ Remove cookies from baking sheets with a metal spatula as soon as they firm up.

✦ Let cookies cool completely on a wire rack and they will be crisp on the bottom.

✦ Store cookies tightly covered but preferably not in any plastic container because it makes the cookies soften.

✦ For best storage, freeze cookies if they will not be eaten in two days.

✦ ✦ ✦

Marbled Cream Cheese Brownies

✦ ✦ ✦

A favorite recipe from my Chocolate Cake Mix Doctor book is now gluten-free. You begin with a gluten-free brownie mix, add a rich cheesecake-like filling, and top everything with miniature semisweet chocolate chips. I bake this in an 8-inch square pan, and it makes twelve to sixteen big delicious brownies.

makes: 12 to 16 brownies

prep: 15 minutes

bake: 40 to 45 minutes

cool: 20 minutes

For the cheesecake filling

6 ounces (three quarters of an 8-ounce package) reduced-fat cream cheese, at room temperature

2 tablespoons (¼ stick) unsalted butter, at room temperature

3 tablespoons granulated sugar

1 large egg

For the brownie layer

1 package (16 ounces) gluten-free brownie mix

¼ cup vegetable oil

2 large eggs

2 tablespoons pure vanilla extract

¼ cup miniature semisweet chocolate chips

1. Place a rack in the center of the oven and preheat the oven to 350°F. Set aside an ungreased 8-inch square metal baking pan.

DAIRY FREE

Substitute a dairy-free cream cheese, such as Better Than Cream Cheese made by Tofutti, for the cream cheese and margarine for the butter in the cheesecake filling and use dairy-free chocolate chips to sprinkle on top before baking.

recipe reminders

Made for:

_____

_____

_____

_____

Prep Notes:

_____

_____

_____

_____

Don't Forget:

_____

_____

_____

_____

Special Touches:

_____

_____

_____

_____

2. Make the cheesecake filling: Place the cream cheese and butter in a medium-size mixing bowl and beat with an electric mixer on low speed until the ingredients are just combined, 30 seconds. Stop the machine and scrape down the side of the bowl. Add the sugar and 1 egg. Increase the mixer speed to medium and beat the filling until smooth, 1 minute. Set the cheesecake filling aside.

3. Make the brownie layer: Place the brownie mix, oil, 2 eggs, and the vanilla in a large mixing bowl. Stir with a wooden spoon until all the ingredients are incorporated and the batter lightens in texture, 50 strokes. Pour the batter into the baking pan and spread it out evenly with a rubber spatula. Dollop tablespoons of the cheesecake filling on top of the brownie layer. Using a dinner knife, swirl the cheesecake filling into the brownie batter to create a marbled effect. Scatter the chocolate chips evenly over the top.

4. Place the pan in the oven and bake the brownies until they are lightly browned around the edges and the center is set, 40 to 45 minutes. Transfer the pan to a wire rack and let the brownies cool for 20 minutes. Cut the brownies into 12 to 16 squares.

KEEP IT FRESH! Store the brownies in the pan, covered with plastic wrap, at room temperature for up to three days. Freeze the brownies in the pan, wrapped in aluminum foil, for up to one month. Let the brownies thaw on the kitchen counter overnight before serving.

✦ ✦ ✦

The Cake Mix Doctor Says

This recipe originally contained Kahlúa. If you like, add a tablespoon of Kahlúa to the cheesecake filling and, if desired, brush another tablespoon of Kahlúa over the top of the baked brownies as they cool.

10 Fast Ways to Doctor a Gluten-Free Brownie Mix

In a hurry to jazz up a gluten-free brownie mix? Make the mix following the directions on the package but before you place the pan in the oven, scatter ½ cup of any of these on top.

✦ Semisweet chocolate chips

✦ Chopped toasted walnuts or pecans

✦ The gluten-free candy of your choice

✦ White chocolate chips and chopped macadamia nuts

✦ Chopped gluten-free caramels

✦ Miniature marshmallows

✦ Fresh raspberries

Or mix a teaspoon of one of these into the batter before baking.

✦ Peppermint extract

✦ Espresso powder

✦ Almond extract

Peanut Butter Brownies

✦ ✦ ✦

makes: 30 brownies

prep: 20 minutes

bake: 30 to 35 minutes

cool: 20 minutes

DAIRY FREE

Because sweetened condensed milk and butter are such crucial components of these brownies, it is not possible to make this recipe dairy-free.

These chocolate and peanut butter brownies get everyone's attention. I recall signing books in a market in Houston late on a Sunday afternoon after the football game was over and people were hurrying in to get the makings for dinner. They saw me and my books and tried to hurry on past but when I mentioned I had samples of peanut butter brownies, well, they stopped in their tracks! This gluten-free version of that peanut butter brownie will make you stop in your tracks, too.

For the brownie layer

1 package (16 ounces) gluten-free brownie mix
¾ cup creamy peanut butter
4 tablespoons (½ stick) unsalted butter, melted
2 large eggs

For the fudge topping

2 cups semisweet chocolate chips
1 can (14 ounces) sweetened condensed milk
2 teaspoons pure vanilla extract
2 teaspoons confectioners' sugar (optional),
   for dusting the top of the brownies

1. Place a rack in the center of the oven and preheat the oven to 350°F. Set aside an ungreased 13 by 9–inch metal baking pan.

2. Make the brownie layer: Place the brownie mix, peanut butter, melted butter, and eggs in a large mixing bowl and beat with an electric mixer on low speed until the ingredients nearly come together into a ball, 1 minute. The mixture will appear crumbly but when pressed with your fingers it will come together. Place the brownie mixture in the baking pan and press it over the bottom. Set the baking pan aside.

3. Make the fudge topping: Place the chocolate chips and condensed milk in a medium-size microwave-safe glass bowl and microwave on high power until the chocolate chips are nearly melted, 1 minute. Stir in the vanilla and continue stirring until the chocolate mixture is smooth. Pour the chocolate mixture into the baking pan, spreading it evenly over the brownie layer. Smooth the top with a rubber spatula and place the pan in the oven.

4. Bake the brownies until they bubble around the edges and the center is set, 30 to 35 minutes. Transfer the pan to a wire rack and let the brownies cool for 20 minutes. Cut the brownies into 30 bars. Dust the brownies with the confectioners' sugar, if desired.

KEEP IT FRESH! Store the brownies in the pan, covered with plastic wrap, at room temperature for up to three days. Freeze the brownies in the pan, wrapped in aluminum foil, for up to one month. Let the brownies thaw on the kitchen counter overnight before serving.

✦ ✦ ✦

The Cake Mix Doctor Says

Substitute white chocolate chips for the semisweet and you have a beautiful color contrast and a chewy, almost caramel-flavored filling.

recipe reminders

Made for:

Prep Notes:

Don't Forget:

Special Touches:

Gluten-Free Magic Brownie Bars

✦ ✦ ✦

makes: About 3 dozen

prep: 10 minutes

bake: 30 to 35 minutes

cool: 1 hour

DAIRY FREE

Since you need sweetened condensed milk to make these brownies, it is not possible make them dairy-free.

You may know these bars by any of a number of names—seven layer, magic, and so on. The idea is that, after melting butter in the pan, you layer in graham cracker crumbs, chocolate, coconut, and nuts and then pour sweetened condensed milk over them all and everything bakes up magically into a delectable bar cookie. With this gluten-free version you pour a box of brownie mix over the butter and then start layering. Add what you like but pour on the sweetened condensed milk last—it is the magic ingredient.

Vegetable oil spray, for misting the pan
Parchment paper, for lining the pan
8 tablespoons (1 stick) unsalted butter
1 package (16 ounces) gluten-free brownie mix
1 cup sweetened flaked coconut
1 cup semisweet chocolate chips
½ cup butterscotch chips (see Note)
1 heaping cup chopped pecans
1 can (14 ounces) sweetened condensed milk

1. Place a rack in the center of the oven and preheat the oven to 350°F. Lightly mist the bottom of a 13 by 9–inch pan with vegetable oil spray. Line the pan with parchment paper so that 3 to 4 inches of the parchment paper extend beyond the long sides of the pan. Place the butter in the pan and place the pan in the oven until the butter melts, 4 to 5 minutes.

2. Transfer the pan with the melted butter to a wire rack. Sprinkle the brownie mix evenly over the melted butter. Scatter the coconut evenly over the brownie mix. Then, scatter the chocolate chips, butterscotch chips, and pecans in layers on top. Drizzle the sweetened condensed milk evenly over the pecans and place the pan in the oven.

3. Bake the bars until they bubble across the top and the edges are lightly browned, 30 to 35 minutes. Transfer the pan to a wire rack and let the brownies cool for 30 minutes. Run a sharp knife around the edge of the pan to loosen the brownies, then carefully lift the parchment paper and brownies out of the pan and place them on a cutting board. Slice the brownies into bars and serve them warm or let them cool to room temperature, 30 minutes longer, before slicing.

NOTE: Hershey's butterscotch chips are gluten-free but Nestlé butterscotch chips are not. Be sure to read the label and, if in doubt, check with the manufacturer.

KEEP IT FRESH! Store the brownies in the pan, covered with plastic wrap, at room temperature for up to three days. Freeze the brownies in the pan, wrapped in aluminum foil, for up to one month. Let the brownies thaw on the kitchen counter overnight before serving.

✦ ✦ ✦

The Cake Mix Doctor Says

Get creative with the layers, using a handful of dried sweetened cranberries or cherries instead of or in addition to one of the ingredients. If you don't care for butterscotch chips, use white chocolate chips instead.

recipe reminders

Made for:

_____

_____

_____

_____

Prep Notes:

_____

_____

_____

_____

Don't Forget:

_____

_____

_____

_____

Special Touches:

_____

_____

_____

_____

Gluten-Free Lemon Bars

✦ ✦ ✦

makes: 30 bars

prep: 20 minutes

bake: 45 to 55 minutes

cool: 30 minutes

DAIRY FREE

Use margarine instead of butter in the crust for the bars.

Brownies may be Americans' favorite bar cookie, but in the South lemon bars are pretty high on the list. With a cookie layer on the bottom and a lemon custard filling on top, they are sheer perfection to eat and suitable most any time of the year. Be sure to read the directions carefully as you need to set aside a little of the cake mix to whisk into the lemon filling. Let the bars cool completely and they will be easier to slice. And to make the bars look their best, dust confectioners' sugar over the top before serving.

For the crust

1 package (15 ounces) yellow gluten-free cake mix
2 tablespoons vanilla instant pudding mix
8 tablespoons (1 stick) unsalted butter, melted
1 large egg

For the lemon filling

2 large lemons
4 large eggs
1½ cups granulated sugar
2 teaspoons confectioners' sugar (optional), for dusting the top

1. Place a rack in the center of the oven and preheat the oven to 350°F. Set aside an ungreased 13 by 9–inch metal baking pan.

2. Make the crust: Measure 2 tablespoons of cake mix and set it aside for the lemon filling. Place the remaining cake mix, pudding mix, melted butter, and 1 egg in the bowl of a food processor fitted with a steel blade. Process until the mixture comes together into a ball, 15 to 20 pulses. Place the crust mixture in the baking pan and press it over the bottom and ¼ inch up the sides. Place the pan in the oven and bake the crust until it turns golden brown, 20 to 25 minutes.

3. Meanwhile, make the lemon filling: Rinse and pat 1 lemon dry with a paper towel, then grate the yellow zest from the lemon onto a plate; you should have about 2 teaspoons. Cut both lemons in half and squeeze the juice through a fine sieve, discarding the seeds and pulp. Measure ½ cup of lemon juice. Place the 4 eggs, granulated sugar, lemon juice, lemon zest, and the reserved cake mix in the same food processor bowl that was used to make the crust (no need to wash the bowl or the steel blade) and process the filling until creamy, 10 to 12 pulses.

4. When the crust is baked, pour the filling over it and return the pan to the oven. Bake the bars until the filling sets, 25 to 30 minutes. Transfer the pan to a wire rack and let the bars cool for 30 minutes. Dust the top with the confectioners' sugar, if desired, then cut the bars and serve.

KEEP IT FRESH! Store the bars in the pan, covered with plastic wrap, at room temperature for up to three days. Freeze the bars in the pan, wrapped in aluminum foil, for up to one month. Let the bars thaw on the kitchen counter overnight before serving.

◆ ◆ ◆

The Cake Mix Doctor Says

Make lime bars by using grated fresh lime zest and freshly squeezed lime juice in place of the lemon. For a twist, add ¼ cup of sweetened flaked coconut to the crust.

Don't Forget the Garnish

Top brownies and bars with a little something extra—fresh berries, a dollop of whipped cream, or a candied citrus zest (see box on page 115). It makes for a pretty finishing touch.

Slice and Bake Sugar Cookies

✦ ◆ ✦

makes: **About 3 dozen cookies**

prep: **15 minutes**

chill: **At least 3 hours**

bake: **6 to 8 minutes**

cool: **10 to 16 minutes**

DAIRY FREE

Use vegetable shortening instead of butter for the cookies.

Come Christmas, my family has a tradition of decorating sugar cookies with red and green sprinkles, and the holiday cookie tray just doesn't seem complete without these cookies. So creating a gluten-free version was at the top of my list. I just can't tell you how wonderful they are! You should bake them at Christmas, but also for other holidays and special days through the year. The dough is easy to make, chill, slice, and bake. And I share all kinds of ways you can dress the cookies up with ingredients from your pantry.

1 package (15 ounces) yellow gluten-free cake mix
8 tablespoons (1 stick) unsalted butter, at room temperature
1 large egg
1 tablespoon pure vanilla extract
Waxed paper, for wrapping the dough
1 egg white, lightly beaten, if topping with
    sugar sprinkles or chopped nuts
Gluten-free sugar sprinkles (see box, page 203),
    cinnamon sugar (see box, page 118), or sliced almonds,
    for sprinkling on top

1. Place the cake mix, butter, egg, and vanilla in a large mixing bowl and beat on low speed with an electric mixer until the ingredients are well combined, 1 minute. Cut a piece of waxed paper about 14 inches long. Place the cookie dough on the waxed paper, then lift one edge of the paper over the dough and press it

10 Ways to Spice up a Sugar Cookie Recipe

Add any of the following ingredients to the basic Slice and Bake Sugar Cookies dough in place of the vanilla. Begin with 1 teaspoon zest and extract, adding up to 1 teaspoon more, to taste. Add chocolate, candies, nuts, and coconut to taste also, beginning with ½ cup and adding up to 1 cup.

1. Grated orange or lemon zest

2. Key lime juice and lime zest

3. Pure almond extract

4. A big pinch of cinnamon

5. A little pinch of nutmeg

6. Miniature semisweet chocolate chips

7. M&M's candies

8. Pistachios and shaved bittersweet chocolate

9. Toasted finely chopped pecans

10. Coconut extract and sweetened flaked coconut

with your hands to form a log about 12 inches long and 2 inches in diameter. Tightly roll the dough in the waxed paper and place it in the refrigerator to chill for at least 3 hours or overnight.

2. Place a rack in the center of the oven and preheat the oven to 350°F. Set aside 2 ungreased baking sheets.

3. Unwrap the waxed paper–covered log of dough and transfer it to a cutting board. Using a sharp knife, slice the dough into slices that are ¼- to ⅜-inch thick. Arrange the slices on the baking sheets 3½ to 4 inches apart. Brush the slices of dough with the egg

recipe reminders

Made for:

_____

_____

_____

_____

Prep Notes:

_____

_____

_____

_____

Don't Forget:

_____

_____

_____

_____

Special Touches:

_____

_____

_____

_____

white and sprinkle your topping choice over them. Place the baking sheets in the oven and bake the cookies until they are lightly browned around the edges, 6 to 8 minutes.

4. Transfer the baking sheets to wire racks and let the cookies cool for 1 minute. Using a metal spatula, transfer the cookies to wire racks to cool completely, 10 to 15 minutes longer. Repeat with the remaining cookie dough.

KEEP IT FRESH! Store the cookies in a cookie jar or tin at room temperature for up to a week. Freeze the cookies, wrapped in aluminum foil or in a resealable plastic bag, for one month. Let the cookies thaw on the kitchen counter overnight before serving.

✦ ✦ ✦

The Cake Mix Doctor Says

Try mixing add-ins into the dough before shaping it into a log. Add ⅔ to ¾ cup of miniature semisweet chocolate chips. Or, fold in 2 teaspoons of grated orange or lemon zest. Add 1 teaspoon of pure almond extract or ½ cup finely chopped candied cherries.

✦ ✦ ✦

Chocolate Slice and Bake Sugar Cookies

Make the Slice and Bake Sugar Cookie dough. Melt 2 squares (2 ounces) of semisweet chocolate and add the melted chocolate and ½ cup of miniature semisweet chocolate chips to the cookie dough, then form a log. The baking time will be the same.

Gingersnaps

✦ ✦ ✦

Who would have thought a gluten-free cake mix could be so perfect for cookies? There is something about the rice flour that makes the crispiest cookies and lends itself to all sorts of flavors. This recipe is a great example. When combined with molasses, vegetable shortening, an egg, and spices, the cake mix turns into crisp and spicy ginger cookies. Pair these with chocolate ice cream, fresh orange slices, lemon curd, or just an afternoon cup of tea or hot chocolate.

makes: **2 dozen cookies**

prep: **10 minutes**

chill: **At least 2 hours**

bake: **9 to 11 minutes**

cool: **10 to 16 minutes**

¼ **cup molasses**
¼ **cup vegetable shortening**
1 **teaspoon pure vanilla extract**
1 **large egg**
1 **package (15 ounces) yellow gluten-free cake mix**
1 **teaspoon ground ginger**
½ **teaspoon ground cinnamon**
¼ **teaspoon ground cloves**
⅓ **cup granulated sugar**

1. Place the molasses, vegetable shortening, and vanilla in a large mixing bowl and beat with an electric mixer on low speed until just combined, 30 seconds. Stop the machine and scrape down the side of the bowl with a rubber spatula. Add the egg. Increase the mixer speed to medium and beat until smooth, 30 seconds. Set the molasses mixture aside.

2. Place the cake mix, ginger, cinnamon, and cloves in a small bowl and stir to combine. Add the cake mix mixture to the

DAIRY FREE

No need to substitute. These cookies are dairy-free.

molasses mixture, a little at a time, beating on low speed until everything is just combined, 30 to 45 seconds. Cover the bowl with plastic wrap and place the cookie dough in the refrigerator to chill for 2 hours or overnight.

3. Place a rack in the center of the oven and preheat the oven to 350°F. Set aside 2 ungreased baking sheets.

4. Place the sugar in a shallow bowl. Form the cookie dough into generous 1-inch balls. Roll the balls of dough in the sugar and arrange them on the baking sheets, about 4 inches apart.

5. Place the baking sheets in the oven and bake the cookies until they are crisp around the edges, 9 to 11 minutes. Transfer the baking sheets to wire racks and let the cookies cool for 1 minute. Using a metal spatula, transfer the cookies to wire racks to cool completely, 10 to 15 minutes longer. Repeat with the remaining cookie dough, if any.

KEEP IT FRESH! Store the cookies in a cookie jar or tin at room temperature for up to a week. Freeze the cookies, wrapped in aluminum foil or in a resealable plastic bag, for one month. Let the cookies thaw on the kitchen counter overnight before serving.

✦ ✦ ✦

The Cake Mix Doctor Says

While these cookies are delicious on their own, you can dress them up with an easy lemon glaze. Place 1 cup of confectioners' sugar in a small mixing bowl and whisk in 2 tablespoons of lemon juice. Drizzle or spread some of the glaze over the tops of the cookies after they have cooled completely. Let the cookies rest for 20 minutes for the glaze to set.

Gingerbread Boys and Girls

✦ ✦ ✦

These cookies are not only adorable, they are crisp, gingery, and delicious. In order to make about eighteen large (6-inch) cookies or three to four dozen smaller ones (3½ inches), you need two boxes of cake mix, plus the add-ins. The tricks to rolling out perfect cookies are to use rice flour for dusting the counter and rolling pin, to keep the dough really cold, and to cut out as many cookies as possible from the dough without rerolling the scraps. Then, turn the scraps into free-form cookies by pressing them onto the baking sheet.

makes: **18 to 24 large gingerbread boys and girls, plus extra cookies from the scraps**

prep: **30 minutes**

chill: **At least 3 hours**

bake: **7 to 9 minutes**

cool: **15 to 16 minutes**

2 packages (15 ounces each) yellow gluten-free cake mix
2½ teaspoons ground ginger
1 teaspoon ground cinnamon
½ teaspoon ground cloves
½ cup molasses
½ cup vegetable shortening
1 tablespoon pure vanilla extract
1 tablespoon water
1 large egg
Rice flour, for rolling the dough
½ cup currants or gluten-free Red Hots candy, for garnish

DAIRY FREE

No need to substitute. These cookies are dairy-free.

1. Place the cake mixes, ginger, cinnamon, and cloves in a medium-size mixing bowl and stir to combine. Set the bowl aside.

recipe reminders

Made for: _____

_____

_____

_____

Prep Notes: _____

_____

_____

_____

_____

Don't Forget: _____

_____

_____

_____

_____

Special Touches: _____

_____

_____

_____

_____

2. Place the molasses, vegetable shortening, vanilla, and water in a large mixing bowl and beat with an electric mixer on low speed until the ingredients are just incorporated, 30 seconds. Stop the mixer, scrape down the side of the bowl with a rubber spatula, and add the egg. Increase the mixer speed to medium and beat the molasses mixture until smooth, 30 seconds. Add the cake mix mixture to the molasses mixture a little at a time, beating on low speed, until everything is just incorporated. The cookie dough will be very thick. Cover the bowl with plastic wrap and place the cookie dough in the refrigerator to chill for 3 hours, or overnight.

3. Place a rack in the center of the oven and preheat the oven to 350°F. Set aside 2 ungreased baking sheets.

4. Spoon about 1 teaspoon of rice flour on a board or clean kitchen counter. Rub some rice flour on a rolling pin. Divide the cookie dough into 4 portions. Working with one portion at a time, form the dough into a ball and roll it out about ¼-inch thick. Cut out cookies using gingerbread boy and girl cutters. Using a metal spatula, transfer the cut-outs to a baking sheet, spacing the cookies at least 2 inches apart. Press the currants into the dough using 2 currants for the eyes and 4 currants for the smile. Place 3 small gluten-free Red Hots as buttons down the center of the body, if desired.

5. Place the baking sheets in the oven and bake the cookies until they are lightly browned, 7 to 9 minutes. The cookies may crack a little as they bake. Transfer the baking sheets to wire racks and let the cookies cool for 1 minute. Using a metal spatula, transfer the cookies to wire racks to cool completely, 15 minutes longer.

6. Repeat with the remaining dough. Take care not to reroll scraps. The cookies will be best looking if they are cut from freshly rolled dough. Use the scraps to make free-form ginger cookies and bake these alongside the gingerbread boys and girls. If the dough seems dry and difficult to roll, gather it up into a ball and work in a little water.

KEEP IT FRESH! Store the cookies in a cookie jar or tin at room temperature for up to a week. Freeze the cookies, wrapped in aluminum foil or in a resealable plastic bag, for one month. Let the cookies thaw on the kitchen counter overnight before serving.

3 Cookie Tools I Love

1. Silpat baking mats, handy nonstick fiberglass and silicone pan liners that let me bake lots of cookies without having to wash a lot of baking sheets

2. Mini scoops for measuring cookie dough evenly

3. Small metal spatulas for removing cookies from the baking sheets

✦ ✦ ✦

The Cake Mix Doctor Says

If you prefer, create a cookie smile with a little piped icing on the cooled cookies.

Snickerdoodle Cookies

✦ ◆ ✦

makes: **3½ dozen cookies**

prep: **15 minutes**

bake: **8 to 12 minutes**

cool: **15 minutes**

DAIRY FREE

Substitute vegetable shortening for the butter in the cookies.

Developing recipes is part science and part mad science. Seriously, you can have an idea for a recipe you'd like to concoct and for many reasons it just does not work. So you learn and try again, or you just wing it. Such was the case with this cookie recipe. I had an inkling that if I reduced the number of eggs I use in the cake recipes I could get a dough stiff enough to turn into cookies. But the proportions took a little tinkering . . . and after a half-dozen tries, I had a cookie dough. When I spiced the dough with cinnamon, I baked crisp, irresistible snickerdoodles. My son prefers these snickerdoodles to any he has tasted, and considering he's twelve, he's something of a cookie connoisseur!

1 package (15 ounces) yellow gluten-free cake mix
¼ cup lightly packed light brown sugar
½ teaspoon ground cinnamon
8 tablespoons butter (1 stick), cut into tablespoons
1 large egg
1 tablespoon pure vanilla extract
1 tablespoon cinnamon sugar (see box, page 118)

1. Place a rack in the center of the oven and preheat the oven to 375°F. Set aside 2 ungreased baking sheets.

2. Place the cake mix, brown sugar, and cinnamon in the bowl of a food processor fitted with a steel blade and pulse once to combine. Add the butter to the processor and pulse until the mixture is crumbly, 15 to 20 pulses. Add the egg and vanilla and pulse until the dough comes together in a large ball, 10 pulses.

3. Scoop the cookie dough into 1-inch balls and arrange 12 balls on each baking sheet, 2 to 3 inches apart. Sprinkle the top of each ball of dough with a little of the cinnamon sugar. If you want crisp 3-inch cookies, press down on the balls with the bottom of a small glass to flatten them. If you prefer chewy 2½-inch cookies, do not flatten the balls of dough.

4. Place the baking sheets in the oven and bake the cookies until golden brown, 8 to 12 minutes. Using a metal spatula, immediately transfer the cookies to wire racks to cool completely, 15 minutes. Repeat with the remaining dough.

KEEP IT FRESH! Store the cookies in a cookie jar or tin at room temperature for up to a week. Freeze the cookies, wrapped in aluminum foil or in a resealable plastic bag, for one month. Let the cookies thaw on the kitchen counter overnight before serving.

✦ ✦ ✦

The Cake Mix Doctor Says

Do you like cakelike cookies? Use 2 eggs in the dough and bake the cookies at 350°F until puffy, 12 to 15 minutes.

recipe reminders

Made for:

Prep Notes:

Don't Forget:

Special Touches:

Peanut Butter Cookies

✦ ◆ ✦

makes: 3 dozen cookies

prep: 10 minutes

bake: 10 to 12 minutes

cool: 15 minutes

DAIRY FREE

Substitute vegetable shortening for butter in this recipe. Use 4 tablespoons of plain, unsweetened almond milk instead of the 2 tablespoons of cow's milk. Vegetable shortening and Crisco butter-flavored vegetable shortening sticks tend to have less water than butter, so you may need to add a little extra liquid to the cookie dough when making it dairy-free.

Peanut butter cookies are such a favorite, and just because you are following a gluten-free diet it doesn't mean you should forgo them. Bake up this recipe and you'll find that this American cookie classic is now okay for you to eat and share with anyone who is gluten-free or just loves peanut butter cookies.

1 package (15 ounces) yellow gluten-free cake mix
⅔ cup creamy peanut butter
6 tablespoons (¾ stick) butter, at room temperature
1 large egg
2 tablespoons milk
2 tablespoons pure vanilla extract
¼ cup granulated sugar

1. Place a rack in the center of the oven and preheat the oven to 375°F. Set aside 2 ungreased baking sheets.

2. Place the cake mix, peanut butter, butter, egg, milk, and vanilla in a large mixing bowl and beat with an electric mixer on low speed until the ingredients just come together and the cookie dough is smooth, 45 seconds. The dough will be stiff. Place the sugar in a shallow bowl. Form the dough into 1-inch balls. Roll each ball of dough in the sugar and arrange 12 balls on each baking sheet 2 to 3 inches apart. If desired, press down on the balls of dough twice with a fork to make the classic cross-hatch pattern.

3. Place the baking sheets in the oven and bake the cookies until golden brown, 10 to 12 minutes. Using a metal spatula, immediately transfer the cookies to wire racks to cool completely, 15 minutes. Repeat with the remaining dough.

KEEP IT FRESH! Store the cookies in a cookie jar or tin at room temperature for up to a week. Freeze the cookies, wrapped in aluminum foil or in a resealable plastic bag, for one month. Let the cookies thaw on the kitchen counter overnight before serving.

✦ ✦ ✦

The Cake Mix Doctor Says

Try crunchy peanut butter for—what else? A crunchy peanut butter cookie.

recipe reminders

Made for:

_____

_____

_____

_____

Prep Notes:

_____

_____

_____

_____

Don't Forget:

_____

_____

_____

_____

Special Touches:

_____

_____

_____

Peanut Butter Whoopie Pies

makes: **15 to 18 whoopie pies**

prep: **25 minutes**

bake: **12 to 15 minutes**

cool: **20 minutes**

What a difference an egg makes! Add one more egg (plus a little instant pudding mix) to the peanut butter cookie recipe and you have soft, pillowy cookies perfect for filling and turning into whoopie pies.

1 package (15 ounces) yellow gluten-free cake mix
2 tablespoons instant vanilla pudding mix
8 tablespoons butter (1 stick), at room
   temperature
½ cup creamy peanut butter, plus more peanut butter
   for filling the whoopie pies (optional)
¼ cup milk
2 large eggs
2 tablespoons pure vanilla extract
Nutella, marshmallow creme, or Chocolate
   Buttercream Frosting (page 287),
   for filling the whoopie pies

1. Place a rack in the center of the oven and preheat the oven to 350°F. Set aside 2 ungreased baking sheets.

2. Place the cake mix, pudding mix, butter, peanut butter, milk, eggs, and vanilla in a large mixing bowl and beat with an electric mixer on low speed until the ingredients are just incorporated, 30 seconds. Stop the machine and scrape down the side of the bowl with a rubber spatula. Increase the mixer speed to medium and beat the cookie dough until smooth, 30 seconds longer.

DAIRY FREE

Substitute margarine or vegetable shortening for the butter in this recipe. Use plain, unsweetened almond milk instead of the cow's milk, adding more as needed to make the cookie dough soft enough to scoop into balls.

3. Scoop the cookie dough into 1-inch balls and arrange them on the baking sheets 3 inches apart. Place the baking sheets in the oven and bake the cookies until they are golden brown and spring back when lightly pressed with a finger, 12 to 15 minutes. Using a metal spatula, immediately transfer the cookies to wire racks to cool completely, 20 minutes. Repeat with the remaining cookie dough.

4. Sandwich 2 cookies, flat sides together, with Nutella, marshmallow creme, chocolate frosting, or more peanut butter inside. Repeat with the remaining cookies.

KEEP IT FRESH! Depending on the filling you have used, the whoopie pies can be stored in a tin at room temperature for up to 4 days. Freeze the unfilled cookies, wrapped in aluminum foil or in a resealable plastic bag, for one month. Let the cookies thaw on the kitchen counter overnight before filling them.

✦ ✦ ✦

The Cake Mix Doctor Says

Gotta have more peanut butter? Sandwich Peanut Butter Frosting (see page 283) between the cookies.

recipe reminders

Made for:

Prep Notes:

Don't Forget:

Special Touches:

Almond Sugar Cookies

✦ ✦ ✦

makes: 3 to 4 dozen cookies

prep: 10 minutes

bake: 8 to 10 minutes

cool: 10 to 12 minutes

DAIRY FREE

Use vegetable shortening instead of the butter.

Reminding me of a crisp and buttery cookie my aunt used to bake, these cookies are a snap to make. You grind whole almonds in a food processor to make a coarse meal and combine this with a yellow cake mix, butter, egg, vanilla, and almond extract. What results is a crisp and nostalgic cookie best eaten freshly baked with a cup of tea.

1 cup whole almonds
1 package (15 ounces) yellow gluten-free cake mix
12 tablespoons (1½ sticks) unsalted butter, melted
1 large egg
1 tablespoon pure vanilla extract
1 teaspoon pure almond extract

1. Place a rack in the center of the oven and preheat the oven to 375°F. Set aside 2 ungreased baking sheets.

2. Place the almonds in the bowl of a food processor fitted with a steel blade and pulse until the almonds form a coarse meal, 45 seconds. Place the almond meal in a large mixing bowl. Add the cake mix, melted butter, egg, and vanilla and almond extracts and beat with an electric mixer on low speed until the ingredients just come together, 30 seconds. Stop the machine and scrape down the side of the bowl with a rubber spatula. Increase the mixer speed to medium and beat the cookie dough until well combined, 30 seconds longer.

3. Spoon the cookie dough by heaping teaspoons onto the baking sheets 3 inches apart. Press down on the dough gently with clean fingers. Place the baking sheets in the oven and bake the cookies until they are lightly browned around the edges and not doughy in the center, 8 to 10 minutes. Transfer the baking sheets to wire racks and let the cookies cool for 1 minute. Using a metal spatula, transfer the cookies to wire racks to cool completely, 10 minutes longer. Repeat with the remaining cookie dough.

KEEP IT FRESH! Store the cookies in a cookie jar or tin at room temperature for up to a week. Freeze the cookies, wrapped in aluminum foil or in a resealable plastic bag, for one month. Let the cookies thaw on the kitchen counter overnight before serving.

✦ ✦ ✦

The Cake Mix Doctor Says

Other nuts work as well as the almonds in these cookies. Try a cup of pecans or pistachios instead of the almonds.

recipe reminders

Made for:

Prep Notes:

Don't Forget:

Special Touches:

Chocolate Cloud Cookies

✦ ✦ ✦

makes: 3½ dozen cookies

prep: 15 minutes

bake: 10 to 12 minutes

cool: 20 minutes

DAIRY FREE

Substitute vegetable shortening for the butter in the cookies.

Anything that is chewy and chocolate is dear to my heart, and these sweet little cookies don't disappoint. Made with a chocolate mix, a little instant pudding, some butter, and an egg, they could not be simpler. You roll the balls of cookie dough in confectioners' sugar before they go into the oven, and when they bake they puff up before your eyes, like chocolate clouds.

1 package (15 ounces) chocolate gluten-free cake mix
2 tablespoons chocolate instant pudding mix
8 tablespoons (1 stick) unsalted butter, melted
1 large egg
⅓ cup confectioners' sugar

1. Place a rack in the center of the oven and preheat the oven to 350°F. Set aside 2 ungreased baking sheets.

2. Place the cake mix, pudding mix, melted butter, and egg in a large mixing bowl and beat with an electric mixer on low speed until the ingredients nearly come together in a ball, 45 seconds. Place the confectioners' sugar in a shallow bowl. With your hands form the cookie dough into 1-inch balls. Roll each ball of dough in the confectioners' sugar and arrange 12 balls on each baking sheet 2 to 3 inches apart.

3. Place the baking sheets in the oven and bake the cookies until they are puffed up, firm around the edges, but still slightly soft in the center, 10 to 12 minutes. Transfer the baking sheets to wire racks and let the cookies cool for 5 minutes. Using a metal spatula, transfer the cookies to wire racks to cool completely, 15 minutes longer. Repeat with the remaining dough.

KEEP IT FRESH! Store the cookies in a cookie jar or tin at room temperature for up to a week. Freeze the cookies, wrapped in aluminum foil or in a resealable plastic bag, for one month. Let the cookies thaw on the kitchen counter overnight before serving.

✦ ◆ ✦

The Cake Mix Doctor Says

Want more chocolate? Fold ½ cup of miniature semisweet chocolate chips into the cookie dough before rolling it into balls.

recipe reminders

Made for: _____

_____

_____

_____

_____

Prep Notes: _____

_____

_____

_____

_____

_____

Don't Forget: _____

_____

_____

_____

_____

Special Touches: _____

_____

_____

_____

_____

FROSTINGS

✦ ✦ ✦ ✦ ✦

I've always said the frosting is the first and last bite you taste on a cake. It needs to be good. It needs to be homemade, and it needs to be simple to prepare. So the recipes in this chapter contain just a handful of ingredients and can be whipped up in minutes. You either beat them in a mixing bowl or stir them in a saucepan over low heat. The only crucial step is to read the ingredient list to make sure the ingredients are at the right temperature.

*Pretty in Pink Strawberry
Cupcakes (page 205)*

For buttercream and cream cheese frostings, make sure the butter or cream cheese is soft enough to blend well with a mixer. If not, place it in a microwave oven until it's soft to the touch, ten to fifteen seconds. For caramel and chocolate pan frostings, make sure you spread the frosting on while it is still warm and allow it to set as it cools on the cake. And when whipping cream, place the beaters and mixing bowl in the freezer fifteen minutes ahead of time to get them nice and cold so your cream whips to the highest heights.

Feel free to switch the frostings around, slathering a chocolate layer cake with chocolate buttercream instead of vanilla or spreading caramel frosting on the hummingbird cake instead of the traditional cream cheese. And if you are following a dairy-free diet, go ahead and substitute the ingredients I have suggested to make these recipes in your kitchen.

If you are pressed for time when making a Bundt or cupcakes, just dust the tops with confectioners' sugar. With layer cakes, however, there really is no substitution for a terrific homemade frosting. The cake depends on the frosting, so read the recipe through, gather the ingredients on the counter, and plunge right on in. You will find that

How Much Frosting Is Enough?

I don't like to run out of frosting when I am frosting a cake, and I'm sure you don't, either. Here is how much frosting you need to have on hand to frost a variety of different size cakes.

✦ At least 1 cup of frosting for every dozen cupcakes

✦ 1 to 2 cups to cover a cake in an 8-inch square pan

✦ 1½ cups to glaze a Bundt or tube cake

✦ 1½ to 2 cups to cover a cake in a 13 by 9–inch pan

✦ 2½ to 3 cups to frost the top and sides of a cake from a 13 by 9–inch pan

✦ 3 to 4 cups to frost a two-layer 8- to 9-inch cake

preparing your own frosting is very simple, takes less time that you thought, and the taste? It's infinitely better than bakery frosting or anything out of a can. It's worth it!

✦ ✦ ✦

Vanilla Buttercream Frosting

✦ ✦ ✦

The most basic frosting of all, this Vanilla Buttercream Frosting is so much better than what is sold in the supermarket. Spread it on the Georgia Peach Cupcakes (page 211), Devil's Food Cake (page 64), or the Chocolate Sour Cream Cupcakes (page 220).

8 tablespoons (1 stick) butter, at room temperature
3¾ cups confectioners' sugar, sifted
3 tablespoons milk, or more as needed
2 teaspoons pure vanilla extract

Place the butter in a medium-size mixing bowl and beat with an electric mixer on low speed until fluffy, 30 seconds. Stop the machine and add the confectioners' sugar, milk, and vanilla a bit at a time, beating with the mixer on low speed until the confectioners' sugar is well incorporated, 1 minute. Increase the mixer speed to medium and beat the frosting until light and fluffy, 1 minute longer. Beat in up to 1 tablespoon more milk if the frosting seems too stiff. Use the frosting at once.

Devil's Food Cake (page 64)

makes: 3½ cups, enough to frost a 2-layer cake, a 13 by 9–inch cake, or 24 or more cupcakes

prep: 10 minutes

DAIRY FREE

Substitute margarine for the butter and plain, unsweetened almond milk for the milk. If you are frosting a layer cake, double the recipe.

recipe reminders

Made for:

_____

_____

_____

_____

Prep Notes:

_____

_____

_____

_____

Don't Forget:

_____

_____

_____

_____

Special Touches:

_____

_____

_____

_____

The Cake Mix Doctor Says

For a low-fat buttercream, use half of the butter and increase the milk to 4 to 5 tablespoons.

Steps to a Perfect Buttercream

Be prepared. Sounds like the scout motto, doesn't it? Well, it's the motto for making top-notch frostings, too!

1. Soften butter by leaving it on the counter or by warming it in the microwave on high power for ten seconds.

2. Sift the confectioners' sugar after measuring to rid it of lumps.

3. Don't add all the liquid called for at once, just as needed. For buttercreams, a good ratio is one tablespoon of liquid for each cup of confectioners' sugar used.

Cream Cheese Frosting

✦ ✦ ✦

Why mess with tradition when it comes to making the perfect frosting to be spread on a carrot cake? It's got to be a cream cheese frosting and it's got to be full fat because you don't get carrot cake with cream cheese frosting every day.

1 package (8 ounces) cream cheese,
   at room temperature
4 tablespoons (½ stick) butter, at room temperature
3 cups confectioners' sugar, sifted
1 teaspoon pure vanilla extract

Place the cream cheese and butter in a medium-size mixing bowl and beat with an electric mixer on low speed until combined, 30 seconds. Stop the machine and add the confectioners' sugar and vanilla a bit at a time, beating with the mixer on low speed until the confectioners' sugar is well incorporated, 30 seconds. Increase the mixer speed to medium-high and beat the frosting until fluffy, 1 to 1½ minutes longer. The frosting can be made a day ahead and refrigerated, covered. Let the frosting return to room temperature before using.

The Cake Mix Doctor Says

When frosting a cake in warm weather, spread a thin coat of Cream Cheese Frosting on the cake first and chill it for 15 minutes. Then generously frost the cake and return it to the refrigerator. It's best to refrigerate cakes with cream cheese frostings until it's time to serve them.

makes: 3 cups, enough to frost a 2-layer cake, a 13 by 9–inch cake, or 24 or more cupcakes

prep: 10 minutes

DAIRY FREE

Substitute an 8-ounce package of dairy-free cream cheese, such as Better Than Cream Cheese made by Tofutti, for the cream cheese and use margarine instead of the butter. Increase the amount of confectioners' sugar to 4 cups.

Classic Carrot Cake (page 52)

Lighter Cream Cheese Frosting

✦ ✦ ✦

makes: 3 cups, enough to frost a 2-layer cake, a 13 by 9–inch cake, or 24 or more cupcakes

prep: 10 minutes

You will not miss the fat in this variation of the classic Cream Cheese Frosting on page 273. This recipe uses half of the cream cheese and half of the butter. And yet it is plenty rich and complements cakes of all kinds, especially the Hummingbird Cake (page 49).

4 ounces (half of an 8-ounce package) reduced-fat cream cheese, at room temperature
4 tablespoons (½ stick) unsalted butter, at room temperature
2 teaspoons pure vanilla extract
3 cups confectioners' sugar, sifted

Place the cream cheese and butter in a medium-size mixing bowl and beat with an electric mixer on low speed until combined, 30 to 45 seconds. Stop the machine and add the vanilla and 1 cup of the confectioners' sugar. Beat with the mixer on low speed until combined, 30 seconds. Add another cup of sugar and beat on low speed until combined, 15 seconds. Add the remaining 1 cup of confectioners' sugar and beat until smooth, 15 to 30 seconds. Increase the mixer speed to medium and beat the frosting until fluffy, 30 seconds longer.

*Hummingbird Cake
(page 49)*

How I Frost a Layer Cake

No one mentioned I might be in front of five hundred people telling them how to frost a cake. It isn't something I thought about when writing my first frosting recipe, but it certainly is something I think about these days. After multiple book tours and appearances, hand me two cake layers, a bowl of frosting, and a spatula—preferably metal—and I will give you back a pretty cake.

I begin with cooled cake layers that I brush free of crumbs on the tops and sides. I place the larger or the least attractive layer on the cake plate first. Then I top that layer with a big dollop of frosting, about ½ cup, and I spread that out nice and smooth with the metal spatula, all the way to the edge. If I need more frosting, I add it. This depends on a couple of factors—is the room warm or is it cool? If it's summer and the room is warm and the frosting is sticky and loose, I will add just enough frosting to stick the layers together. But if the room is cool and the amount of frosting is ample, I will go ahead and add another big stroke of frosting, feeling generous. Now, I place the second layer on top of the first, lining it up as best I can.

If I'm given the luxury of time and a refrigerator, I might place the two layers sandwiched together by the frosting in the fridge to chill for fifteen minutes. If not, I proceed. Frosting the top before the side is my plan of action because I like to make sure the top of the cake is gorgeous. I add ½ cup of frosting, and then I spread it out. I add another full cup of frosting and decorate the top in curls and waves, using the end of the metal spatula or the back of a spoon or whatever comes to mind, spreading the frosting all the way to the edge.

Now, I focus on the side and gather a couple of big tablespoons of frosting with the spatula. I carefully place this on the side of the cake and pull the spatula round the cake, working toward me. I repeat this process, pulling the spatula and the frosting around the cake again until all the crumbs have been covered. With what is left of the frosting, I retrace my steps and frost the side once more.

Holding the cake on its plate in my left hand and the frosting spatula with my right, I am able to frost a cake without a turntable, without an assistant, without any fuss. I can do this at home, in a TV studio, in a car, and in front of five hundred people on a warm, muggy Los Angeles afternoon. It's called practice makes perfect. And I love it.

Strawberry Cream Cheese Frosting

✦ ✦ ✦

makes: 3 cups, enough to frost a 2-layer cake, a 13 by 9–inch cake, or 24 or more cupcakes

prep: 15 minutes

What else for the Pretty in Pink Strawberry Cupcakes or the strawberry layer cake but a picture-perfect strawberry frosting? Choose the ripest strawberry you can find when making this cream cheese frosting.

1 large strawberry
4 ounces (half of an 8-ounce package) cream cheese, at room temperature
4 tablespoons (½ stick) unsalted butter, at room temperature
3½ cups confectioners' sugar, sifted

Fresh Strawberry Cake (page 22)

Rinse and pat the strawberry dry. Cut the green cap off the strawberry and chop the berry into small pieces. Place the chopped strawberry in a medium-size mixing bowl and mash it with a fork until pureed. Add the cream cheese and butter and beat with an electric mixer on low speed until combined, 20 seconds. Stop the machine and add the confectioners' sugar. Beat with the mixer on low speed until the confectioners' sugar is well incorporated, 15 seconds. Increase the mixer speed to medium-high and beat the frosting until fluffy, 2 minutes longer. The frosting can be made a day ahead and refrigerated, covered. Let the frosting return to room temperature before using.

Pretty in Pink Strawberry Cupcakes (page 205)

✦ ◆ ✦

The Cake Mix Doctor Says

You want just a whisper of strawberry in this frosting recipe because if you add too much strawberry you have to add more sugar to get the frosting to pull together. This frosting needs a large strawberry without a lot of juice. Save the juicy strawberries for slicing and serving on top of the cake.

recipe reminder

Made for:

_____

_____

_____

_____

Prep Notes:

_____

_____

_____

_____

Don't Forget:

_____

_____

_____

_____

Special Touches:

_____

_____

_____

_____

Orange Cream Cheese Frosting

✦ ✦ ✦

makes: 2½ cups, enough to thinly frost a 2-layer cake or a 13 by 9–inch cake, and to generously frost an 8-inch square cake in the pan or 24 or more cupcakes

prep: 15 minutes

Substitute an 8-ounce package of dairy-free cream cheese, such as Better Than Cream Cheese made by Tofutti, for the cream cheese and use margarine instead of the butter. Increase the amount of confectioners' sugar to 4 cups.

This frosting is made for orange cakes and also for cakes that benefit from an orange flavor, such as the pumpkin spice cake. The zest of the orange gives this frosting its fresh orange flavor. For lemon cake lovers, I've also included a lemon frosting variation. Rinse and pat the fruit dry before using.

4 ounces (half of an 8-ounce package) cream cheese, at room temperature
4 tablespoons (½ stick) butter, at room temperature
3 cups confectioners' sugar, sifted
1 teaspoon grated orange zest
1 teaspoon orange juice (fresh or from a carton), or more as needed

Place the cream cheese and butter in a medium-size mixing bowl and beat with an electric mixer on low speed until combined, 30 seconds. Stop the machine and add 2¾ cups of the confectioners' sugar and the orange zest and orange juice a bit at a time, beating with the mixer on low speed until the confectioners' sugar is well incorporated, 30 seconds. Increase the mixer speed to medium and beat the frosting until fluffy, 1 to 1½ minutes longer, adding up to ¼ cup more confectioners' sugar if the frosting is too thin or

Pumpkin Spice Cake (page 181)

1 teaspoon more orange juice if the frosting is too stiff. The frosting can be made a day ahead and refrigerated, covered. Let the frosting return to room temperature before using.

✦ ✦ ✦

The Cake Mix Doctor Says

For an easy orange buttercream frosting, omit the cream cheese and use from 6 to 8 tablespoons of butter, 2½ to 3 cups confectioners' sugar, and 2 to 3 tablespoons of orange juice.

✦ ✦ ✦

Lemon Cream Cheese Frosting

4 ounces (half of an 8-ounce package) reduced-fat cream cheese, at room temperature
8 tablespoons (1 stick) butter, at room temperature
4 cups confectioners' sugar, sifted
1 teaspoon grated lemon zest
2 teaspoons fresh lemon juice

Place the cream cheese and butter in a medium-size mixing bowl and beat with an electric mixer on low speed until combined, 30 seconds. Stop the machine and add 2 cups of the confectioners' sugar and the lemon zest and lemon juice a bit at a time, beating with the mixer on low speed until the confectioners' sugar is well incorporated, 30 seconds. Add 1½ cups of the remaining confectioners' sugar and beat until smooth and spreadable, 30 seconds. Increase the mixer speed to high and beat the frosting until fluffy, 1 minute longer, adding up to ½ cup more confectioners' sugar if the frosting is too thin.

White Chocolate Cream Cheese Frosting

✦ ✦ ✦

makes: 3 cups, enough to frost a 2-layer cake, a 13 by 9–inch cake, or 24 or more cupcakes

prep: 20 minutes

You will need to find dairy-free white chocolate and melt it over very low heat. Substitute an 8-ounce package of dairy-free cream cheese, such as Better Than Cream Cheese made by Tofutti, for the 4 ounces of reduced-fat cream cheese and use margarine instead of the butter. Increase the amount of confectioners' sugar to 3½ to 4 cups.

By adding melted white chocolate to a cream cheese frosting you make the frosting richer and more dramatic, perfect for frosting the apricot cake or any other special-occasion cake.

6 ounces white chocolate
4 ounces (half of an 8-ounce package) reduced-fat
   cream cheese, at room temperature
4 tablespoons (½ stick) unsalted butter, at room temperature
3½ cups confectioner' sugar, sifted
2 teaspoons pure vanilla extract

1. Chop the white chocolate into pieces and place it in a small microwave-safe glass bowl and microwave it on high power until melted, 1 minute. Remove the bowl from the oven and stir the white chocolate with a wooden spoon or a rubber spatula until it is smooth. Set the chocolate aside to cool.

2. Place the cream cheese and butter in a medium-size mixing bowl and beat with an electric mixer on low speed until combined, 30 seconds. Stop the machine and add the melted white chocolate. Beat with the mixer on low speed until just combined, 30 seconds. Add 3 cups of the confectioners' sugar and the vanilla a bit at a time, beating on low speed until the confectioners' sugar is well incorporated, 30 seconds. Increase the mixer speed to medium and beat the frosting until fluffy, 1 minute longer, adding up to ½ cup more confectioners' sugar if the frosting is too thin. The frosting can be made a day ahead and refrigerated, covered. Let the frosting return to room temperature before using.

✦ ✦ ✦

The Cake Mix Doctor Says

To make frosting a cake easier in warm weather, spread just a small amount of frosting on the top and side of the cake, as a skim coat, and place the cake in the refrigerator to chill for 5 minutes. Then spread the remaining frosting in decorative swirls over the top and side for a decorative final coat.

*Apricot Cake
(page 39)*

Fluffy Marshmallow Frosting

✦ ✦ ✦

makes: 4½ cups, enough to generously frost a 2- or 3-layer cake

prep: 10 minutes

DAIRY FREE

As long as the marshmallow creme you use is dairy-free, this frosting will be dairy-free.

When you don't want a buttercream or a cream cheese frosting, try this. It's frosting that will remind you of frostings your grandmother made—or you wished she made!

½ cup granulated sugar
2 tablespoons water
3 large egg whites
1 jar (13 ounces) marshmallow creme
1 teaspoon pure vanilla extract

1. Place the sugar, water, and egg whites in a large, heavy saucepan over low heat. Cook, beating continuously with an electric hand mixer on high speed, until soft peaks form, 2 to 3 minutes. If your hand mixer has a cord, make sure to keep it away from the burner.

2. Remove the pan from the heat. Add the marshmallow creme and vanilla and beat the mixture with the mixer on high speed until stiff peaks form, 2 minutes. Use the frosting at once or chill for easiest spreading, especially in warm weather.

The Cake Mix Doctor Says

Check the label to make sure that the marshmallow creme you are using is gluten-free.

Peanut Butter Frosting

✦ ◆ ✦

Peanut butter lovers will tell you this frosting would be sublime on most any cake, be it vanilla, chocolate, pineapple, or pistachio. But my favorite peanut butter match-up is bananas and chocolate. Frosting the chocolate banana cake with this fluffy peanut confection creates a heavenly combination.

makes: 3 cups, enough to frost a 2- or 3-layer cake or the top of a 13 by 9–inch cake

prep: 5 minutes

1 cup creamy peanut butter

8 tablespoons (1 stick) unsalted butter, at room temperature

2½ cups confectioners' sugar, sifted

2 tablespoons milk, or more as needed

2 teaspoons pure vanilla extract

Chocolate Banana Cake (page 85)

DAIRY FREE

Substitute margarine for the butter and use 3 tablespoons of plain, unsweetened almond milk instead of the cow's milk. Increase the amount of confectioners' sugar to 3 cups.

recipe reminders

Made for:

_____

_____

_____

_____

Prep Notes:

_____

_____

_____

_____

Don't Forget:

_____

_____

_____

_____

Special Touches:

_____

_____

_____

_____

Place the peanut butter and butter in a medium-size mixing bowl and beat with an electric mixer on low speed until fluffy, 30 seconds. Stop the machine and add 2 cups of the confectioners' sugar and the milk and vanilla a bit at a time, beating with the mixer on low speed until the confectioners' sugar is well incorporated, 1 minute. Increase the mixer speed to medium and beat the frosting until light and fluffy, 1 minute longer, adding up to ½ cup more confectioners' sugar if the frosting is too thin or up to 1 tablespoon more milk if the frosting is too stiff. Use the frosting at once.

✦ ✦ ✦

The Cake Mix Doctor Says

One of my favorite garnishes for cakes with this frosting is banana chips. They are found in the produce section of supermarkets and are delicious on banana, chocolate, or spice cakes.

Quick Caramel Frosting

✦ ✦ ✦

This has to be one of my favorite frosting recipes of all time. It is a recipe my mother shared with me many years ago, a Southern mother to daughter culinary secret. Instead of caramelizing granulated white sugar, my mom added light and dark brown sugars. I don't know why anyone would want to make caramel frosting the old-fashioned way except to say that they make it the old-fashioned way! The frosting is de rigueur on the banana layer cake and also the Easy One-Pan Caramel Cake (page 156). And it is optional but appreciated on just about any other cake in this book.

makes: 3 cups, enough to frost a 2-layer cake, the top of a 13 by 9–inch cake, or 24 or more cupcakes

prep: 8 to 10 minutes

8 tablespoons (1 stick) butter
½ cup lightly packed light brown sugar
½ cup lightly packed dark brown sugar
¼ cup plus 2 tablespoons milk (see Note), or more
    as needed
2 cups confectioners' sugar, sifted
1 teaspoon pure vanilla extract

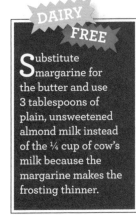

DAIRY FREE

Substitute margarine for the butter and use 3 tablespoons of plain, unsweetened almond milk instead of the ¼ cup of cow's milk because the margarine makes the frosting thinner.

1. Place the butter and brown sugars in a heavy medium-size saucepan over medium heat. Cook, stirring, until the mixture comes to a boil, about 2 minutes. Add the milk, stir, and let the mixture return to a boil, then remove the pan from the heat. Add 1½ cups of the confectioners' sugar and the vanilla and whisk until the frosting is smooth. Add up to ½ cup more confectioners' sugar

Half Recipe Quick Caramel Frosting

This smaller recipe will glaze the top of a Bundt cake, frost an 8-inch square cake, or frost twelve to fourteen cupcakes. And it's still delicious. For a half recipe follow the Quick Caramel Frosting recipe instructions, but use:

4 tablespoons (½ stick) butter
¼ cup lightly packed light brown sugar
¼ cup lightly packed dark brown sugar
3 tablespoons milk, plus another tablespoon if needed
1 cup confectioners' sugar, sifted

but not so much that the frosting thickens and hardens. It should be smooth enough to spread.

2. Ladle the frosting over the cake while it is still warm. It will set as it cools. For a 13 by 9–inch cake, just pour the frosting over the top and spread it with a metal spatula to smooth the top. For cupcakes, spoon the frosting on top while it is warm and it will set. If the frosting hardens too much, place the saucepan back over low heat and stir in 1 or 2 tablespoons of milk.

NOTE: Use whole milk if possible in this recipe because it makes a smoother, richer frosting. The 2 percent milk works okay, but don't use fat-free milk.

✦ ✦ ✦

The Cake Mix Doctor Says

I experimented with different measurements when making this frosting for gluten-free cakes. Because these cakes are slightly smaller than their counterparts with gluten, they sometimes need less frosting. But this frosting might be the exception because you can always use a little extra caramel frosting by spreading it on the top more thickly or adding extra between the layers. I decided to go with my original recipe plus a bit more milk to make the frosting thinner and a little easier to spread on the cake. As for the half recipe, it is perfect for topping a Bundt cake, a square cake, or for frosting a dozen cupcakes.

Easy One-Pan Caramel Cake (page 156)

Chocolate Buttercream Frosting

✦ ✦ ✦

A wonderful go-to frosting, this is the classic frosting for birthday cakes, chocolate chip cakes, even strawberry-flavored layers. Use this also to frost the Favorite Yellow Birthday Cupcakes (page 201) and the Chocolate Espresso Buttermilk Cake (page 193). To jazz up the flavor, add a teaspoon of espresso powder, a pinch of cinnamon, or make this with Dutch-processed cocoa powder, which has a darker color and deeper flavor.

makes: 2½ cups, just enough to frost a 2-layer cake, an 8-inch square cake, or 24 or more cupcakes

prep: 10 minutes

6 tablespoons (¾ stick) butter, at room temperature
½ cup unsweetened cocoa powder
2½ cups confectioners' sugar, sifted
3 tablespoons milk, or more as needed
1 teaspoon pure vanilla extract

Place the butter in a medium-size mixing bowl and beat with an electric mixer on low speed until fluffy, 30 seconds. Stop the machine and add the cocoa, confectioners' sugar, milk, and vanilla a bit at a time, beating with the mixer on low speed until the confectioners' sugar is well incorporated, 1 minute. Increase the mixer speed to medium and beat the frosting until light and fluffy, 1 minute longer. Beat in up to 1 tablespoon more milk if the frosting seems too stiff. Use the frosting at once.

DAIRY FREE

Substitute margarine or butter-flavored Crisco vegetable shortening sticks for the butter. Use 4 tablespoons of plain, unsweetened almond milk instead of the cow's milk and increase the amount of confectioners' sugar to 3½ cups. If you are frosting a layer cake, double the recipe.

✦ ✦ ✦

recipe reminders

Made for: _____

_____

_____

_____

_____

Prep Notes: _____

_____

_____

_____

_____

Don't Forget: _____

_____

_____

_____

Special Touches: _____

_____

_____

_____

The Cake Mix Doctor Says

When making this recipe dairy-free, you can use margarine or Earth Balance butter-flavored spread. Substitute unsweetened plain almond milk for the cow's milk and be aware you may need more milk than the original recipe calls for. If you are making a large two-layer or a three-layer cake you may need to double a dairy-free buttercream frosting recipe because butter substitutes don't whip to the volume that butter does.

Favorite Yellow Birthday Cupcakes
(page 201)

Chocolate Pan Frosting

✦ ✦ ✦

Many times all of this chocolate frosting doesn't make it to the cake. It is stolen from the pan by my children or poured over vanilla ice cream. It, too, is one of my mother's recipes and I have fond memories of her standing over the stove, her left hand on her hip, her right hand stirring the pan of frosting with a wooden spoon. Use the frosting on my Chocolate Chip Pistachio Cake (page 70) or the Boston Cream Pie Your Way (page 82), on any of my cupcakes, or really on any chocolate or yellow cake in this book. Enjoy!

makes: 3 cups, enough to frost a 2-layer cake, a 13 by 9–inch cake, or 24 or more cupcakes

prep: 10 to 15 minutes

8 tablespoons (1 stick) butter
4 tablespoons unsweetened cocoa powder
⅓ cup milk, or more if needed (see Note)
3½ cups confectioners' sugar, sifted

1. Melt the butter in a medium-size saucepan over low heat, 2 to 3 minutes. Stir in the cocoa powder and milk. Cook, stirring, until the mixture thickens and just begins to come to a boil, 1 minute longer. Remove the pan from the heat. Stir in 3 cups of the confectioners' sugar a bit at a time, adding up to ½ cup more sugar or more milk if needed, until the frosting is thickened and smooth and the consistency of hot fudge sauce.

2. Ladle the warm frosting over the top of cooled cake layers, then spread the side of the cake with more frosting, smoothing it out with a long metal spatula as you go. For a 13 by 9–inch cake, just pour the frosting over the top and spread it with a metal

DAIRY FREE

Use margarine instead of butter in both the Chocolate Pan Frosting and the Warm Chocolate Glaze. Use 3 to 4 tablespoons of plain, unsweetened almond milk instead of the cow's milk in the frosting and use 2 to 3 tablespoons of almond milk instead of the milk in the glaze.

Substitutes for Milk in Frostings and Glazes

In the movies, actors who replace the stars are called doubles. In dairy-free baking, the ingredients that replace cow's milk are called invaluable. Here are some ingredient doubles to keep on hand for making dairy-free frostings.

✦ Plain, unsweetened almond milk

✦ Coconut milk

✦ Rice milk

✦ Soy milk

✦ Brewed coffee

✦ Orange juice

✦ Lemon juice

As a rule, for buttercreams and cooked frostings, use almond milk, coconut milk, or rice or soy milk. For cream cheese frostings and for glazes use coffee, orange juice, or lemon juice.

spatula to smooth the top. And for cupcakes, spoon the frosting on while it is warm. The frosting will harden as it cools.

NOTE: Any milk works in this recipe, but for the best result use whole milk or even half-and-half.

✦ ✦ ✦

The Cake Mix Doctor Says

Go ahead and sift the powdered sugar, but do this after measuring. Sifting will remove the lumps that might otherwise show up in this frosting.

✦ ✦ ✦

VARIATION:
HALF RECIPE CHOCOLATE PAN FROSTING

A half recipe of the Chocolate Pan Frosting, this is perfect to top a Bundt cake, spread over an 8-inch square cake right from the oven, or frost just a dozen cupcakes or the Boston Cream Pie Your Way (page 82). Follow the recipe directions on page 289 but make these adjustments to the ingredient amounts, using:

4 tablespoons (½ stick) butter
2 tablespoons unsweetened cocoa powder
3 tablespoons milk
1½ to 1¾ cups confectioners' sugar, sifted

To make the frosting even more interesting, add ½ teaspoon of almond extract or a pinch of espresso powder.

Caramel Glaze

✦ ✦ ✦

Spoon this glaze over the banana bread cake, Southern Sweet Potato Pound Cake (page 129), or the Almond Cream Cheese Pound Cake (page 101). Or don't spoon it over cake at all—just eat it from the spoon!

makes: ½ cup, enough to lightly glaze a Bundt or tube cake

prep: 10 minutes

3 tablespoons butter
3 tablespoons lightly packed light brown sugar
3 tablespoons granulated sugar
3 tablespoons heavy (whipping) cream
½ teaspoon pure vanilla extract

Place the butter, brown sugar, granulated sugar, and cream in a medium-size saucepan over medium heat and let come to a boil, stirring. Let the butter mixture boil for 1 minute, stirring constantly. Remove the pan from the heat and stir in the vanilla. Pour the glaze over the cooled cake of your choice.

Caramel Melted Ice Cream Cake (page 107)

✦ ✦ ✦

The Cake Mix Doctor Says

Don't have any heavy cream? If you have evaporated milk in your pantry you can substitute it for the cream.

DAIRY FREE

Substitute margarine for the butter and coconut milk for the cream. Refrigerate the Caramel Glaze for 30 minutes before using so that it sets.

Sweetened Whipped Cream

✦ ✦ ✦

makes: 2 cups, enough to serve with a 13 by 9–inch cake or to top a 2-layer cake or 18 to 20 cupcakes

prep: 5 to 7 minutes

Cakes with fruit or vegetables baked in them don't always need a frosting, but they do need a topping of some sort, such as this whipped cream that has been lightly sweetened and flavored with vanilla. Serve it on the Chocolate Zucchini Snack Cake (page 187).

1 cup heavy (whipping) cream, chilled
¼ cup confectioners' sugar, sifted
½ teaspoon pure vanilla extract

Place a large mixing bowl and electric mixer beaters in the freezer for a few minutes while you assemble the ingredients. Pour the cream into the chilled bowl and beat it with an electric mixer on high speed until the cream has thickened, 1½ minutes. Stop the machine and add the confectioners' sugar and vanilla. Beat on high speed until stiff peaks form, 1 to 2 minutes longer. The Sweetened Whipped Cream can be made 3 to 4 hours ahead and refrigerated, covered.

✦ ✦ ✦

DAIRY FREE

Purchase a dairy-free whipped dessert topping at the supermarket or natural foods store.

The Cake Mix Doctor Says

For a real treat, make chocolate whipped cream. Melt 1 cup (6 ounces) of semisweet chocolate chips in a microwave oven on high power for 45 seconds or over low heat on the stove, then let the chocolate cool. Whip 2 cups (1 pint) of cold heavy (whipping) cream until firm peaks form. Don't add sugar or vanilla, just fold the whipped cream into the cooled chocolate.

*Holy Cow Cake
(page 195)*

recipe reminder

Made for:

_____

_____

_____

_____

_____

Prep Notes:

_____

_____

_____

_____

Don't Forget:

_____

_____

_____

_____

Special Touches:

_____

_____

_____

_____

Julie's Lemon Curd

✦ ✦ ✦

makes: 1⅓ cups, enough to fill a 2-layer cake or top 24 cupcakes

prep: 20 minutes

DAIRY FREE

Sorry, it's not dairy-free. You need to use butter to make Julie's recipe. As a substitute, look for jars of prepared lemon curd made with margarine.

My friend Julie Buchanan in England makes this luscious lemon curd in a snap. She is brilliant, and so is her recipe!

2 large lemons
¾ cup granulated sugar
2 large eggs
6 tablespoons (¾ stick) unsalted butter, melted and slightly cooled

1. Rinse and pat the lemons dry with paper towels. Grate the yellow zest onto a plate; you should have about 1 tablespoon. Cut the lemons in half and squeeze the juice through a fine sieve, discarding the seeds; you should have about ¼ cup of juice. Place the lemon juice and zest in a medium-size mixing bowl. Whisk in the sugar and eggs and beat until well combined, 2 minutes. Whisk in the melted butter until incorporated.

Lemon Lover's Chiffon Cake (page 31)

2. Pour the lemon mixture into a heavy medium-size saucepan set over medium heat. Whisk constantly until the mixture gradually thickens and comes to a boil, 5 to 7 minutes.

3. Strain the lemon curd through a fine-mesh sieve to remove the zest, if desired. Pour the lemon curd into a glass bowl or jar, cover it with plastic wrap or a lid, and refrigerate it. Lemon curd can be refrigerated for up to 1 week.

✦ ✦ ✦

The Cake Mix Doctor Says

Make lime curd with Persian or key limes. Make tangerine curd with tangerines. Vary the citrus fruit, but keep the measurements the same.

recipe reminder

Made for: _____

_____

_____

_____

_____

Prep Notes: _____

_____

_____

_____

_____

Don't Forget: _____

_____

_____

_____

_____

Special Touches: _____

_____

_____

_____

_____

Gluten-Free Online: Where to Go for Help

Websites for Diet, Health, and Gluten-Free Recipe Information

• • •

Celiac Disease Center at Columbia University—www.celiacdiseasecenter.columbia.edu

Celiac Disease Foundation—www.celiac.org

Celiac Sprue Association—www.csaceliacs.org

Gluten Intolerance Group of North America—www.gluten.net

The University of Chicago Celiac Disease Center—www.celiacdisease.net

The University of Maryland Center for Celiac Research—www.celiaccenter.org

www.celiac.com—a longtime site that offers advice and recipes

www.liveglutenfreely.com—General Mills' gluten-free site

www.zeer.com—lets you check more than 30,000 foods for their gluten content, including specific brands

Blogs and Websites for Recipes and Fellowship

• • •

Here are some blogs and websites I have enjoyed reading and visiting while working on this book.

www.beyondricecakes.com—Celiac Princess

www.bookofyum.com

www.celiacchicks.com

www.flour-arrangements.com

www.gingerlemongirl.blogspot.com

www.glutenfreeeasily.com

www.glutenfreegirl.blogspot.com—gluten-free girl and the chef

www.glutenfreegoddess.blogspot.com

www.glutenfreetasteofhome.blogspot.com

www.glutenhatesme.com

www.heythattastesgood.com—Hey, that tastes good!

www.holdthegluten.net

www.simplygluten-free.blogspot.com—Simply . . . gluten-free

Local Clubs and Organizations

• • •

The best way to eat well gluten-free is to find friends in your area who are also following a gluten-free diet. Join a local support group; take a cooking class; start a gluten-free supper club. There are many chapters of the international support group called R.O.C.K. (Raising Our Celiac Kids). Search celiac.com online to see if one is in your area.

Magazines

• • •

You might want to subscribe to a magazine specializing in gluten-free cooking and baking. Check out:

Living Without—www.livingwithout.com

Delight gluten free—
www.delightgfmagazine.com

Gluten-Free Living—
www.glutenfreeliving.com

Hard-to-Find Baking Ingredients

• • •

I made my best effort in this book to call for ingredients that are available in most supermarkets. You'll find many gluten-free products at Whole Foods. Go to www.wholefoodsmarket.com for information about the store nearest you. But should you need to shop online, here are two sources:

The Gluten-Free Pantry—
www.glutenfree.com

The Gluten-Free Mall—
www.glutenfreemall.com

Conversion Tables

✦ ✦ ✦ ✦ ✦

Liquid Conversions

U.S.	IMPERIAL	METRIC
2 tbs	1 fl oz.	30 ml
3 tbs	1½ fl oz	45 ml
¼ cup	2 fl oz.	60 ml
⅓ cup	2½ fl oz	75 ml
⅓ cup + 1 tbs.	3 fl oz.	90 ml
⅓ cup + 2 tbs.	3½ fl oz.	100 ml
½ cup	4 fl oz.	125 ml
⅔ cup	5 fl oz.	150 ml
¾ cup	6 fl oz.	175 ml
¾ cup + 2 tbs.	7 fl oz.	200 ml
1 cup	8 fl oz.	250 ml
1 cup + 2 tbs	9 fl oz.	275 ml
1¼ cups	10 fl oz.	300 ml
1⅓ cups	11 fl oz.	325 ml
1½ cups	12 fl oz.	350 ml
1⅔ cups	13 fl oz.	375 ml
1¾ cups	14 fl oz.	400 ml
1¾ cups + 2 tbs	15 fl oz.	450 ml
2 cups (1 pint)	16 fl oz.	500 ml
2½ cups	20 fl oz (1 pint)	600 ml
3¾ cups	1½ pints	900 ml
4 cups	1¾ pints	1 liter

Weight Conversions

US/UK	METRIC	US/UK	METRIC
½ oz.	15 g	7 oz.	200 g
1 oz	30 g	8 oz.	250 g
1½ oz.	45 g	9 oz.	275 g
2 oz	60 g	10 oz.	300 g
2½ oz.	75 g	11 oz.	325 g
3 oz	90 g	12 oz.	350 g
3½ oz.	100 g	13 oz.	375 g
4 oz	125 g	14 oz.	400 g
5 oz	150 g	15 oz.	450 g
6 oz	175 g	1 lb	500 g

Oven Temperatures

FAHRENHEIT	GAS MARK	CELSIUS
250	½	120
275	1	140
300	2	150
325	3	160
350	4	180
375	5	190
400	6	200
425	7	220
450	8	230
475	9	240
500	10	260

Note: Reduce the temperature by 20°C (68°F) for fan-assisted ovens.

Approximate Equivalents

1 stick butter = 8 tbs = 4 oz = ½ cup

1 cup all-purpose presifted flour or dried bread crumbs = 5 oz

1 cup granulated sugar = 8 oz

1 cup (packed) brown sugar = 6 oz

1 cup confectioners' sugar = 4½ oz

1 cup honey or syrup = 12 oz

1 cup grated cheese = 4 oz

1 cup dried beans = 6 oz

1 large egg = about 2 oz or about 3 tbs

1 egg yolk = about 1 tbs

1 egg white = about 2 tbs

Please note that all conversions are approximate but close enough to be useful when converting from one system to another.

ℋ

ℐ ✦ ℐ ✦ ℋ

ℒ